South Asia Economic and Policy Studies

Series editors

Sachin Chaturvedi, RIS for Developing Countries, New Delhi, India
Mustafizur Rahman, Centre for Policy Dialogue (CPD), Dhaka, Bangladesh
Abid Suleri, Sustainable Development Policy Institute, Islamabad, Pakistan
Saman Kelegama (1959–2017), Institute of Policy Studies of Sri Lanka (IPS), Colombo, Sri Lanka

The Series aims to address evolving and new challenges and policy actions that may be needed in the South Asian Region in the 21st century. It ventures niche and makes critical assessment to evolve a coherent understanding of the nature of challenges and allow/facilitate dialogue among scholars and policymakers from the region working with the common purpose of exploring and strengthening new ways to implement regional cooperation. The series is multidisciplinary in its orientation and invites contributions from academicians, policy makers, practitioners, consultants working in the broad fields of regional cooperation; trade and investment; finance; economic growth and development; industry and technology; agriculture; services; environment, resources and climate change; demography and migration; disaster management, globalization and institutions among others.

More information about this series at http://www.springer.com/series/15400

Debashis Bandyopadhyay

Securing Our Natural Wealth

A Policy Agenda for Sustainable Development in India and its Neighboring Countries

 Springer

Debashis Bandyopadhyay
Council of Scientific and Industrial
 Research/CSIR-CGCRI
Kolkata, West Bengal
India

ISSN 2522-5502　　　　　　　　ISSN 2522-5510　(electronic)
South Asia Economic and Policy Studies
ISBN 978-981-13-4262-2　　　　ISBN 978-981-10-8872-8　(eBook)
https://doi.org/10.1007/978-981-10-8872-8

© Springer Nature Singapore Pte Ltd. 2018
Softcover re-print of the Hardcover 1st edition 2018
This work is subject to copyright. All rights are reserved by the Publisher, whether the whole or part of the material is concerned, specifically the rights of translation, reprinting, reuse of illustrations, recitation, broadcasting, reproduction on microfilms or in any other physical way, and transmission or information storage and retrieval, electronic adaptation, computer software, or by similar or dissimilar methodology now known or hereafter developed.
The use of general descriptive names, registered names, trademarks, service marks, etc. in this publication does not imply, even in the absence of a specific statement, that such names are exempt from the relevant protective laws and regulations and therefore free for general use.
The publisher, the authors and the editors are safe to assume that the advice and information in this book are believed to be true and accurate at the date of publication. Neither the publisher nor the authors or the editors give a warranty, express or implied, with respect to the material contained herein or for any errors or omissions that may have been made. The publisher remains neutral with regard to jurisdictional claims in published maps and institutional affiliations.

Printed on acid-free paper

This Springer imprint is published by the registered company Springer Nature Singapore Pte Ltd. part of Springer Nature
The registered company address is: 152 Beach Road, #21-01/04 Gateway East, Singapore 189721, Singapore

To my parents (Mani and Baba)

Foreword

Identifying policy instruments and institutions meant to secure environmental and natural wealth is both complex and difficult when economic growth is being led by globalization, liberalization and consumerism. Even when properly identified, effective implementation is likewise difficult because stakeholders must navigate conflicts in the overall impact on associated areas; intellectual property rights (IPR); issues of governance; plant variety protection; farmers' rights; traditional knowledge and geographical indications; as well as access to genetic resources.

In turn, each issue provides substantially different impacts on both developing and developed countries, thereby creating additional conflict situations needing to be studied and resolved if the associated international agreement on Trade-Related Aspects of Intellectual Property Rights (TRIPS), the Convention on Biological Diversity and other treaties/protocols is to be respected.

The above-referenced issues are especially complex, but extremely important for a developing country like India and its neighbours, particularly considering that all have large agricultural sectors, dynamic and modern non-agricultural sectors and an emphasis on trade. Poverty and food in-security, however, still exist reminding policy makers that an 'all-inclusive development' strategy is not yet complete. Securing environment and natural resources in such a context is therefore a challenging task for scientists, policy makers and activists.

Nevertheless, brave scientists like Debashis Bandyopadhyay are accepting the challenge head-on while also looking for opportunities to contribute towards their resolution. In his book 'Securing Our Natural Wealth: A Policy Agenda for Sustainable Development in India and its Neighboring Countries', Dr. Bandyopadhyay systematically flags and analyses issues associated with the emergence of IPR regimes and international conventions like TRIPS and CBD, as well as their impact on food security and conservation in developing countries. The most striking and innovative contribution of the author comes from his ability to contextualize TRIPS and CBD while articulating the developing country's perspective on food security, plant protection and farmers' rights, protection of traditional and indigenous knowledge, genetically modified crops and biosafety.

In short, the most resounding message proffered by the author is that by taking advantage of abundant natural resources, biodiversity and improved agricultural prospect, many economic activities are moving to developing countries. In this situation, it is all the more important that efforts are taken to secure such comparative advantage for sustaining the pace of growth and development. Debashis Bandyopadhyay's technical expertise and his extensive policy research in this area are both important contributions to existing literature and will ultimately prove useful for a range of present and future stakeholders interested in sustainable growth and development.

Bangkok, Thailand

Hiren Sarkar
Former Chief, Development Policy Section
UNESCAP

Preface

The year 2017 marked the twenty-fifth anniversary of the Rio Summit and birth of the Convention on Biological Diversity (CBD). The CBD is unique in many aspects. One of its most noteworthy aspects is the interpretation about how we view natural resources. From the doctrine of 'mankind's common heritage', the Convention has ensured that they are subjected to sovereign rights of countries that harbour them. It has also advocated regulating developmental and industrial laws that are likely to be prejudicial to the environment. The CBD has thus emerged as an important tool for driving social equity across the world through its inclusive nature and fair disposition. Needless to say, the Convention has thus been largely accepted by the developing countries amid a vastly exclusive set-up. It has also nucleated creation of numerous other protocols on key issues concerning natural resources such as Cartagena Protocol on Biosafety; Nagoya Protocol on Access to Resources and Benefit Sharing etc.

Two years after the Rio Summit, the Trade-Related Aspects of Intellectual Property Rights (TRIPS) was adopted as an annex to the Marrakesh Agreement. It advocated a rule-based trading system and an intellectual property regime that would balance the rights and obligations of the member countries. The Agreement was largely viewed as a handle for the developed countries to harmonize international trade laws.

TRIPS and CBD with their mutually conflicting provisions (in many cases) are currently shaping the global scenario. The conflicts and debates regarding the provisions of TRIPS and CBD have arisen from the claims of a strong IPR regime by the former vis-a-vis the strong conservation claims by the latter. Ironically, what seems to have been ignored is the underlying synergy between the two in promoting an equitable world.

Intellectual property rights have long been viewed as an element of the capitalist world. It is considered as a tool to exert influence over the 'have-nots' and to extend the reach of transnational corporations across the world. Developing countries are considered to be on the receiving end, often paying royalties for resources that originate in their own territories. Yet, little effort has been expended to understand the pivotal role IPR can play in protecting the economic sovereignty of the developing world—be it through commodity trade or through exploitation of natural resources which most of the developing world is richly endowed with.

The scenario, however, is beginning to change. Since the economic recession of 2008, economic growth and development is shifting southwards with more and more production and economic activities moving to developing countries. This is largely because of the advantage from economies of scale and availability of raw materials. A significant portion of such productive endeavours rely on natural resources, biodiversity and agriculture. For example, pharmaceutical companies are increasingly focusing on bioprospecting natural resources, be it in the Amazon rainforests or in the slopes of the Himalayas. Manufacturing industries are looking towards nature-derived raw materials, and innovation industries are relying on traditional knowledge held by indigenous communities. The importance of intellectual property rights in developing countries, especially the ones protecting natural resources, has become imperative in the current context than ever before.

Let us return to the TRIPS and the CBD. While the former advocates balancing rights and obligations, the latter prohibits any such intervention that is considered prejudicial to the environment. And TRIPS does provide an option for the developing countries to protect their plant resources through systems aligned to the specific requirements of the country. We have thus begun to realize and appreciate the fact that IPR is just not an instrument of expanding capitalist hegemony of the west, but also an enabling tool for developing countries to build a world based on sustainability and equity. Thus, while intellectual property protection laws and policies of various countries are different and evolve at varying paces, the global governance frameworks should be adequately tweaked so as to accommodate this changing paradigm of international relationships. This also involves a multitude of other treaties and conventions regulating plant variety protection, geographical indications, access and benefit sharing and so on.

Sustainable development is the organizing principle that focuses on meeting human development goals while conserving natural resources. However, a question that is commonly asked is that since any value creation out of limited resources would definitely use up the resource, what exactly should be sustained in sustainable development? Assuming that sustainable development should be looked into through a wider perspective and that it should also include sustaining the tacit elements that underlie development (apart from the tangible resources that make up the world), aspects such as traditional human practices and knowledge, creations of human mind and the ability of human to manage such resources begin to emerge. It is through such perspective that intellectual property rights get firmly embedded into the mandate of sustainable development. Traditional knowledge is perpetual; agriculture is renewable through human effort. Any policy agenda for sustainable development should thus invariably focus on conserving traditional knowledge, indigenous practices, agricultural methods and access to knowledge to all of these. It is thus fair to argue that ensuring security to our natural wealth through legally binding frameworks that cover not only tangible natural assets but also intangible intellectual assets held by communities, forms the crux of achieving sustainable development and equity.

In this book, I have tried to provide a glimpse of the above, restricted to a small region of the world, namely a group of countries bordering the Bay of Bengal in South Asia. My aim has been not to provide prescriptions or solutions, but to flag problems and challenges that need to be addressed while working towards IPR-based sustainable development. The overview of governance frameworks in the countries and at the international levels gives an indication of the gaps that need to be bridged and strengths that can be leveraged. The various issues and implications, challenges and opportunities associated with the region unequivocally reflect that it is a long way to conform the mandate and that a concerted regional initiative would be much more effective than national efforts in achieving our goal.

A few aspects of the organization of the work might prove useful. Firstly, throughout this book, there is a preponderance of comparison between developed and developing countries. This is not with an intention of compartmentalizing the world into two poles or to draw a positive or negative picture about two categories of the world economies. This is essentially to highlight the fact that the global debates and policy challenges relating to IPR are to a large extent about dichotomy, interpretation and trade-offs on various issues among these two groups of countries. Secondly, the region being discussed here witnesses an increasing focus on food security, agricultural production and agro-based livelihood. This is probably why we have talked more about the plant genetic resources and farmers' rights and related aspects compared to other facets of natural resource-based IPR instruments. And thirdly, this book is more a book in the context of India, or rather on the enabling role of India in the region. This is reflected in discussion of other countries being undertaken after a preliminary discussion of the relevant instrument for India.

I am thankful to several individuals, ranging from teachers to friends and colleagues who had given valuable suggestions and insightful comments. Sukanya Datta, a seasoned writer herself, and Dipankar Basu have prodded me for years to begin the task of writing a book. Swati Roy Gangopadhyay made a preliminary review of the concept and provided useful comments. Santanu Sengupta and Suman Kundu have been instrumental in nucleating the proposal and connecting me with the publishers. I have greatly benefited from the discussions with and expert advice from Subhashis Mukhopadhyay, Ashoke Ranjan Thakur and Ajitava Raychaudhuri for fine-tuning the contents of this book.

The present work matured during a year I spent on deputation from CSIR at the pristine environs of the Indian Institute of Technology Kanpur. It is a pleasure for me to acknowledge the moral support of Indranil Manna and K. Muraleedharan, Directors of IIT Kanpur and CSIR-CGCRI, respectively. I am particularly grateful to Hiren Sarkar, former Chief of Development Policy at United Nations Economic and Social Commission for Asia and Pacific, Bangkok, for agreeing to write an insightful foreword to this work. I am also particularly thankful to my wife Oishila for painstakingly going through the manuscript, especially the tables and references, often with the messy WDI data and flagging places where corrections were needed, and to my son Aritra for his assistance in finalizing the manuscript. Finally, I am grateful to Springer's Executive Editor Sagarika Ghosh and her colleague Nupoor Singh for their suggestions and comments and to Springer's Production Editor Smilin Prince Nelson and his associate Jayanthi Narayanaswamy for seeing this work to completion.

Kolkata, India   Debashis Bandyopadhyay

Contents

1	**Introduction**			1
	1.1	Background		1
	1.2	South and Southeast Asia: Trade and Cooperation		2
	1.3	Coverage and Scope		2
	1.4	Defining Natural Wealth		3
	1.5	Facets of Natural Wealth Protection		3
	1.6	The Agenda-21 for Sustainable Development		4
	1.7	Evolving Integrated Solutions and Policies		5
	1.8	New Vistas in South–South Cooperation		5
	1.9	Structure of the Book		5
	1.10	Epilogue		6
	References			6
2	**Emergence of IPR Regimes and Governance Frameworks**			7
	2.1	Overview		7
	2.2	Evolution of IPR Regimes		8
		2.2.1	The Paris Convention	8
		2.2.2	The Berne Convention	8
		2.2.3	Categories of Multilateral Industrial Property Treaties	8
		2.2.4	Regional Industrial Property Treaties	9
		2.2.5	World Trade Organization and the TRIPS Agreement	10
	2.3	Governance Frameworks for IPR Protection of Life Forms		10
		2.3.1	Trade-Related Aspects of Intellectual Property Rights (TRIPS)	10
		2.3.2	Convention on Biological Diversity (CBD)	11
		2.3.3	Cartagena Protocol	12
		2.3.4	International Treaty on Plant Genetic Resources for Food and Agriculture (ITPGRFA)	13

		2.3.5	International Union for Protection of New Plant Varieties (UPOV).	14
		2.3.6	Budapest Treaty	15
		2.3.7	Lisbon Agreement for Appellation of Origin	16
	2.4	Major Issues of Protection		16
	2.5	Protection vis-a-vis Access		17
	2.6	The Middle Path: Achieving a Balance in Intellectual Property Protection and Public Access		18
	2.7	Conclusion		19
	References			19
3	**TRIPS, CBD and Developing Countries: Implications on Food Security and Conservation**			**21**
	3.1	Overview		21
	3.2	Agriculture and Food Security		22
	3.3	Biodiversity and Conservation		23
	3.4	Traditional Knowledge, Indigenous Knowledge and Traditional Cultural Expressions		24
	3.5	The Enigma of Article 27.3(b) of the TRIPS		25
	3.6	Plant Variety Protection and Biodiversity: Biased Stand of the TRIPS		25
	3.7	Options Under the CBD		26
	3.8	Options Under a *Sui generis* System		26
		3.8.1	What Constitutes an Effective *Sui generis* System	26
	3.9	Addressing the Concerns of Developing Countries		27
	3.10	UPOV's Bias Against Developing Countries and Evolution of *Sui generis* System at Global Level		29
	3.11	Addressing Conflict of Compliance		29
	3.12	Conclusion		30
	References			30
4	**The South Asian Perspective**			**31**
	4.1	Background		31
	4.2	Overview of the Bay of Bengal Initiative for Multi-Sectoral Technical and Economic Cooperation (BIMSTEC)		32
		4.2.1	Trade Dimension of the BIMSTEC	33
		4.2.2	Land Use	34
		4.2.3	Human Development	35
	4.3	Country Profiles of Selected Countries of South Asia		35
		4.3.1	Bangladesh	36
		4.3.2	Bhutan	37
		4.3.3	India	38
		4.3.4	Myanmar	39

		4.3.5	Nepal	40
		4.3.6	Sri Lanka	41
		4.3.7	Thailand	42
	4.4	Why Natural Wealth Protection in South Asia is Important?		42
	4.5	Conclusion		43
	References			44
5	**Plant Variety Protection and Farmers' Rights**			45
	5.1	Background		45
	5.2	Possible Fall Out of Plant Variety Protection		46
	5.3	Privilege for the Farmers		46
	5.4	PVP vis-a-vis Patents: What Developing Countries Stand to Gain		47
	5.5	PVP in South Asian Countries		48
		5.5.1	India	48
		5.5.2	Bangladesh	50
		5.5.3	Bhutan	51
		5.5.4	Nepal	52
		5.5.5	Myanmar	54
		5.5.6	Thailand	54
		5.5.7	Sri Lanka	56
	5.6	Conclusion		57
	References			57
6	**Protection of Traditional Knowledge and Indigenous Knowledge**			59
	6.1	Background		59
	6.2	Protection of Traditional Knowledge		60
	6.3	Misappropriation of Traditional Knowledge		60
		6.3.1	Examples of Misappropriation of TK in India	60
	6.4	International Instruments for Protecting Traditional Knowledge		61
	6.5	Protection of TK/IK in South Asian Countries		61
		6.5.1	India	61
		6.5.2	Bangladesh	64
		6.5.3	Bhutan	64
		6.5.4	Myanmar	65
		6.5.5	Nepal	65
		6.5.6	Sri Lanka	66
		6.5.7	Thailand	66
		6.5.8	Challenges to TK/IK Protection in South Asian Countries	67

	6.6	Traditional Cultural Expressions	68
		6.6.1 Protection of TCEs: Initiatives of WIPO	68
		6.6.2 Using Certification Marks and Labels of Authenticity to Protect TCEs	68
		6.6.3 Success Story of 'One Tambon One Product' Project in Thailand	69
	6.7	Conclusion	69
	References		69
7	**Geographical Indications and Appellation of Origin**		**71**
	7.1	Background	71
	7.2	Origins of the Concept of Appellation of Origin	72
		7.2.1 The Madrid Agreement for Repression of False or Deceptive Indications of Source of Goods, 1891	72
		7.2.2 The Lisbon Agreement for the Protection of Appellations of Origin and their Registration, 1958	72
	7.3	The TRIPS and TRIPS Plus Provisions for Geographical Indications	73
		7.3.1 Limitations Under TRIPS	73
		7.3.2 Alternative Bilateral and Multilateral GI Protection	74
	7.4	Geographical Indications and Equitable Development	74
	7.5	Protection of Geographical Indications in South Asian Countries	75
		7.5.1 India	75
		7.5.2 Bangladesh	77
		7.5.3 Bhutan	77
		7.5.4 Myanmar	78
		7.5.5 Nepal	78
		7.5.6 Sri Lanka	78
		7.5.7 Thailand	78
		7.5.8 Challenges to Protection of Geographical Indication in South Asian Countries	79
	7.6	Conclusion	79
	References		80
8	**Genetically Modified Crops, Agriculture and Biosafety**		**81**
	8.1	Background	81
	8.2	The Cartagena Protocol on Biosafety	82
		8.2.1 Salient Features of the Protocol	82
	8.3	The Nagoya-Kuala Lumpur Supplementary Protocol on Liability and Redress	83

	8.4	The Global Concerns on Use of Genetically Modified Organisms in Food and Agriculture	84
	8.5	GM Crops and Biosafety in South Asian Countries	84
		8.5.1 India	84
		8.5.2 Bangladesh	86
		8.5.3 Bhutan	87
		8.5.4 Myanmar	88
		8.5.5 Nepal	88
		8.5.6 Sri Lanka	89
		8.5.7 Thailand	90
	8.6	Conclusion	91
	References		91
9	**Access to Genetic Resources and Sharing of Benefits**		**93**
	9.1	Background	93
	9.2	The Issue of Access and Benefit Sharing	93
	9.3	The Case of Ayahuasca Patent Revocation: Why Do We Need a Harmonious ABS Regime	94
	9.4	Evolution of International Protocols for ABS	95
		9.4.1 The Bonn Guidelines	95
		9.4.2 The Nagoya Protocol	96
	9.5	ABS in South Asian Countries	97
		9.5.1 India	97
		9.5.2 Bangladesh	99
		9.5.3 Bhutan	100
		9.5.4 Myanmar	102
		9.5.5 Nepal	102
		9.5.6 Sri Lanka	103
		9.5.7 Thailand	103
	9.6	Conclusion	105
	References		105
10	**Cross Country Comparisons**		**107**
	10.1	Introduction	107
	10.2	Economic Profiles of the BIMSTEC Countries	107
	10.3	Status of Accession to International Treaties	109
	10.4	Comparison of the Natural Wealth Protection Frameworks at National Levels	110
		10.4.1 Plant Variety Protection and Farmers' Rights	110
		10.4.2 Traditional and Indigenous Knowledge	112
		10.4.3 Geographical Indications	113
		10.4.4 Genetically Modified Crops	114
		10.4.5 Access to Genetic Resource and Sharing of Benefits	115

	10.5	Conclusion	116
	References		116
11	**IPR and Development in South Asia: Issues and Implications**		**119**
	11.1	Introduction	119
	11.2	Imminent Threats to Conservation	119
		11.2.1 Patterns of Land Use	120
		11.2.2 Depleting Water Resources	120
		11.2.3 Unsustainable Livelihood Practices	120
		11.2.4 Loss of Biodiversity	121
		11.2.5 Climate Change	121
	11.3	Imperatives of Regional Cooperation	121
	11.4	Key Issues for IPR-Based Development in South Asia	122
		11.4.1 The Transition from Common Heritage to Secured Wealth	122
		11.4.2 Legislation Versus Livelihood	123
		11.4.3 Safeguarding Rights of Farmers	123
		11.4.4 Loss of Plant Biodiversity	125
		11.4.5 Achieving a Balance Between Conservation and Development	125
		11.4.6 Arresting Erosion in Traditional and Community Knowledge	126
		11.4.7 The Farm–Forest Nexus	127
	11.5	Effects of Harmonization of Intellectual Property Norms and Standards	128
	11.6	Implications of the TRIPS Plus Standards	128
		11.6.1 Examples of the TRIPS Plus and the Doha Declaration	129
		11.6.2 TRIPS Plus in Plant Varieties	130
	11.7	Multilateral and Bilateral Access and Benefit-Sharing Mechanisms: Implications of a Mutually Supportive System	131
		11.7.1 The Multilateral System of ABS Under ITPGRFA	131
		11.7.2 The Bilateral System of ABS Under CBD and Nagoya Protocol	132
		11.7.3 Challenges for the Mutually Supportive System	132
		11.7.4 A Middle Path Again Through Regional Protocols?	132
	References		133
12	**The Road Ahead: Challenges and Opportunities**		**135**
	12.1	Introduction	135
	12.2	Trade and Regional Value Chains in the BIMSTEC	135

12.3	Development Priorities		136
12.4	Achieving the Priorities: Activism Versus Rationality		137
12.5	The Importance of Regional Initiatives		139
12.6	The Centrality of India's Role		140
12.7	Reforms to the TRIPS		140
12.8	International Negotiations for TRIPS Reforms		143
12.9	Revisiting the ITPGRFA: Challenges of Evolving a Multilateral Conservation System		144
	12.9.1	Interdependence of Countries on Crop Varieties	144
	12.9.2	Sustainable Use of PGR Through Conservation	145
	12.9.3	What Is the Advantage of a Multilateral System?	146
	12.9.4	Expanding Scope of the Multilateral System	146
	12.9.5	Addressing a Policy Bottleneck: Unauthorized Access Versus Legitimate Exchange of PGR	147
12.10	Regional Imbalance as a Consequence of National Laws		147
12.11	Evolving Regional IPR Protocols		148
	12.11.1	Lessons from the MERCOSUR	148
	12.11.2	Lessons from the ASEAN	149
	12.11.3	Prospects of the BIMSTEC	149
12.12	Policy Challenges for Agenda 21 Compliance		150
References			151
Appendix A: Statistical Tables and Additional Information			153
Glossary			171
Index			177

About the Author

The original version of this book was revised. The version supplied here includes correct About the Author information.

Dr. Debashis Bandyopadhyay is a molecular biologist subspecialized in intellectual property rights and has been working in the domains of S&T management, technology transfer and S&T dissemination since 2005 with institutions under Department of Science and Technology (DST) and Council of Scientific and Industrial Research (CSIR) of the Ministry of Science & Technology, Government of India. Most of his professional assignments are focused on fine-tuning institutional policies, frameworks and systems to facilitate linking R&D outcomes in laboratories to a cross section of stakeholders. His research interests cover sustainable development, public policy and IPR governance with a special focus on cross-country comparisons of various development policy frameworks, technology transfer regimes and innovation clusters. He also works on studying the implications of emerging IPR and technology transfer regimes on the developing countries from both the positive and negative perspectives.

Acronyms

ABS	Access and Benefit Sharing
AIA	Advanced Information Agreement
AO	Appellation of Origin
ARIPO	African Industrial Property Organization
ASEAN	Association of Southeast Asian Nations
ASSINSEL	International Association for Plant Breeders for Protection of Plant Varieties
BIMSTEC	Bay of Bengal Initiative for Multi-sectoral Technical and Economic Cooperation
CBD	Convention on Biological Diversity
CBM	Community Biodiversity Management
CBR	Community Biodiversity Register
CGIAR	Consultative Group for International Agricultural Research
CIR	Community Intellectual Rights
COP	Conference of Parties
EPC	European Patent Convention
FAO	Food and Agricultural Organization
FR	Farmers' Rights
FTA	Free Trade Agreement
GDP	Gross Domestic Product
GEAC	Genetic Engineering Approval Committee
GI	Geographical Indication
GM	Genetically Modified
GMO	Genetically Modified Organism
HDI	Human Development Index
IGC	Inter-Governmental Committee on Intellectual Property and Genetic Resources, Traditional Knowledge and Folklore
IK	Indigenous Knowledge
IPR	Intellectual Property Rights

ITPGRFA	International Treaty on Plant Genetic Resource for Food and Agriculture
LDC	Least Developed Country
LMO	Live Modified Organism
MERCOSUR	Mercado Comun del Sur
MFN	Most Favoured Nation
MTA	Material Transfer Agreement
NAFTA	North American Free Trade Association
NBF	National Biosafety Fund
NGO	Non-Governmental Organization
OAPI	Organization of African Industrial Property
OECD	Organization of Economic Cooperation and Development
PBR	Plant Breeder's Rights
PBR	Public Biodiversity Register
PIC	Prior Informed Consent
PVP	Plant Variety Protection
RVC	Regional Value Chain
SAARC	South Asian Association for Regional Cooperation
SAFTA	South Asian Free Trade Association
SAPTA	SAARC Preferential Trading Arrangement
SAR	South Asian Region
TK	Traditional Knowledge
TKDL	Traditional Knowledge Digital Library
TKRC	Traditional Knowledge Resource Classification
TRIPS	Trade-Related Aspects of Intellectual Property Rights
UN	United Nations
UPOV	Union Internationale pour la Protection des Obtentions Vegetales
WIPO	World Intellectual Property Organization
WTO	World Trade Organization

Chapter 1
Introduction

1.1 Background

The extensive resource-rich status of the developing countries, particularly with respect to biodiversity, makes them vulnerable to various forms of exploitation. This vulnerability and the historical trend of economic and social marginalization have made conservation one of the principal issues for these countries. Conservation issues in developing countries comprise not only initiatives for the sustenance of biodiversity in terms of flora and fauna, but also the protection of indigenous human communities, their customs, practices, folklore and traditional knowledge along with the regulation of access to the above resources.

Intellectual property rights (IPR) protection is an effective means of achieving conservation. Conservation-related IPR issues centres around protection of plant varieties, protection of life forms, protection of traditional knowledge, protection of farmers' rights, regulation of access to biological resources and equitable sharing of benefits with local communities. Nevertheless, more often than not, IPR regimes continue to remain unequivocally biased towards the interests of the developed countries and therefore need to be substantially tuned to suit the requirements and aspirations of the developing economies.

Majority of the countries are signatories and thus members of the World Trade Organization (WTO) [1]. Regulatory mechanisms under the WTO primarily centres around Trade-Related Aspects of Intellectual Property Rights (TRIPS), which happens to be the only most comprehensive framework. However, TRIPS is deficient in several aspects such as provision for protecting the indigenous or local community knowledge; or equitable sharing of benefits related to biodiversity. Provisions available under other agreements/protocols aimed towards conservation such as the Convention on Biological Diversity, Cartagena Protocol and the International Treaty on Plant Genetic Resources for Food and Agriculture are also fraught with vagaries and inconsistencies. The fundamental question thus remains as to how developing countries could device policies that incorporates conservation, sustainable use and equitable benefit sharing from natural resources while engaging in trade and economic progress.

As developing countries continue to grapple with poor IPR regimes and governance frameworks, geopolitical obligations from memberships and access to various trading agreements both regional and beyond emerge as a new challenge. Regional integration and trade agreements aim to facilitate economic growth through mutual cooperation by making use of regional resources and demographic advantages. Trade and development often rely significantly on use of natural resources, indigenous knowledge and cultural practices. Thus it is imperative that trade agreements take into consideration the conservation requirements of natural and cultural resources.

1.2 South and Southeast Asia: Trade and Cooperation

Most of the countries of South and Southeast Asia are members of the World Trade Organization that influence trade, technology transfer and materials transfer including those derived from natural resources. The region is additionally organized under multiple trade blocks through free trade agreements (FTA). Typically, there are overlaps between such blocks that make a water-tight demarcation of South and Southeast Asia impossible.

The South Asian Association for Regional Cooperation (SAARC), Bay of Bengal Initiative for Multi-Sectoral Technical and Economic Cooperation (BIMSTEC) and the Association of Southeast Asian Nations (ASEAN) are major examples. While SAARC and BIMSTEC mostly encompass South Asia, ASEAN covers south-eastern countries. Obligations under such agreements need to be appropriately dovetailed with those of conservation issues of the countries concerned. Moreover, it is essential to address conflicts of compliance and also device an effective hierarchy among the governance frameworks to determine which provision would supersede others during such conflicts. Sustainable development priorities of India and its neighbours are thus increasingly being influenced by the need to address the intertwined issues of IPR, trade and conservation. This broad ambit covers aspects such as informed access to biodiversity and equitable sharing of benefits; protection of the rights of farmers; mechanisms to safeguard traditional and community knowledge; and developing enabling policy frameworks and institutional mechanisms to achieve a coherent regime incorporating all the above parameters.

1.3 Coverage and Scope

Among the various economic blocs mentioned above, in view of the similarity in country settings and also renewed political considerations to enhance cooperation, the BIMSTEC is particularly noteworthy of attention for several reasons [2]. Firstly, the countries comprising of BIMSTEC are the home to one-fourth of the world population and witness impressive growth above 6%; however, it contributes only 4% of world GDP (BIMSTEC GDP is roughly USD 3 trillion; against approximately USD 78 trillion world GDP). Secondly, for all countries in the bloc, agriculture and natural resources are significant providers of national income thereby making these sectors important foci for targeting IPR-based conservation. Thirdly, a strong BIMSTEC group, with a coherent and mutually synergistic IPR regime, would provide a unique advantage to the region not only with respect to economic stability, but also an effective way of countering the developed country bias in the WTO.

Amidst the aforesaid backdrop, the present work envisages to enumerate the provisions and gaps vis-a-vis challenges and opportunities arising from various international agreements and treaties relating to the relevant intellectual property rights; and to evaluate the existing provisions and arrangements relating to bioprospecting, farmers' rights, plant variety protection, traditional knowledge, indigenous and community practices, etc., in India, Bangladesh, Nepal, Bhutan, Sri Lanka, Myanmar and Thailand.

1.4 Defining Natural Wealth

Natural wealth is customarily defined as the sum total of the resources of a country that is derived from nature either in its endemic form or in such forms that are modified by human. Thus, while biodiversity and forests comprise of the first component, the latter comprise of elements such as agriculture, fisheries. In whichever component we choose to focus, they constitute wealth in so far as their ability to generate economic returns and prosperity.

In the present discussion of natural wealth, we have adopted a broader view. We consider apart from the above endemic and man-made components, another component that includes human tacit knowledge usually derived from nature and handed down over generations. Such knowledge, so-called the traditional and indigenous knowledge, represents a unique canvas of a country that substantially influence livelihood. Traditional knowledge comprises of elements such as medicinal use of plants and natural products; local varieties of seeds and farming practices used in agriculture; and even traditional cultural expressions such as indigenous community practices, handicrafts and folklore.

1.5 Facets of Natural Wealth Protection

The extant rule-based approaches to protection and IPR identify some specific facets around which natural wealth in countries is sought to be protected. There are overarching treaties and conventions that provide international frameworks within which countries are obliged to create enabling legislation and policies. The former includes frameworks like Convention on Biological Diversity (CBD) [3],

Trade-Related Aspects of Intellectual Property Rights (TRIPS) [4] and so on. The latter consist of multiple legislations related to protection of plants, life forms, traditional knowledge, etc., that widely vary among countries both in terms of enactment and compliance.

As we shall discuss in course of the chapters, the countries under consideration in the present work are essentially agrarian (i.e. agriculture comprise the mainstay in their economies) and also they are hot spots of biodiversity and demographic diversity. Thus, the principal facets of natural wealth in these countries that are sought to be protected include plant varieties, biodiversity, traditional knowledge, community practices, and access to genetic resources. Concomitant to this is the need to protect farmers' rights, cultural heritage and to device policies for equitable sharing of benefits resulting from access to biodiversity and policies for genetically modified organisms. These are some of the key aspects that we shall discuss in course of this book.

1.6 The Agenda-21 for Sustainable Development

The UN Conference on Environment and Development (Earth Summit) held at Rio de Janeiro in 1992 unfurled a non-binding agenda for UN organizations, national and local governments and other multilateral organizations aimed at promoting sustainable development during the twenty-first century. Known as Agenda-21, this declaration aims to combat poverty (especially in developing countries), alter consumption patterns, promote health, achieve a more sustainable population, and promote sustainable practices to safeguard the planet [5]. The preamble of Agenda-21 highlights its salient feature as follows:

'Agenda-21 addresses the pressing problems of today and also aims at preparing the world for the challenges of the next century. It reflects a global consensus and political commitment at the highest level on development and environment cooperation. Its successful implementation is first and foremost the responsibility of Governments'

The Agenda comprises of two important components as follows:

1. Conservation and Management of Resources for Development: This includes atmospheric protection, combating deforestation, protecting fragile environments, conservation of biological diversity (biodiversity), control of pollution and the management of biotechnology, and radioactive wastes.
2. Strengthening the Role of Major Groups: This includes the roles of children and youth, women, NGOs, local authorities, business and industry, and workers; and strengthening the role of indigenous peoples, their communities, and farmers towards promotion of sustainability.

The fundamental vehicles of implementation of the provision include but not restricted to science, technology transfer, education, international institutions and financial mechanisms.

The Agenda-21 was signed and supported by 178 countries; however being a non-binding declaration, there was no obligation of the respective governments to implement provisions set out by the Agenda. We shall discuss about the Agenda-21 implications in greater details later in the book.

1.7 Evolving Integrated Solutions and Policies

The countries discussed in the present work have several commonalities and differences. They are subjected to the same governance frameworks as far as the international treaties are concerned. However, there are differences in patterns of accession and ratification to some of them. Further, as we shall see, with the exception of India, most of them are yet to evolve comprehensive internal mechanisms to address the obligations of such treaties.

It is important thus to devise integrated policies and evolve integrated solutions that suffice in protecting natural wealth of the countries.

1.8 New Vistas in South–South Cooperation

Trade and investment linkages coupled with an integrated regional intellectual property regime have the potential to play a pivotal role in south–south collaboration. Prospects of such cooperation in South Asia are large for several reasons. Firstly, all the countries are experiencing robust economic growth and thus have a vibrant market value chain. Secondly, there are complementary national priorities and geopolitical considerations that can be effectively leveraged (e.g. the Look East policy of India vis-a-vis Look West policy of Thailand). Thirdly, given the geographical proximity, there is a larger scope of people–people contact to leverage synergies. Fourthly, some countries such as India or Thailand have developed institutional frameworks to build capacities that can be used by other countries to jump-start their own skills and capabilities. Taken together, the regional blocs suffice in significantly bolstering economic growth through technology transfer, capacity building and technical cooperation.

1.9 Structure of the Book

The book broadly deals with the subject in three parts. The first part takes a look at the historical development of intellectual property regimes, explores the various frameworks and treaties, and finally takes a look at some of them in the light of food security, conservation and development policy. In the second part, we explore the five major facets of IPRs that are instrumental in protecting natural wealth, namely plant variety protection, protection of traditional knowledge, protection of geographical indications, regulation of genetically modified crops and finally frameworks for regulating access to genetic resources. Legislative instruments, policy frameworks and challenges in implementation for each of the above are discussed for individual countries. In the third and final part, we take an integrative viewpoint. We make a cross-country comparison of the various instruments and discuss the key issues concerning IPR in the development of South Asia and finally policy alternatives that could spur sustainable development of the region.

1.10 Epilogue

In the present work, we have avoided providing detailed analysis and comprehensive review of the literature available in the domain. It is intended to be a broad discussion that might facilitate policy dialogues at greater depths.

References

1. World Trade Organisation, Geneva (2017). http://www.wto.org. Accessed 25 Sept 2017
2. Bay of Bengal Initiative for Multi-sectoral Technical and Economic Cooperation (2004). http://bimstec.org. Accessed 25 Sept 2017
3. Convention for Biological Diversity, Statute of Convention of Biological Diversity, Annex-I (1992). http://www.cbd.int. Accessed 25 Sept 2017
4. Trade Related Aspects of Intellectual Property Rights (1992). http://www.wto.org/english/tratop_e/trips_e.htm. Accessed 25 Sept 2017
5. Agenda-21: Sustainable Development Knowledge Platform (1992). https://sustainabledevelopment.un.org/outcomedocuments/agenda21. Accessed 08 Oct 2017

Chapter 2
Emergence of IPR Regimes and Governance Frameworks

2.1 Overview

The origin of an international regime to protect intellectual property dates back to the Industrial Revolution during the latter half of the eighteenth century. With a massive increase in the types of manufacturing techniques and industrial products along with concomitant export and trade, the commercial and cultural relations between countries were on a rise. Such interaction necessitated development of a more organized structure to deal with the modalities of such interactions and to protect the intellectual labour that went into the development of such products and processes. As time progressed, the concept of intellectual property became closely associated with a means to protect the creations of mind and human innovation. Technology became linked with development paradigms. More industrial, public and private players began to invest in technology development and used this intellectual property protection as a means to reap the benefits of the investment. Needless to say, the balance of technology providers and users was unequivocally tilted towards the developed countries.

Thus, while on one side globalization opened up free trade and seamless movement of knowledge across the world, protectionist IPR regimes imposed a restriction on trans-boundary movement of technology. One of the most significant impacts of such a scenario was a new form of exclusion that widened the rift between developing and developed countries.

Against the above backdrop emerged the new rule-based trading system that sought to balance the rights of the technology developers with obligations of the users and vice versa. However, much ground needed to be covered to make the system equitable and aligned with the global development needs.

2.2 Evolution of IPR Regimes

2.2.1 The Paris Convention

The need for protecting foreign inventors in a country was voiced during the Vienna International Exposition in 1873. The Vienna Congress, which formed part of this exposition, resolved to put in place a mechanism to accord legal protection for intellectual pursuits. A series of conferences were held in Paris during 1878, 1880 and 1883 that culminated with the Paris Convention for the Protection of Industrial Property (March 1883). The Convention came into force in 1884 with 14 signatory states. Currently, 186 states are contracting parties to the Paris Convention. Paris Convention was the first attempt to establish a trans-national common platform for evolving a common intellectual property protection practice. Prior to this, protection in different countries was a matter of compliance with individual national requirements [1].

2.2.2 The Berne Convention

Following the Paris Convention, the field of literary and artistic works was also sought to be protected. This was formulated through a series of conferences in 1858, 1878, 1883 and 1884. It eventually culminated in the Berne Convention of 1886 with adoption of the first international copyright treaty in the world. The Berne Convention for the Protection of Literary and Artistic Works (September, 1886) became effective in 1887 with nine signatory countries. Today, 157 states are contracting parties in the Berne Convention [1].

The Paris Convention (through Article 19) and the Berne Convention (through Article 20) have in course of time evolved into the primary legal basis of all subsequent multilateral intellectual property treaties.

2.2.3 Categories of Multilateral Industrial Property Treaties

Rapid institutionalization of global IPR regimes saw evolution of multilateral treaties. We have three principal categories of multilateral treaties as follows:

1. Treaties providing ad hoc forms of protection: examples in this category include Madrid Agreement, Budapest Treaty, Nairobi Treaty.
2. Treaties that establish classification systems: examples in this category include Nice Agreement, Strassborg Agreement, Vienna Agreement.
3. Treaties providing a procedure for the grant of industrial property rights in multiple countries: examples in this category include Hague Agreement, Lisbon Agreement, Patent Cooperation Treaty.

2.2.4 Regional Industrial Property Treaties

The latter part of the twentieth century witnessed an attempt to evolve intellectual property protection systems that were common to a group of countries. This culminated in regional networks that spread across Africa, North America, South America, Europe and Asia. In this context, the following regional set-ups were established [2]:

2.2.4.1 Africa

The relevant provisions include Bangui Agreement on the creation of an African Intellectual Property Organization (OAPI) in 1977 linking the French-speaking countries; and Agreement on the Creation of African Industrial Property Organization (ARIPO) in 1976 linking the English-speaking countries

2.2.4.2 Eurasia

It includes the European Patent Convention (1994) set up as an interstate system for the protection of inventions and the Agreement on the Measures for the Prevention and Repression of the Use of False Trade Marks and Geographical Indications (1999)

2.2.4.3 North America

It includes the North America Free Trade Agreement (NAFTA) in 1992 between Canada, USA and Mexico to liberalize investments.

2.2.4.4 South America

It includes the Andean Subregional Integration Agreement (Cartagena Agreement) in 1969 that links Bolivia, Colombia, Ecuador, Peru and Venezuela.

Additionally there is the Protocol for Harmonization of Intellectual Property Provisions (1995) within the MERCOSUR, linking Argentina, Brazil, Paraguay and Uruguay

2.2.4.5 Europe

It includes the European Patent Convention (1973) providing an uniform procedure for the filing of patent applications and for the grant of patents in one or more member states. Council Regulation on Community Trade Marks (1993)

2.2.5 World Trade Organization and the TRIPS Agreement

In the backdrop of the above diverse set up of the international intellectual property regimes, the World Trade Organization (WTO) was established in 1994 under the Marrakesh Agreement [3]. The Agreement on Trade-Related Aspects of Intellectual Property Rights (TRIPS) was formulated as an annex of the Marrakesh Agreement, which has assumed integral importance in the current intellectual property scenario. The TRIPS was the maiden global initiative to protect intellectual property rights. It also integrated into a single instrument the basic tenets of a number of existing multilateral treaties about the protection of intellectual property rights. TRIPS provides the minimum standard of protection within the broader ambit of trade and commercial relation among the member states [4].

2.3 Governance Frameworks for IPR Protection of Life Forms

Life forms have become a subject of intellectual property protection. These essentially cover micro-organisms, genetically modified organisms (GMOs) and plant varieties. Although the Agreement on Trade-related Aspects of Intellectual Property Rights (TRIPS) of the World Trade Organisation (WTO) provides for a general exclusion to patentability of life forms (except micro-organisms), the same Agreement also provides for the protection of new plant varieties through patents or an effective *sui generis* system or a combination of the two. In the light of this rather controversial setting, IPR regimes with respect to life forms are governed by a number of national and international frameworks. Lack of clear definitions of the basic tenets of the protection regimes has resulted in most of the matters being left open to interpretation and subject to the laws of the respective countries. Cases concerning protection of life forms have therefore been interpreted and resolved differently in different jurisdictions and countries. In the section below, we discuss the salient features of governance frameworks of the various treaties/legislations that have implications in protection of life forms.

2.3.1 Trade-Related Aspects of Intellectual Property Rights (TRIPS)

The Trade-Related Aspects of Intellectual Property Rights (TRIPS) constitutes Annex-1C of the Marrakesh Agreement establishing the World Trade Organization (WTO). The negotiations for the establishment of TRIPS began with the Uruguay Round of the GATT and were essentially in response to the US complaint that America was losing out on royalties of its products as a result of poor IP frameworks in

2.3 Governance Frameworks for IPR Protection of Life Forms

the developing countries. It represents a minimum standard agreement as it sets out the minimum protection that must be given for each category of intellectual property rights in the national law of each WTO member country. The countries were left with their own choice of determining the appropriate method of implementation of the Agreement. The Agreement also lays down the procedures and remedies to be provided by each country for intellectual property rights enforcement. It reaffirms the practice of national treatment which means that the nationals of any member country would be treated in the same way as nationals of the country where protection is granted. The TRIPS Agreement comprises of 73 articles in seven parts [4]. The parts include:

1. General provisions and basic principles
2. Scope and use of intellectual property rights
3. Enforcement of intellectual property rights
4. Acquisition and maintenance of intellectual property rights
5. Dispute prevention and settlement
6. Transitional arrangement
7. Institutional arrangements and final provisions

The agreement focuses on the specific areas of intellectual property rights like copyrights, trademarks, geographical indications, patents, layout designs, trade secrets and anti-competitive practices. Protection of geographical indications has become mandatory under this Agreement, and also, there has been a change in the scope of non-patentable inventions.

With regard to biotechnology and life forms, the complexity of the issues has resulted in divided opinion among the member countries. The Agreement provides only a transitional arrangement that would be reviewed four years after entry.

2.3.2 Convention on Biological Diversity (CBD)

The Convention on Biological Diversity (CBD) was acceded to in 1992 during the Rio Summit and comprises one of the major umbrella conventions for the protection of natural heritage of the world [5]. The objectives of CBD are stated in Article-1 as:

'the conservation of biological diversity, the sustainable use of its components and the fair and equitable sharing of the benefits arising out of the utilization of genetic resources, including by appropriate access to the generic resources and by appropriate transfer of the relevant technologies, taking into account all rights over those resources and to technologies, and by appropriate funding.'

As per terms of reference of the convention, biological resources include genetic resources, organisms or parts thereof, populations or any other biotic components of the ecosystems with actual or potential use or value for humanity. CBD has in all 42 articles, of which seven are of particular relevance as instruments of the intellectual property regimes. These include:

Article 6:   General measures for conservation and sustainable use
Article 8:   In situ conservation
Article 9:   Ex situ conservation
Article 10:   Sustainable use of the components of biological diversity
Article 15:   Access to genetic resources
Article 16:   Access to and transfer of technology
Article 22:   Relationship with other international conventions

It might be pertinent to discuss some of the key features of the above articles:

In situ Conservation:

Article 8 of the CBD advocates protection of natural habitats and ecosystems to conserve the diversity of plants, animals and micro-organisms contained therein so that a viable population of species can be maintained. This is also supplemented by promotion of environmentally sustainable practices of regulation, management and risk reduction in the use of live modified organisms (LMOs) as a result of biotechnology. The article also has provision for conservation of indigenous knowledge and practices of local communities. Thus, traditional lifestyle and innovations relevant to conserving biological diversity are protected.

Ex situ Conservation:

Article 9 of the CBD envisages to complement the in situ practices with appropriate ex situ approaches where components of biological diversity are preserved preferably in country of origin. As per the provisions, contracting parties adopt measures to recover and rehabilitate threatened species with an objective of reintroducing them into their natural habitats. The approach also results in maintenance of a gene pool that might be useful in recovering the germplasm in event of some calamity.

Access to Genetic Resources:

CBD enhances the sovereign rights of the contracting parties by authorizing the national governments to frame national level legislation to govern access to the country's genetic resources. Such an access would be subject to prior informed consent and a fair and equitable sharing of benefits by putting in place an appropriate financial mechanism.

2.3.3 Cartagena Protocol

The Cartagena Protocol for Biosafety evolved as an annex to the CBD in accordance with the precautionary approach contained in Principle-15 of the Rio Declaration on Environment and Development [6]. The objective of this protocol is:

'*to contribute to ensuring an adequate level of protection in the field of safe transfer, handling and use of live modified organism resulting from modern biotechnologies that may have adverse effects on the conservation and sustainable use of biological diversity, taking also into account risks to human health, and specifically focusing on trans-boundary movements.'*

Biosafety is one of the major issues that arise out of the development and use of live modified organisms in food and agriculture (including new varieties of plants and crops). The Cartagena Protocol, with its provision for regulating trans-boundary movement, controls the process of intentional introduction to the environment that is effected through an advance informed agreement procedure. The parties are obliged to take appropriate measures in case of any release that might lead to an unintentional trans-boundary movement of live modified organisms. The Protocol lays adequate emphasis on the socio-economic considerations, especially with regard to the value of biological diversity to the indigenous and local communities.

Being one of the pivotal frameworks regulating the trans-boundary movement of GM products, the Cartagena Protocol is one of the major collateral instruments that govern the life form protection regimes, where movement, containment and use of LMOs constitute essential features.

2.3.4 International Treaty on Plant Genetic Resources for Food and Agriculture (ITPGRFA)

The need was felt for having a framework that would serve as an enabler of national provisions that would facilitate access to in situ plant genetic resources and associated sharing of benefits. As such, there was evolution of a multilateral system that covered 35 crop genera and 29 forage species. This treaty known as the International Treaty on Plant Genetic Resources for Food and Agriculture was adopted in Rome during 2001 and came into force in June 2004. The ITPGRFA also provides intellectual property protection of the communities concerned [7].

Debates and deliberations in the FAO underpinned the fact that there existed a definite dichotomy between intellectual property rights that was provided to breeders and farmers. Interestingly, although most of the breeders varieties were derived from those that were initially produced by farmers, it was the former who had an edge in the protection regime. The unequivocal contribution of farmers in supplying plant genetic resources was appreciated, and thus, need was felt to accord appropriate farmers' rights as an intellectual property right to correct this imbalance. The basic doctrine of this protection was incorporated in Article 9 of the ITPGRFA that encourage countries to protect farmers' rights. Such rights also included protection of traditional knowledge and participation in the decision making process for equitable sharing of benefits, improvements in conservation and sustainable use of the resources.

As the contribution of local communities and farmers in conservation and development of plant genetic resources has been adequately recognized under the ITPGRFA, the treaty contends that subject to national legislation, each country would take appropriate measures to achieve the following:

a. Protection of traditional knowledge relevant to plant genetic resources for food and agriculture;
b. The right to equitably participate in sharing benefits arising from the utilization of plant genetic resources for food and agriculture;
c. The right to participate in making decisions, at national level, on matters related to the conservation and sustainable use of plant genetic resources for food and agriculture.

In this connection, it is pertinent to mention that none of the above farmers' rights provisions under ITPGRFA shall be interpreted to limit any rights that farmers have to save, use, exchange and sell farm-saved seed/propagating material, subject to national law and as appropriate.

ITPGRFA also keeps an open-ended issue in terms of germplasm that are held in CGIAR depositories and other international organizations and do not form part of the treaty. As per extant arrangement, they are held in trust for the originating countries. Nevertheless, should the CGIAR or the organizations wish to enter into agreements with third parties in terms of IPR for products developed from such germplasm, they are likely to lead to important ownership dilemmas and issues.

2.3.5 International Union for Protection of New Plant Varieties (UPOV)

The International Union for the Protection of New Varieties of Plants (UPOV) is envisaged to provide an effective *sui generis* mechanism for plant variety protection. The objective of UPOV is to encourage development of new varieties of plants for the benefit of the society. UPOV represents an inter-governmental organization that was adopted in Paris in 1961 and subsequently revised in 1972, 1978 and 1991 [8]. However, as we shall see later in the discussion, provision under the UPOV is highly biased towards the interests of developed countries that has been a major impediment in its adoption as an effective *sui generis* system by the developing world. The various versions of UPOV along with their salient features are as follows

UPOV-61:

A patent or a special title was the two different ways of granting breeders rights that was allowed to member states under the UPOV 1961. Technically, a state was allowed to use both; however, for a given genera or species only one of them could be used. UPOV 61 was intended to be complied with in a phased manner and eventually covering all genera of plants. Five genera were to be chosen during joining; two more added over three years; four more within another three years; and inclusion of all genera within another two years (i.e. eight years in total). Protection and commercial marketing of reproductive materials and the new variety would require prior authorization from the breeder, and the rights of breeders were also extended to ornamental plants or its parts thereof. UPOV 61-based protection has a duration of 18 years for vines, fruit trees (including root stocks), and 15 years for all other varieties of plants.

UPOV-78:

UPOV 78 sought to expand the scope of protection of plant varieties to cover even those that were discovered, unlike patents that could be granted only when there was an inventive step involved. Any variety that was new; distinct from other varieties in common knowledge; homogeneous; and relatively stable in their essential characters qualified for protection under UPOV 78. Inclusion of varieties was also in a phased manner like the UPOV 61 with five genera to begin with at the time of joining; ten genera within another three years; eighteen genera within another three years; and twenty-four genera within a total of eight years. Provisions under Article 4 also allowed reduction in the number of genera to be complied with in case of countries that experience any special economic or ecological condition that would make such inclusions untenable. This provision was by far the biggest difference UPOV 78 introduced over UPOV 61 that addressed some of the concerns of developing countries by providing flexibility in compliance and moving the framework significantly away from the interests of European countries.

UPOV-91:

UPOV 1991 strengthened the breeders rights even further. Coverage of varieties that qualified protection, nature of breeders rights and rights over essentially derived varieties were significantly different under UPOV 91 from previous versions of the convention. UPOV 91 advocated a more comprehensive coverage of varieties although not immediately. New members are, however, obliged to protect 15 genera or species on accession and include all genera and species within a period of 10 years [9].

2.3.6 Budapest Treaty

The Budapest Treaty on the International Recognition of the Deposit of Microorganism (1980) was a special agreement under the Paris Union and administered under the International Bureau of WIPO [10]. Fundamental to the patent law is the requirement of a disclosure of an invention sufficient to enable one skilled in the field to reproduce the same. Normally, such a disclosure is a written one. However, in case of micro-organisms, this is implemented with deposit of a sample of the concerned microorganism with a specialized institution. Budapest Treaty provides for this deposition in any International Depository Authority, rather than each individual country. The Treaty increases the security of the depository because it would be a uniform system of deposit, recognized and furnished of a sample of microorganism.

2.3.7 Lisbon Agreement for Appellation of Origin

The Lisbon Agreement concerns protection of the appellations of origins and their international registration [11]. Appellations of origin cover the geographical names of a country, region or locality which serves to designate a product originating therein, the quality and characteristics of which are due exclusively or essentially to the geographical environment, including natural and human factors. The Protocol requires the contracting parties to protect the appellations of origins of other contracting parties recognized and protected in the country of origin. Appellations of origin encompass life forms as well as non-living products that belong to a particular geographical region. Its association with life forms makes the Lisbon Agreement an important collateral instrument.

2.4 Major Issues of Protection

Intellectual property protection regimes concerning life forms continue to remain rather ill-defined in the context of the existing frameworks. The provisions of the TRIPS are far from being equitable, and this has resulted in a significant imbalance of the concepts and mechanisms contained therein. Member countries of the WTO are therefore faced with unacceptable scenarios during the implementation process that are often difficult to resolve within the ambit of TRIPS [12]. Some of the key issues underlying the intellectual property protection of life forms are as follows:

1. There is no basis for distinguishing between plants and animals (that come under exclusion under the patent laws) and micro-organisms (that are patentable under the same laws).
2. The same discrepancy holds true while distinguishing essentially biological processes from microbiological processes.
3. This apart, plants/animals/micro-organisms are components of nature and therefore ideally represent discovery rather than invention. Thus, the rationale of granting patent for the same remains debatable.

2.4 Major Issues of Protection   17

4. As plants are not patentable, there seems to be no basis for the requirement of mandatory IPR protection of plant varieties.
5. TRIPS do not define the meaning of an effective *sui generis* system. No provisions exist under the Agreement for protecting farmers' rights and the rights of local communities.

2.5 Protection vis-a-vis Access

Genetic engineering applications have caused this trend to progressively shift towards a scenario where the majority of biological resources be it natural or man-made are faced with a regime of exhaustive intellectual property protection. Allowing such trends to continue, we might arrive at a point where the entire biological world with all biodiversity slips into the domain of proprietary knowledge. This would be a completely contrasting scenario to that of a world where no biological material is protected, i.e. everything relating to plants, animals, micro-organisms remains part of the public domain that could be used by one and all. It is thus interesting to envision an everything protected versus nothing protected biological world.

Possible fall-out of a 'no protection of life forms' system

This would be the same from where we began. Biological resources, plant and animal varieties, etc., would comprise part of the public domain that could be used by one and all. This would lead to the scenario which triggered the signing of the Rio Declaration that all natural resources irrespective of their region of location represents common heritage of mankind. Developed countries, powered by their technological prowess, easy access to far-off countries and an open system, would rapidly take control over the entire biological domain. As there would be no instrument for the developing countries to protect their natural heritage, traditional knowledge or local products, there would be extensive biopiracy and cultural piracy (interestingly we would not be able to dub it as piracy as it would represent public property!!). The large population diversity of the developing countries, which reflects enormous genetic diversity and gene polymorphisms, would be indiscriminately used to isolate and identify new disease genes and new generation of genomic medicines, without any recognition given to the local populations. Drugs generated thus would nevertheless remain out of the economic reach of the people of the developing countries as there would be no provision for compulsory licensing of public health care products (which is provided by the patent system). It would thus be a re-run that would resemble the era of colonization that had impoverished Asia, Africa and Latin America.

Possible fall-out of a 'complete protection of life forms' system

In this type of a system, the entire gamut of biological knowledge would become a part of the protected domain. Thus, all plant varieties of medicinal plants and specialty crop plants would be under protection. The seed sector would be completely formal.

As the strength of the intellectual property protection systems of the developing countries would continue to remain weak and subject to bilateral agreements with different developed countries, the latter would largely control the sector through assignment of rights, compulsory licensing and sharing of resources. Agricultural costs would increase because of royalties to be paid to the breeders and the total number of endemic varieties would diminish, as the farmers would be forced to cultivate only the specified high-yielding or specific-quality varieties. High cost of medical research as a result of use of patented micro-organisms and model animals would result in a manifold increase in economic externalities associated with R&D, particularly in the developing countries. The world would experience alarming ethical and moral conflicts as critical factors such as human genome information and cell lines would pass onto the proprietary domain.

2.6 The Middle Path: Achieving a Balance in Intellectual Property Protection and Public Access

The scenarios discussed above are largely under idealized conditions unlikely to be operative in the global settings. Practically, it seems that the current regimes would eventually lead to a situation where there would be substantial intellectual property protection in the domain of life forms that would be substantially biased towards the developed countries. The developing countries would experience large difficulties in compliance that would eventually result in large erosion of natural and cultural heritage.

Nevertheless, as evident from the discussion above, intellectual property regimes are of particular relevance to the developing economies to safeguard their knowledge capital and natural resources. It would thus be imperative that the global intellectual property scenario should be made to undergo a change to adequately accommodate the interests of the developing countries. Arguably, this would require major changes to be implemented.

Some scholars feel that one of the options is to scrap TRIPS altogether and replace it with an instrument that is more balanced towards the trade needs of the developed countries and the conservation needs of the developing countries. At least what might be settled for is incorporation of some radical changes in the TRIPS. Further, the numerous bilateral agreements that exist under the TRIPS could be done away altogether as most of these provide for protection that is far in excess of what TRIPS mandates for.

It is also felt that establishment of primacy of CBD over TRIPS through international negotiations would address the issues of safeguarding the biodiversity of developing countries. Article-22 of the CBD states,

'The provisions of this Convention shall not affect the rights and obligations of any Contracting Party deriving from any existing international agreement, except

where the exercise of those rights and obligations would cause a serious damage or threat to biological diversity.'

It is clear that the implementation of the provisions of the TRIPS would be detrimental to the biological diversity; as such, the primacy of the CBD needs to be invoked.

2.7 Conclusion

The global IPR regimes thus underwent a progressive evolution from the Paris Convention and Berne Convention. In the process, it had transformed from a purely industrial property instrument to an instrument that safeguards several other facets of intellectual creations that have an implication on trade. Multiple governance frameworks emerged to cover international regimes encompassing trade, biodiversity, plant varieties, appellations of origin, protection of micro-organisms and so on. Through provisions of achieving a balance between protection and access, such IPR regimes shaped the global scenarios as we see it today.

References

1. Myeneni S (2001) Laws of Intellectual Property. Asia Law House, Hyderabad
2. Ilardi A (2005) Origin and development of international protection of intellectual property. St Peters College, Oxford
3. World Trade Organisation, Geneva (2017). http://www.wto.int. Accessed 25 Sept 2017
4. Trade Related Aspects of Intellectual Property Rights, World Trade Organisation, Geneva (1992). http://www.wto.int/TRIPS. Accessed 25 Sept 2017
5. Convention for Biological Diversity, Statute of Convention of Biological Diversity Annex I (1992). http://www.cbd.int. Accessed 25 Sept 2017
6. Cartagena Protocol on Biosafety, Annex to the Convention of Biological Diversity (2006). http://www.cbd.int/cartagena. Accessed 25 Sept 2017
7. International Treaty on Plant Genetic Resources for Food and Agriculture, Food and Agricultural Organization, Rome (2017). http://www.fao.org. Accessed 25 Sept 2017
8. International Convention for the Protection of New Plant Varieties (1961) UPOV. http://www.upov.int/upovlex/en/upov_convention. Accessed 25 Oct 2017
9. Adhikari R, Adhikari K (2003) UPOV: Faulty agreement and coercive practices. SAWTEE Policy Brief No 05
10. Budapest Treaty on the International Recognition of the Deposit of Microorganisms for the purposes of patent procedure (1977) WIPO. http://www.wipo.int/treaties/en/registration/budapest/. Accessed 25 Oct 2017
11. The Lisbon Agreement for the protection of appellations of origin and their registration (1958) WIPO. http://www.wipo.int/treaties/en/registration/lisbon/. Accessed 25 Sept 2017
12. Watal J (2001) Intellectual property rights in the WTO and developing countries. Oxford University Press, New Delhi

Chapter 3
TRIPS, CBD and Developing Countries: Implications on Food Security and Conservation

3.1 Overview

The ambit and coverage of intellectual property evolved steadily since its inception during the Paris Convention. It transformed as an instrument for protecting industrial property to one that provides protection to innovations. Soon, intellectual property rights emerged as principal drivers of technology development, transfer and use. During the latter part of the last century, advent of biotechnology and genetic engineering saw intellectual property rights being applied to living organisms.

The scope of intellectual property protection of life forms covers micro-organisms, genetically modified organisms/plants and plant varieties. The right of property flows from the concept of ownership. Its possession and value depend on the knowledge of use associated with it. Increased knowledge about life forms and the advent of biotechnology has led to an era where mankind is capable of modifying and tinkering with living systems. As such, there has been creation of new organisms and new forms of life that hitherto did not exist in nature. Associated with this emerged the concept of proprietary right over these life forms in terms of the product, the process, the protocol or the combination thereof.

Natural resources were for long, considered to constitute public property that was jointly held and nurtured by communities. Such property is increasingly being converted into private and proprietary property, thereby requiring its protection for the benefit of the local communities. However, the intellectual property regimes seem to be extremely inadequate and undefined with respect to life forms. As such, vagaries and conceptual differences in the instruments underlying such protection abounds.

TRIPS sets out the minimum standards that countries are mandated to provide in the newly evolved global intellectual property regimes. As we have seen in the previous chapter, there is however a significant crosstalk with other frameworks especially when it comes to protection of natural resources and life forms.

The TRIPS and Convention on Biological Diversity (CBD) with mutually conflicting approaches are now shaping the domestic regimes of member states with respect to biological resources. While the TRIPS provides for allowing patents on biological materials and associated indigenous knowledge, the CBD acknowledges that local communities have rights over bioresources and indigenous knowledge, which implies that it belongs to the public domain and hence must be excluded from the intellectual property right protection. This dichotomy is at the heart of all the debates and discourses being held on the subject.

3.2 Agriculture and Food Security

The inclusion of agriculture and agricultural practices within the ambit of intellectual property rights has a far-reaching implication. While on one hand it has direct effect on food security, on the other hand it also provides the impetus to the private sector to invest and innovate in technologies to enhance crop yield. Developing countries, where agriculture continues to be the mainstay of the economy, are particularly sensitive to the enforcement of such IPR regimes.

Traditionally, adherence to an open system was considered conducive to food security. Access to food, access to seeds and other attributes of agricultural production without restrictions keep costs low thereby making food crops universally available and affordable. In contrast, proprietary systems through enforcement of IPRs would push up costs and make crops limited to access by a large section of population. This in turn would have deleterious implication on food security.

Proponents of agricultural IPR argue that adequate protection to seeds and plant varieties would ensure availability of better quality of crops, e.g. those with special disease-resistant traits; higher nutritional values; high-yielding varieties; and so on. Large scale adoption of such varieties, according to such proponents, would enhance crop yield and farmer income.

During the past three decades, explosive increase in knowledge and application of agro-biotechnology has permeated intellectual property rights into the very roots of the agricultural sector. A vast majority of crops are products of genetic engineering. Improvements that can be brought about by agro-biotechnology include plant varieties that produce higher yields; varieties that have the capacity to combat pests and varieties modified to grow faster through enhanced efficiency in the use of inputs such as fertilizers, pesticides and water. From a food security point of view, another potentially revolutionary feature of agro-biotechnology is the possibility to modify varieties to improve their nutritional value, such as in the case of the pro-vitamin A rice.

Notwithstanding the potential benefits stated above, introduction of IPRs in agriculture raises major concerns for developing countries. The primary contention is about the farmer's control of their resources and knowledge, and their freedom of planting, saving and re-planting seeds that have their origins in proprietary technologies. Majority of existing agricultural products have evolved through selection and collection of endemically growing species called landraces. Introduction of IPRs has tended to obliterate and replace landraces by the protected varieties which are superior in their qualities of yield and value. Such displacements lead to homogenization of agricultural fields leading to severe loss of biodiversity, along with its centuries-old community knowledge and practices. As the world struggles to strike a balance between necessity to grow more food using less resources vis-a-vis obligations to conserve biodiversity and traditional practices, the debate on protection versus public access assumes pivotal importance. We shall discuss in greater details about the policy implications of IPR and food security later in the book.

3.3 Biodiversity and Conservation

The developing countries including those in South Asia are rich in biodiversity, with several mega-diverse hot spots falling within their ambit. The forest and mountainous regions of South Asian countries abound in flora and fauna that produce a very large number of medicinal and aromatic plants; several varieties of crop plants, e.g. tea, spices and fruits; and in addition more than 100 varieties of rice. This is supplemented with a wealth of traditional and indigenous knowledge of the numerous commercial uses of these products; farming practices; and traditional cultural expressions. Conservation issues in these countries thus comprise not only initiatives in the sustenance of this vast spectrum of biodiversity but also the protection of associated indigenous human communities, their customs, folklore and traditional knowledge along with the regulation of access to the above resources.

Instances of biopiracy and patenting of products derived from indigenously occurring natural resources abound in the patent literature. Some notable examples include patenting of the healing property of turmeric (US Patent 5,401,504); patent for the ayahuasca vine of the Amazon forests (US Patent 5,751); patent on the crop variety of Basmati (US Patent 5,663,484); patent on the cell line derived from the Hagahai tribesmen of Papua New Guinea (US Patent 5,397,696) and many more. The challenge before the developing countries thus is to ensure exhaustive documentation of its natural heritage and device ample legislative frameworks to enable intellectual property rights protection and thereby conservation.

Intellectual property rights (IPR) protection could provide with one of the effective means of achieving conservation. Conservation-related IPR issues happen to centre around four major foci. These include protection of plant varieties, protection of traditional knowledge, and regulation of access to biological resources and equitable sharing of benefits. Nevertheless, more often than not, IPR regimes continue to remain unequivocally biased towards the interests of the developed north and therefore needs to be substantially modified so as to suit the requirements and aspirations of the developing economies. Kothari and Anuradha (1997) [1] have identified three important ways in which the misuse of IPR regimes could detrimentally affect the developing countries. These include:

1. Industrial countries exploiting the resource-rich economically poor countries;
2. Intensification of the trend to homogenize agricultural production through promotion of new protected varieties, thereby damaging the indigenous varieties; and
3. Enforcing species-wide IPRs as in the case of soya bean and cotton.

Ironically, enforcement of IPRs through strong regimes structured in tune with their own interests happens to be the only effective way of prevention of IPR misuse and misappropriation.

3.4 Traditional Knowledge, Indigenous Knowledge and Traditional Cultural Expressions

Developing countries in Asia, Africa and Latin America are seats of historical civilizations rich in their own culture, tradition and practices. The World Intellectual Property Organization established the Intergovernmental Committee on Intellectual Property and Genetic Resources, Traditional Knowledge and Folklore (IGC) in 2000 and in 2009 proceeded to develop legal instruments to bestow traditional knowledge, genetic resources and folklore (traditional cultural expressions) appropriate protection under intellectual property regimes.

Present intellectual property regimes including patents provide for protection of original works and inventions by named individuals for a limited period of time. Traditional knowledge, indigenous knowledge and folklore in contrast are often held by communities, passed on from generation to generation through oral transmission and most often are not documented. Thus, current systems of IPR protection are inadequate to protect such expressions. It is thus imperative to devise methods to accord protection to such practices so as to enable the concerned communities to control and benefit through commercial exploitation of such knowledge and also safeguard against its misappropriation. The Ayahuasca vine episode of the Amazon is a glaring example of how misappropriated traditional knowledge can lead to extraordinary harm to local communities in developing countries. Further, when local communities innovate within a traditional knowledge/indigenous knowledge framework, the new inventions can be protected through patents. Thus, it is important to inculcate a new international legal framework to support such initiatives.

Traditional cultural expressions or folklore also constitute integral part of cultural diversity and social identities of indigenous communities. Protecting folklore promotes economic development, preserves cultural heritage and encourages cultural diversity. While geographical indications, appellation of origin, trademarks and certification marks under the existing IPR systems are often used to protect such expressions, it is imperative to devise frameworks beyond these to enable a more comprehensive and equitable protection regime.

3.5 The Enigma of Article 27.3(b) of the TRIPS

Article 27.3 (b) in the TRIPS Agreement provides for the products that can be excluded from patentability by the member countries and by far comprise of possibly the most controversial clauses of the WTO [2]. It states:

'Members shall exclude from patentability plants and animals other than microorganisms and essentially biological processes for the production of plants or animals other than non-biological and microbiological processes. However, Members shall provide for the protection of plant varieties either by patents or by an effective sui generis system or by any combination thereof. The provisions of this subparagraph shall be reviewed four years after the date of entry into force of the WTO Agreement'

It is thus left for the contracting parties to judge what is to be considered as an essentially biological process; what should be the separating line between a plant and a plant variety; and what should constitute an effective *sui generis* system. As we shall see later in this book, these three contentions have fuelled most of the biases that have increasingly divided developed and developing countries.

3.6 Plant Variety Protection and Biodiversity: Biased Stand of the TRIPS

The TRIPS framework covering bioresources is against the interests of indigenous communities and the farmer-centric agriculture sector that characterizes developing countries [3]. It does not provide any recognition to local communities and their rights over bioresources and associated knowledge. It fails to acknowledge farmers' rights that are expressly provided by the CBD and ITPGRFA. It does not have any provision for ensuring benefit sharing from technology and innovation or require prior informed consent of the people whose knowledge is tapped for technological innovation. Patents on seeds and varieties would take away the indigenous communities rights to breed and propagate their locally adapted varieties for food, healing and rituals. The TRIPS do not have any obligation to divulge the source from which a variety is derived, and therefore, there is no safeguard against biopiracy.

It has often been felt that provision of information and disclosure of source of biological resources (including country of origin) should form an essential prerequisite for any patent application if biological materials are used. Moreover, there should be satisfactory evidence of provision for prior informed consent and equitable sharing of benefits in the respective national laws. Several countries like India, Brazil, China, Cuba, Dominican Republic, Ecuador, Pakistan, Thailand, Venezuela, Zambia and Zimbabwe have urged the TRIPS Council to include additional clauses in the Agreement.

3.7 Options Under the CBD

The Convention on Biological Diversity (CBD) is by far the most important instrument addressing the issue of IPR and conservation. Three articles under the CBD are of particular relevance with respect to IPRs [4].

Article 8(j): protection of traditional and local knowledge relating to conservation of biodiversity

Article 16.5: cooperation of contracting parties to ensure that IPRs are *'supportive of and do not run counter to its (CBDs) objectives'*

Article 22: provisions laid down in the CBD *'will not affect the rights and obligations of countries to other international agreements, except where the exercise of those rights and obligations would cause a serious prejudice to environment'*.

3.8 Options Under a *Sui generis* System

Article 27.3 provides for signatory countries to adopt an effective *sui generis* system for protecting plant varieties. In the absence of a proper definition of what constitutes an effective system, UPOV is touted by the developed countries as being the most effective *sui generis* mechanism. UPOV has more contradictions than not regarding the interests of the developing countries [5].

3.8.1 What Constitutes an Effective Sui generis System

The TRIPS Agreement mentions that member countries might protect plant varieties either by patents or by an effective *sui generis* system or by a combination thereof. In context of the above, most of the developing countries are inclined to opt for a *sui generis* mechanism. What then would actually be implied to satisfy that the adopted *sui generis* system is effective?

In a commentary, Biswajit Dhar has illustrated three interpretations as to what constitutes effectiveness [6]:

Effective Enforcement:

The effectiveness of the system is reflected by effective enforcement at national level of the rights and procedures. The formulation argues that the system should allow effective action against any acts of infringement. A major criticism of this approach is that it does not depend on the requirement for or on the level of protection.

Compliance to UPOV:

The WTO has often considered that the UPOV represents the only most comprehensive and internationally accepted *sui generis* system for protecting plant varieties. As such, the effectiveness of a *sui generis* mechanism under this context would be judged by the degree of compliance with UPOV. The International Association for Plant Breeders for the Protection of Plant Varieties (ASSINSEL) contends that the *sui generis* protection regime could operate only if varieties are defined in terms of uniformity, stability and distinctness. In absence of these, any variety would be vague, quite unsuitable for being a subject matter of legal right. A major criticism of this approach is that the UPOV is unmistakably biased towards the interests of the developed countries and multinational seed companies.

Protection Available as an Indicator of Effectiveness:

Under this approach, the extent of protection available to new plant varieties is the sole determinant to assess effectiveness. Thus, a legal framework that can provide protection to the largest range of new varieties developed can alone be dubbed as effective. Understandably, these criteria can only be met if protection is extended to a cross section of stakeholders in plant breeding, i.e. formal breeders (belonging to the TNC seed companies) and traditional farmers who continue to play a significant role in the development of agriculture across countries.

Incidentally, India has followed this third interpretation with enactment of the Plant Variety and Farmers Rights Act. Arguably, it represents the only *sui generis* system outside the purview of UPOV that has been enacted by law.

3.9 Addressing the Concerns of Developing Countries

Developing countries around the world are characterized by their own set of externalities and diversities [5] that make them distinct not only from developed countries but also among themselves. However, they also possess some striking commonalities apart from the economic indicators that have particular relevance to the outcome of protection of intellectual property rights with respect to natural resources and life forms.

First, most of the developing countries are rich in natural resources which make most of the biodiversity hot spots that can be commercially exploited to their advantage. Second, most of them are predominantly agriculture dependent although there has certainly been a rapid industrialization in some of them. Third, developing countries harbour 90% of the world's genetic resources and traditional/indigenous knowledge which serve as treasure troves for new innovations based on this community knowledgebase. Fourth, developing countries without exception depend upon inward technology flow, foreign direct investment and global market access to drive their economies.

With the above said, developing countries have inherent deficiencies in enforcing intellectual property regimes to the minimum standards as warranted under TRIPS to match with the level of protection in developed countries. However, as we have discussed briefly in the previous chapter, IPRs seem to benefit developing countries more than the developed countries especially when it comes to natural resources, agriculture, traditional knowledge and life forms.

Intellectual property rights are envisaged to balance the benefits of rights provided to the IPR holder and the broader requirements of social welfare. The objectives clause of the TRIPS elucidate the above concept succinctly as:

'The protection and enforcement of intellectual property rights should contribute to the promotion of technological innovation and to the transfer and dissemination of technology, to the mutual advantage of the producers and users of technological knowledge and in a manner conducive to social and economic welfare, and to a balance of rights and obligations'.

Notwithstanding the perspective set forth by the TRIPS, enforcement of IPR regimes under the WTO has widened the gap among developed and developing nations and thus added a new factor of exclusion. Among the myriad of contentions that fuel this divide, one of the major aspects is the distinction being created between farmers and breeders, which is likely to have far-reaching consequences if implemented in the manner warranted under TRIPS.

On-farm innovation by farmers has been a trend for long, although recognition of this as an intellectual attainment is a relatively recent phenomenon. The farmer innovation process, in which the farmer adopts clearly defined criteria for generating improved variety of plants, is essentially similar to what is adopted by the professional breeders. Nevertheless, while the knowledge of the breeders is extensively codified and documented, there is little or no codification or documentation available to the farmer's innovation process. While specific innovations can be attributed to one or a group of breeders, similar attribution is not possible for farmers as the knowledge is essentially acquired over generations. Thus, innovations could at best be associated with a given community. This has been the chief impediment why the farmers have been left out in the intellectual property rights scenario.

While disregarding the contribution of the farmers, TRIPS has coined a new category of individuals known as breeders who are responsible for generating new plant varieties and as such claimants of the intellectual property rights associated with it. In this context, the act of production or multiplication, conditioning for the purpose of propagation, marketing, stocking, etc., all comprise of exclusive rights of the breeders.

The major concern among developing countries thus is to protect the rights of farmers in an era of formal seed sector and adopt mechanisms that offset the breeder's rights to levels of the pre-TRIPS era. Adopting a *sui generis* system has thus appeared as the most acceptable alternative. As we shall explore later, such a *sui generis* system would also have to be beyond the UPOV framework. We shall further see that India's landmark Farmers' Rights Act has emerged as an excellent *sui generis* system that is being adopted by other developing countries to safeguard their interests.

Yet another major concern for developing countries is the enforcement of an IPR regime that safeguards the country's traditional knowledge, indigenous knowledge and biodiversity associated with natural resources. Obligations under TRIPS do not require stating the origin of the natural product for application of patents derived from them. Similarly, there is no provision of acknowledging the local community whose indigenous innovations are sourced to generate new innovations that could be patented. Such discrepancies always run the risk of misappropriation of knowledge of indigenous and local communities, biopiracy and deprivation of local communities from their legitimate dues arising out of commercialization of their knowledge.

Developing countries have thus consistently voiced concerns about prior informed consent of access to resources and equitable sharing of benefits arising from their use as essential amendments in the current intellectual property legislation.

3.10 UPOV's Bias Against Developing Countries and Evolution of *Sui generis* System at Global Level

Influential international bodies including the WTO itself is pushing to restrict the *sui generis* option to a single legislative model provided by UPOV. The UPOV system promotes commercially bred plant varieties for industrial agricultural mechanisms. The farmers would thus need to pay royalties on seeds. Plant breeding is undertaken with patented genes at the expense of more indigenous sustainable systems. The impact of such regimes would be highly detrimental to developing country interests. Firstly, the farmers who contribute varieties on which the breeders develop have no rights. Secondly, UPOV conditions are tailored for industrial economies. India and Philippines for instance have tabled legislation on community intellectual rights (CIRs) that aim to protect the rights of communities with knowledge of biodiversity and are involved in maintaining, innovating and utilizing such knowledge.

Comprehensive biodiversity legislation has been approached in Costa Rica, Thailand, Ethiopia and South Africa and also probably advocated in India. The fundamental aim of such legislation is to elaborate mechanisms of access to bioresources, biosafety concerns, intellectual property rights associated with them and frameworks for national action plan for achieving conservation and sustainable use of biodiversity.

Sectoral community right's regimes have been practised in Laos and Thailand, with enactment of Community Forestry Acts.

3.11 Addressing Conflict of Compliance

The parallel occurrences of a number of frameworks that govern intellectual property management have often led to conflicting situations. Most of the countries are signatories of multiple treaties and protocols and thereby are obliged to implement the principles of all of them. These conflicts, coupled with relatively vague dispositions and polarized nature of the governance frameworks, have impeded compliance, particularly among developing countries.

Interestingly, TRIPS and the CBD are seemingly in conflict on certain key issues. For example, under the CBD all signatory countries have sovereignty over their genetic resources, while TRIPS is extremely vague in such provision. Again, CBD warrants that all parties must protect and promote local communities while TRIPS provide no obligation towards local communities and traditional knowledge. Finally, access to genetic resources requires prior informed consent and sharing of benefits under the CBD with no such provision under the TRIPS.

There seems to exist no clear and easy mechanism to resolve such conflicts although Article 22 of the CBD is often considered to be crucial in this regard. The Article 22 states:

'The provisions of this Convention shall not affect the rights and obligations of any Contracting Party deriving from any existing international agreement, except where the exercise of those rights and obligations would cause a serious damage or threat to biological diversity'.

It is often argued that establishment of primacy of CBD over TRIPS through international negotiations would address the issues of safeguarding the biodiversity of developing countries. It is clear that the implementation of the provisions of the TRIPS would be detrimental to the biological diversity and prejudicial to the environment. As such, the primacy of the CBD warranted under Article 22 needs to be invoked in such a scenario.

3.12 Conclusion

The TRIPS and the CBD have thus played a major role in shaping the IPR regimes. While the provisions under TRIPS for plant varieties with associated traditional knowledge and access to genetic resources had a direct implication on food security, the complementary approach of CBD had a significant implication on conservation. Developing countries were more to gain from this balancing stand of the two instruments, although a clear and consistent hierarchical arrangement is lacking. As we shall see later, it is important to have this hierarchy in place to enable a more judicious implementation.

References

1. Kothari A, Anuradha R (1997) Biodiversity, intellectual property and the GATT Agreement: how to address the conflicts. Econ Polit Wkly 32(43)
2. Dhar B (2002) Sui generis systems of plant variety protection: options under trips. Quaker United Nations Office. http://www.quno.org/. Accessed 25 Sept 2017
3. Dhar B (2003) The Convention on Biological Diversity and the TRIPS Agreement: Compatibility or conflict. In: Bellmann C, Dutfield G, Melendez-Ortiz R (eds) Trading in Knowledge: Development Perspectives on TRIPS, Trade and Sustainability. ICTSD, London, pp 77–87
4. Secretariat CBD (2008): Biodiversity and Agriculture – Safeguarding Biodiversity and Securing Food for the World, Secretariat of CBD, Montreal
5. Mashelkar R (2002) Intellectual Property Rights and the Third World. J Intellect Prop Rights 7:308–323
6. Sahai S (2003) Indigenous knowledge and its protection in India. In: Bellmann C, Dutfield G, Melendez-Ortiz R (eds) Trading in knowledge: Development perspectives on TRIPS, Trade and Sustainability. ICTSD, London, pp 166–174

Chapter 4
The South Asian Perspective

4.1 Background

South Asia comprises one of the fastest growing regions of the world. Endowed with an extraordinary natural resource diversity, historically evolved economies and vibrant livelihoods, the region is also fraught with multitude of challenges. Poverty, inequality, environmental degradation, vulnerability to natural disasters, high population pressure are some of the key challenges faced by the region. Agriculture is the mainstay of most of the South Asian economies, contributing a significant percentage of GDP, and also employing a significant proportion of labour. Addressing the need and challenges of sustainable development of South Asia would thus require a systematic effort to understand and address the concerns related to biodiversity, agriculture, culture and socio-economic status of the region.

Development paradigms of South Asia thus rely upon one or all of the following attributes:

(a) Addressing poverty alleviation and reducing inequality
(b) Addressing the issue of food security
(c) Strengthening trade and economic policies
(d) Effectively sharing and managing natural resources

Technically, the South Asian Region (SAR) comprises of eight countries, namely Afghanistan, Bangladesh, Bhutan, India, Maldives, Nepal, Pakistan and Sri Lanka. Nevertheless, in its journey towards economic integration, there has over the years, emerged multiple trade blocs, namely the SAARC and BIMSTEC [6]. While SAARC comprises of the above-stated countries, the BIMSTEC makes an overlap with two countries belonging to the ASEAN bloc, namely Myanmar and Thailand, while leaving out Afghanistan, Maldives and Pakistan. Both SAARC and BIMSTEC nonetheless represent high potential, high-stake partnerships that are poised to play a pivotal role in driving the developmental challenges mentioned above [10].

BIMSTEC has a wider contour especially in view of its multisectoral set-up. This makes some of the collateral components that influence trade, namely technology, agriculture, public health, environment, energy and so on more central players in the partnership. Trade for instance cannot flourish without regard to environment or public health concerns; or countries comprising the partnership need to pay unequivocal attention to technological progress [3]. As such, we have used BIMSTEC as the focal region for evolving a policy agenda for sustainable development.

4.2 Overview of the Bay of Bengal Initiative for Multi-Sectoral Technical and Economic Cooperation (BIMSTEC)

Regional integration is an accepted mechanism globally to accelerate growth through cooperation in areas of common interest, making use of regional resources and geopolitical and socio-economic advantages. As a sequel of Bangkok Declaration (1997), a regional cooperation grouping was established to spur economic development comprising of Bangladesh, India, Sri Lanka and Thailand. This was designated as the Bangladesh–India–Sri Lanka–Thailand Economic Cooperation (BISTEC). Later during the same year, the grouping was expanded with inclusion of Myanmar, with changed nomenclature of Bangladesh–India–Myanmar–Sri Lanka–Thailand Economic Cooperation (BIMSTEC). In 2004, the grouping underwent further expansion with Nepal and Bhutan joining the bloc. The predominant distribution of the countries encircling the Bay of Bengal led to the new bloc comprising of the seven countries to be designated as the Bay of Bengal Initiative for Multi-Sectoral Technical and Economic Cooperation (BIMSTEC) [6].

As evident from the above, the cooperation within the BIMSTEC was essentially sectoral. Trade, technology, energy, transport, tourism and fisheries were the initial six sectors with which the cooperation began. Eventually, as the group built up, nine more sectors were progressively added that covered agriculture, public health, poverty alleviation, counter-terrorism, environment, culture, people-to-people contact and climate change [1].

The BIMSTEC represents an economically and demographically high-potential bloc, comprising of around 1.6 billion people (representing a hefty 22% of the world population) and having a combined GDP of USD 2.8 trillion growing at an average of 6%. It is also strategically and geopolitically important as it forms a bridge between the SAARC and the ASEAN [9].

The following table provides the macroeconomic profile of the countries comprising the BIMSTEC (Table 4.1).

Table 4.1 Macroeconomic and trade data of the BIMSTEC (2014)

Country	Population (million)	GDP (billion $)	Export (million $)	Import (million $)
Bangladesh	159	173.8	30,131.6	42,267.6
Bhutan	0.80	0.8	534.7	900.5
India	1295.3	2066.9	329,633	405,122
Myanmar	53.4	64.3	8860.1	12,749.5
Nepal	28.2	19.6	901.5	6614.7
Sri Lanka	20.6	74.9	11,767.1	17,475.1
Thailand	67.7	373.8	224,777	200,217

4.2.1 Trade Dimension of the BIMSTEC

The BIMSTEC accounted for 3.7% of world trade in 2014, experiencing a robust growth. Total exports from the BIMSTEC grew from USD 113.5 billion in 2001 to USD 608 billion in 2014. Total imports into the BIMSTEC similarly witnessed a growth from USD 118.4 billion in 2001 to USD 685 billion in 2014. Despite the above, intra-regional trade within the BIMSTEC was a mere USD 37 billion in 2014. In percentage terms, it is around 2.86% that is significantly lower than intra-regional trade among similar blocs, e.g. SAARC (7%), APTA (7.5%), MERCOSUR (16%) and ASEAN (29%) [2] (Tables 4.2 and 4.3).[1]

Table 4.2 Intra-BIMSTEC Trade: Exports FOB 2016[a]

	Bangladesh	Bhutan	India	Myanmar	Nepal	Sri Lanka	Thailand	China
Bangladesh	–	2.60	642.80	26.54	36.40	20.54	29.63	716.12
Bhutan	12.49	–	468.81	na	1.95	na	0.10	0.32
India	5711.64	429.59	–	1156.35	4614.51	3910.61	2962.11	8946.78
Myanmar	21.48	na	1038.11	–	0.87	6.38	2241.50	4766.68
Nepal	360.44	1.55	360.44	0.02	–	4.60	0.90	11.94
Sri Lanka	118.87	0.02	753.48	1.67	1.40	–	36.32	107.75
Thailand	933.32	na	5119.75	4157.55	66.29	428.75	–	23615.00

[a]Source: Calculated from Direction of Trade Statistics, 2016, *International Monetary Fund*

---

[1]FOB stands for 'free on board' that is used to refer to export data. CIF stands for 'cost with insurance and freight' that is used to refer to import data. While FOB does not factor in insurance and freight charges for tradable commodities, CIF factors in the aforesaid costs. At the country level, usually there is a mismatch between export FOB and import CIF in most cases, as evident from table above (Tables 4.2 and 4.3). The corresponding figures for China are provided as reference in order to compare the relative trade preferences of the partners. Barring the trade with India, majority of the countries (with some exception of Thailand) exhibit very meagre trading both in terms of exports and imports.

Table 4.3 Intra-BIMSTEC trade: imports CIF 2016[a]

	Bangladesh	Bhutan	India	Myanmar	Nepal	Sri Lanka	Thailand	China
Bangladesh	–	23.78	5530.18	43.36	12.63	44.83	731.67	1028.79
Bhutan	2.93	–	1537.54	na	3.89	na	19.99	8.38
India	711.67	220.06	–	1086.54	407.50	631.95	5316.77	60539.52
Myanmar	19.45	na	1094.70	–	0.01	0.12	1985.91	5403.10
Nepal	40.59	2.82	5569.96	8.16	–	1.03	104.31	817.41
Sri Lanka	29.35	0.00	3824.97	31.87	0.28	–|	514.46	2135.38
Thailand	56.17	0.00	2587.36	2368.64	0.60	40.19	–	42239.00

[a]Source: Calculated from Direction of Trade Statistics, 2016, *International Monetary Fund*

4.2.2 Land Use

All the countries of the BIMSTEC region are essentially agrarian and therefore agriculture comprises of one of the major economic activities. Moreover, the region is typified by dense population that makes demographic pressure on land among the highest and most challenging in the world. Climatic characteristics and geographical location have historically endowed the countries with large swathes of forested lands with an extraordinary expanse of biodiversity. Over the decades, demographic pressure and compulsions of development have eroded significant portions of these forests and biodiversity.

As the countries continue to grow both economically and in terms of population, they have to continually explore newer options of sustainability that would enable a more judicious use of biodiversity and natural resources.

The table provides a snapshot of the land use pattern among the BIMSTEC countries. As evident from the data, India and Bangladesh (among the two most populous states of the region) show the weakest agriculture–forest ratio with majority of land area being used up for agricultural purposes. Percentage of forests are among the lowest in these countries (23 and 11% respectively) while percentage of arable land among the highest (53 and 59% respectively). In the contrasting other end of the spectrum, Bhutan and Myanmar have a very high agriculture–forest ratio with percentage of forested land being 85 and 48%, respectively, making it the highest in the region. The other countries, namely Nepal, Sri Lanka, Thailand fall somewhat midway between these two extremes with agriculture–forest ratio in the range of 1–1.2 [9] (Table 4.4).

The patterns of land use are important in determining the contours of policy frameworks for conservation and sustainable use of resources contained therein. The distribution is also reflected in the composition of economic activity of the countries concerned.

Table 4.4 Land use in BIMSTEC countries

Country	Area (sq km)	Agricultural land use (%)				Forest land use (%)	Land use ratio (agriculture/forest)
		Arable	Crops	Pasture	Total		
Bangladesh	148,460	59.0	6.5	4.6	70.1	11.1	6.32
Bhutan	38,394	2.6	0.3	10.7	13.5	85.5	0.16
India	3,287,363	52.8	4.2	3.5	60.5	23.1	2.62
Myanmar	676,578	16.5	2.2	0.5	19.2	48.2	0.40
Nepal	147,181	15.1	1.2	12.5	28.5	25.4	1.12
Sri Lanka	65,610	20.7	15.8	7.0	43.5	29.4	1.48
Thailand	513,120	30.8	8.8	1.6	41.2	37.2	1.11

Pressure on land for countries like India and Bangladesh has seriously impeded the expansion of forest cover, initiation of plantation forestry (to supplement production of commercial forest products) and also higher volume farming. Farming communities in these countries thus continue to remain small and marginal farmers with limited landholding. Such externalities have contributed to the inability of the farmers to compete with professional breeders of developed countries in use of advanced technologies and raising the volume of agricultural production.

4.2.3 Human Development

The level of human development is one of the most important determinants of economic and social progresses. The table gives the Human Development Index of the BIMSTEC countries. All of them fall in either high or medium categories. Sri Lanka and Thailand are categorized within the 'high' HDI band, while the others, namely India, Bhutan, Bangladesh, Nepal and Myanmar are categorized within the 'medium' HDI band [4] (Table 4.5).

4.3 Country Profiles of Selected Countries of South Asia

The countries comprising the BIMSTEC are diverse. The following paragraphs provide a broad overview of the countries [7, 9] (Fig. 4.1).

Table 4.5 Human Development Ranking 2016

Country	Rank	Category
Sri Lanka	73	High
Thailand	87	High
India	131	Medium
Bhutan	132	Medium
Bangladesh	139	Medium
Nepal	144	Medium
Myanmar	145	Medium

4.3.1 Bangladesh

Located in the deltaic region of South Asia bordered by India, Myanmar, and Nepal, Bangladesh is among the least developed yet most densely populated countries of the world. The country represents a riverine plain that is criss-crossed by numerous rivers some of them being the largest in the region. The country is also prone to natural disasters in view of its vulnerable location especially through floods and

Fig. 4.1 Geographical location of the BIMSTEC countries in South Asia

cyclones and is also particularly vulnerable to the effects of sea-level rise and climate change. Although poverty is very pronounced, the country has in recent times taken proactive measures to reduce its population growth and also improve education, health and other social indicators. Bangladesh has a land area of 1,47, 570 sq km with a population of 159 million (2015 figure) and a population growth rate of 1.37%. The capital of the country is Dhaka. GDP growth rate is around 6.5% (2015 figure) and population below the poverty line approximately 24.3%. The country is endowed with large reserves of natural gas, coal, limestone, ceramic clay and hard rock.

Agriculture continues to remain the mainstay in the economy. Chief agricultural produce is rice, wheat, jute, tobacco, sugarcane, pulses, oilseeds, spices, potato, vegetables and fruits, e.g. banana and mango. Reduced creation of jobs has resulted in a high degree of skilled migration to other countries in search of livelihood. The economy is undergoing diversification in recent times with industrialization being accorded priority. There has also been a steady growth of foreign direct investment leading to a surge in infrastructure development. The industrial sector of the country comprises of ready-made garments, cotton textiles, jute and jute-diversified products, tea processing, paper, cement and chemicals. Oil refining, steel and shipbuilding are also developing gradually as a result of enhanced investment. Traditional industrial units comprise of carpets, handloom and handicrafts, ceramic ware and brick products. Bangladesh currently has around 22 special economic zones and 8 export processing zones. Exports comprise of garments, jute and leather products and fish, with India, China, Singapore and Europe being principal trading partners. Political stability in Bangladesh has remained elusive since its independence from Pakistan in 1971. There have been stints of military rule with democracy residing since 1990. Political rivalry, tensions and occasional influence of extremist groups have retarded economic progress.

Bangladesh consists of a little over 2500 km of railways (mostly laid during the British colonial period) and around 200,000 km of highways (although only a eighth of which is paved). Despite the extensive riverine systems, the navigable waterways in Bangladesh are relatively less. There are 16 airports [7, 8].

4.3.2 Bhutan

Bhutan is a landlocked Himalayan country bordered by China, India and Nepal. It is a monarchy and is adhered to traditional values. This had resulted in the country being kept cut off from rest of the world till 1970s. The local name of Bhutan is Druk Yul that means Land of the Thunder Dragon. The country is slowly embracing reforms both at governmental as well as economic levels and is also slowly opening itself up to international relations. The country has a land area of 38,364 sq kms and a population of 7,50,000. Of this population, around 50% consist of endemic Bhutia and 35% ethnic Nepalese. The predominant religion is Lamaistic Buddhism although Indo-Nepalese Hinduism is also practiced. Life expectancy is low (around 52 years) and literacy rate is of the order of 42%. The capital city is Thimpu. The country is entirely mountainous interspersed with valleys and jungles and exhibits an alpine temperate climate. Several strategically important mountain passes are controlled by Bhutan.

Hydroelectric power, timber, gypsum are major natural resources. Agriculture and horticulture are major drivers of the economy with fruit and fruit products being important revenue and foreign exchange earners. Agriculture produce comprises of rice, corn, root crops and fruits. Eggs and dairy products are important components of the agro-sector. The country's industrial sector is underdeveloped and is dominated by wood products, fruit processing and alcoholic beverages. Cement industry is the sole exception to the group. India is the country's main trading partner (>80%) followed by Hong Kong (11%). Fifty-eight percentage of Bhutan's labour force is engaged in agriculture with around 20% in industry. Bhutan has, in recent times, shown brisk growth of the technology sector particularly those related to green and nature-derived technologies. Bhutan's infrastructure is severely restrained with no railways, only around 2000 km of highways and two airports.

Bhutan is a biodiversity-rich country and is one of the few places where the majority of land area is covered by forests. Conservation is among the major focus of the government, and Bhutan has endeavoured to develop strong participatory policies of protecting natural habitats, flora and fauna. The location and geographical attributes make Bhutan susceptible to climate change and other environmental issues. The country by virtue of its pristine environment harbours a large and vibrant biodiversity. Plant diversity includes 5603 species of vascular plants and almost 400 species of ferns. There are more than 300 species of medicinal plants found along the slopes of the Himalayas ranging from altitude 200–7800 m. This has led to Bhutan's historical nomenclature as 'Lhomenjong' or the 'valley of medicinal herbs'. As a result of this rich diversity, Bhutan remains a treasure trove of genetic and biological resource, with rich traditional knowledge of local communities on exploitation of these biological resources. ABS thus assumes pivotal significance in Bhutan for safeguarding this natural heritage.

4.3.3 India

Flanked by the Himalayas, Arabian Sea, Bay of Bengal and Indian Ocean, India is the largest country of South Asia and the seventh largest country of the world. It has an approximate land area of 32,87,263 sq km. A seat of ancient civilizations dating back to several thousand years, India has a long history of social, cultural and economic accomplishment. Currently, it represents the second most populous country of the world (with over one billion population) and among the fastest growing economies. The capital of India is New Delhi.

India has a large diversity geographical zones including mountains, river plains, plateaus, forests and deserts and possesses more than 7000 kms of coastline. India has a monsoon type of climate. The climate and natural habitat make the country extraordinarily rich in biodiversity. Hot spots of such diversity exist in the Western Ghats, Himalayas and the north-eastern part of the country. The richly forested regions are endowed with numerous plants and animal species, while the river plains are the regions of bustling economic activities and among the most populous regions of the country. Natural resources of the country include coal, iron ore, manganese ore, mica, bauxite, limestone, gypsum, dolomite and so on. There exists a significant reserve of petroleum and natural gas. The coasts and seas abound with fish, and the country (especially the Himalayan region) also has large resources of medicinal and aromatic plants.

Social indicators in India are not very strong. Life expectancy is around 65 years, and literacy rates are around 75–80%. A significant portion of population continues to remain below poverty line although the figure is undergoing progressive improvement. Infant mortality rate is around 60.8 deaths per thousand live births.

India has a mixed economy. Agriculture is predominant that is made up of both indigenous farming practices as well as modern mechanized agricultural practices. The industrial sector comprises of heavy industries such as automobile, iron and steel, pharmaceuticals, chemicals and also small and cottage industries that comprise of handicrafts and others. Economic liberalization has opened up the economy progressively to international trade and investment. India has a vibrant trade with various countries of the world that especially encompass USA, Japan, China and Europe. Chief exports are textiles, leather goods, engineering goods, chemicals, jewellery, agro-produce, food products and so on. Principal commodities of import include petroleum products, machinery, chemicals and fertilizers.

The chief infrastructural component of India includes nearly 63,000 km of railways (among the largest in the world) that is extensively electrified, and over 3.3 million km of highways. There are several ports and harbours and over 16,000 km of navigable waterways. There are over 200 airports with paved runways.

4.3.4 Myanmar

The South Asian country of Myanmar is bordered by India and Bangladesh in the west, China in the north and Thailand in the east. Originally designated as Burma, it has seen a tumultuous past since securing independence from Britain. The country has for long being controlled and governed by military junta that has led to a serious compromise of human rights and economic progress. Myanmar has recently entered into a transition to democracy since 2016 and is poised for economic and social recovery. Predominance of ethnic majority of Burmans over the other ethnic minorities has been a source of perennial conflicts. Myanmar has a land area of around 6,76,552 sq km and a population of around 53 million. Population growth rate is around 1.6% and life expectancy is low (around 55 years). Religion is dominated by Buddhism with smaller sections of Christians and Muslims. The capital of the country is Yangon. Myanmar is among the poorest countries of the region plagued by decades of economic stagnation. Infrastructure is poor and undeveloped; skilled workforce is lacking, and industries are in a primitive state. The country's mixed terrain comprising of the central lowlands and eastern mountains together with a somewhat tropical monsoon climate has led to the country's population being unevenly distributed and also prone to natural disasters. Agriculture is a chief component of the economy and comprises of rice (>60%). Natural resources of Myanmar comprise of precious stones (rubies, sapphires, pearls and jade), wood products, gems, metals, oil and natural gas. Proximity of the country's coasts to major shipping lane of the Indian Ocean endows a special advantage in terms of leveraging trade.

Myanmar is among the less-developed regions of Asia that have high poverty essentially because of its colonial past and post-independence military rule. Economic liberalization during the recent period has begun to open the industrial and agriculture sector to private and foreign investment, with a significant easing of government control that lasted for almost 35 years. Flow of funds has resulted in slow revival of the economy although civil unrest, corruption and black market have major deleterious effects on a sustained economic growth. Exports from Myanmar consist of rice, beans, rubber, teak and other forms of wood, with China, Japan, India, Thailand and Singapore being major trading partners. Myanmar has a very skewed export control regime, e.g. 70% of pulses exported to India, 90% watermelon to China, 75% onions to Thailand and so on. Agriculture is nevertheless underproductive, and the share of agriculture in GDP has declined from 57% in 2000 to 32% in 2015.

Infrastructure in Myanmar is ill-developed. It has 3,740 km of railways, around 3500 kms of paved roads and 3000 kms of navigable waterways. There are several seaports and airports.

4.3.5 Nepal

Nepal is a landlocked Himalayan country flanked by India, China and Bhutan. Known for its ancient culture, the country was a surviving monarchy that underwent a transition to democracy during the recent past. Nepal ranks among the poorer countries in the world, and its economy is dependent on tourism and external aid. Nepal has a land area of 1,47, 181 sq kms having a population of around 31 million. A Hindu major country Nepal contains several South Asian ethnic groups such as Sherpas, Newars. Literacy rate is extremely low (around 27%), and life expectancy is moderate (around 60 years). Social indicators are not very strong in Nepal making it relatively vulnerable. The economy of Nepal is presently undergoing a growth rate of around 7.5%, with industry sector experiencing a steady upward growth. The capital is Kathmandu. Main natural resources of Nepal include hydropower, timber and deposits of quartz, lignite, copper and iron ore. Overuse of wood and fuel has resulted in enhanced deforestation which is a major environmental challenge.

Nepal's natural habitation comprises of river plains and high mountains, with densely forested foothills. Agriculture is the mainstay of Nepal's economy that employs over 75% of the labour and accounted for around 36% of the national GDP in 2012. The contribution of the service sector is progressively increasing.

Agriculture production is undertaken chiefly in the Terai region and comprises of tea, rice, corn wheat, sugarcane and root crops. The industrial sector consists essentially of food processing, jute products, sugarcane extraction and grain processing. The acute shortage of skilled labour force is one of the chief impediments to Nepal's industrial sector. Remoteness and the landlocked nature have impeded Nepal's development significantly although new government intervention is proactively exploring possibilities for large foreign investment.

Exports are an important component for Nepalese economy and account for a total of around USD 822 million. Principal export items consist of carpets, clothing, leather goods, jute-diversified products, etc. The country imports gold, machinery, petroleum and fertilizers. India, Germany, UK, USA, Japan and Singapore are principal trading partners.

Infrastructure is relatively underdeveloped. There is only around 100 kms of railways. Paved roads comprise of around 3000 kms and five operating airports.

The unique subHimalayan location and climate make Nepal an extraordinarily biodiverse country. There are 862 species of birds, 181 species of mammals, 687 species of ferns, 1500 species of fungi, 465 species of lichens and more than 7000 species of flowering plants. Economically important medicinal and aromatic plants also abound in Nepal with more than 200 identified species. There are more than 300 species of orchids and numerous other agro-horticultural crops. The country is also rich in fruit varieties (more than 60 species are known to occur).

4.3.6 Sri Lanka

Sri Lanka is a distinct example of small-island developing state located in the Indian Ocean with its capital at Colombo. It is separated from the southern tip of India by the narrow channel of Palk Strait. The country has a land area of around 65,610 sq kms and a population of roughly 21 million and is categorized as a lower middle-income country by the World Bank. The population comprised of around 74% Sinhalese and around 18% Tamils. The principal religion is Buddhism along with a significant Hindu population. For decades, the country was torn by ethnic conflict that has impeded growth and economic development. Ever since the civil war ended, Sri Lanka has witnessed rapid growth and significant improvement in social indicators. The population has been progressively transitioning from rural to urban habitats and manufacturing and services are beginning to take up important places in the country's economy.

USA, Japan, India and several European countries are Sri Lanka's chief trading partners. Textiles, apparel, tea, rubber, coconut, diamonds and gems are major items of export. Imports comprise of machinery, equipment, building materials, sugar and petroleum.

Sri Lanka experiences a tropical climate and its terrain comprises of flat plains with mountainous tracts in the south central region. Its secluded ecosystem has put its rate of endemism at 25% (the highest in South Asia). Plant diversity and animal diversity are very large with more than 3000 species of flowering plants, more than 500 species of lower plants and numerous species of ferns, algae and fungi. More than 80 species of mammals, 236 species of birds, 175 species of reptiles and nearly 100 species of fishes have made the country among the biodiversity hot spots of South Asia. Despite the large biodiversity, threats to its survival are large thus making conservation among the important priorities of the country.

Sri Lanka has a good infrastructure of more than 1500 km of railways, 40,000 km of highways, several ports and 12 airports.

4.3.7 Thailand

Thailand shares its borders with Myanmar, Laos and Cambodia and with the Gulf of Thailand. The country is unique in South Asia by being the only example without a colonial history. This has probably led to its higher economic profiles. Thailand has an area of 5,13, 115 sq kms and a population of roughly 70 million people. The capital is Bangkok and country has been ruled by mostly monarchy and the military with interludes of democracy. Thailand is a predominantly Buddhist country and comprises of 75% Thai and around 14% of Chinese origin.

Thailand experienced a fairly brisk and sustained economic growth, except for some slump as a result of the Asian economic crisis. This has resulted in progressive reduction of poverty and also an improvement in various social indicators. Thailand envisages attaining the status of developed country by 2030 and is in the process of reforming its economy in line with this aim. The principal trading partners are USA, Japan, Singapore, Malaysia and Hong Kong. The country's exports comprise of manufactured goods, agriculture and fishery products while imports consist of capital goods and raw materials, various consumer items and petroleum.

Thailand witnesses a tropical climate with mixed terrain that consists of central plains, eastern plateaus and intermittent mountains.

Infrastructure is well developed in Thailand, and the county enjoys a strategic position by being the only land transit route that connects mainland Asia with Malaysia and Singapore. The country has over 60,000 kms of highways and more than 4000 kms railways. There are several ports and around 100 airports [5, 6].

4.4 Why Natural Wealth Protection in South Asia is Important?

The South Asian region contains 4 out of the 34 global biodiversity hot spots and is known for not only its diversity of forest and natural wealth but also demographic diversity. Pristine forests still abound in Bhutan, Nepal and Myanmar. The slopes of the Himalayas continue to be dominated by an extraordinary variety of aromatic and medicinal plants (India's north-eastern regions and the Terai Himalayas need special mention).

In addition to this forest wealth, all the countries exhibit extraordinary agricultural diversity. More than 100 varieties of rice alone grow in the Indo-Gangetic plains; much of which represent farmer-developed varieties. The agricultural diversity is not only related with the genetic diversity of crops but also with the diversity of knowledge pertaining to farming practices among the local and indigenous communities. Historic trends of harbouring ancient civilizations make the region replete with rich cultural diversity and cultural knowledge that are demonstrated through the endemic traditional cultural expressions.

Despite the large natural resources and agricultural production, trade partners of the region mostly consist of USA, China, East Asia and OECD countries. Since historical times, trade occurs with Africa. Needless to say, such global movement of products warrants adequate protection measures being adopted in order to conserve the identity of the region. Moreover, the high population of the region (with special reference to India and Bangladesh) makes it a major market for foreign products, including agricultural products. Thus, it is imperative to adopt safeguards to ensure that the country's genetic diversity and gene pool is not overwhelmed by germplasm originating from outside through uncontrolled introduction of GM technology.

We shall discuss in subsequent sections of the need and priorities of sustainable development options, through adoption of advanced technologies and conservation of endemic resources. It is nevertheless imperative to devise judicious options for the same probably through regional cooperation.

4.5 Conclusion

South Asia thus comprises of an important region in the global intellectual property rights regime. With the emerging importance of the BIMSTEC group of countries, they seem to play an important role in shaping the systems of South Asia. Both economically and in terms of agro-bio resources (including forest resources) and cultural resources, the region is richly endowed. It is thus imperative to develop a system of facilitating this economic progress with concomitant protection of the natural wealth contained therein. BIMSTEC by its unique positioning as a 'bridge bloc' between SAARC and ASEAN is poised for an increasingly important role in this respect.

References

1. BIMST-EC summit declaration (2004) BIMST-EC Summit Declaration, Bangkok
2. Direction of Trade Statistics (2016). International Monetary Fund. https://data.imf.org. Accessed 25 Sept 2017
3. Hossain S (2013) Impact of BIMSTEC Free Trade Area: A CGE analysis. J Econ Sustain Dev 4:16–27
4. Human Development Report (2016). http://hdr.undp.org/en/2016-report. Accessed 25 Sept 2017
5. Kakakhel S (2012) Environmental challenges in South Asia. ISAS insights no 189, Singapore
6. Rahaman MM, Kim C (2016) Prospects of economic integration of BIMSTEC: trade and investment scenario. Int J U E Serv 9:235–248
7. The World Factbook (2016) Central Intelligence Agency. https://www.cia.gov/library/publications/the-world-factbook. Accessed 25 Sept 2017
8. World Bank Open Knowledge Repository (2017) World Bank https://openknowledge.worldbank.org. Accessed 25 Sept 2017
9. World Development Indicators (2017) World Bank. http://wdi.worldbank.org/tables. Accessed 25 Sept 2017
10. Yahya F (2005) BIMSTEC and emerging patterns of Asian regional and inter-regional cooperation. Aust J Polit Sci 40:391–410

Chapter 5
Plant Variety Protection and Farmers' Rights

5.1 Background

The half-century following the Paris Convention witnessed a sway of attempts to extend IP protection to the field of agriculture in the European countries. This included the recognition of seeds and seedlings as items of protection, introduction of the Plant Registry of newly bred strains and also institutional mechanisms to control production and distribution of seeds. The Plant Patent Act (1930) was enacted in the USA to recognize the rights of plant breeders. Although this Act covered plants that were propagated asexually, the legislation coupled with the European initiatives stirred up intense debate regarding the pros and cons of intellectual property protection in agriculture and its subsequent implications on food security [1].

Following such developments, the Strassborg Convention on Unification of Certain Points of Substantive Law on Patents adopted a resolution that plants or animal varieties and essentially biological processes for the production of plants and animals were exceptions to patentable subject matter. Thus, the Parties were not bound to grant patents for protection of plant varieties, animal varieties or essentially biological processes for production of plants and animals. These exceptions provided by the Strassborg Agreement were adopted by the European Patent Convention in 1973 under its Article 53. Incidentally, the TRIPS Agreement in 1995 reproduced this same language of the European Patent Convention in its Article 27.3(b) which we have already discussed in the previous chapter.

The debate however continued. In developing countries, traditional farming methods form the backbone of agriculture. Seed supply takes place essentially through informal innovation and breeding by local farming communities. Provision of intellectual property rights to agriculture was likely to detrimentally affect the rights of farmers. The issue was thus to devise ways to safeguard the rights of farmers amidst an institutional system of seed supply and agricultural production.

5.2 Possible Fall Out of Plant Variety Protection

One of the main concerns about the extension of IP protection to agriculture was that it might take away the right of farmers in developing counties to save, share and exchange the farm produce as well as seeds that they had traditionally enjoyed. Monopoly in agricultural components was also likely to raise the costs. Moreover, developing countries thus far did not have any specific community called 'breeders' as the functions of breeders were traditionally carried out by the farmers themselves. Thus, should farmers in developing countries be considered as breeders? Above all, the contribution of farmers in conservation and preservation of plant varieties and also sustenance of agricultural biodiversity was considered an important feature in the fabric of the agricultural economies of the developing countries [2].

Two options were considered relevant in addressing these concerns. Firstly, it was important to protect the privilege of farmers to save and reuse seeds of protected plant varieties as an exception to plant breeders rights. Secondly, the farmers are entitled to receive a fair and equitable share of benefits derived from the use of plant genetic resources being conserved by them. As we shall see later in this chapter, the first aspect has been sought to be addressed by the UPOV Convention while the second aspect has been sought to be addressed by the International Undertaking on Plant Genetic Resources of FAO, which was later renegotiated and incorporated in the ITPGRFA. Notwithstanding the above, as we shall see, the provisions of the UPOV have been particularly biased against the interests of the developing countries, thereby necessitating separate *sui generis* systems being adopted by such countries.

5.3 Privilege for the Farmers

Since time immemorial, farmers had been associated with informal breeding, conservation and preservation of plant genetic resources around the world. Thus, it is imperative to accept that the farmers deserved to be recognized and rewarded for their contributions [3]. The matter was taken up for deliberation in the 25th FAO Conference in 1989. In a landmark resolution 4/89 in the said conference, the concept of farmers' rights was introduced into the International Union of Plant Genetic Resources. It was underlined that although farmers had been instrumental in conserving, improving and distributing plant genetic resources, their contributions had not been appropriately recognized. The FAO Conference adopted and defined farmers rights as 'rights arising from the past, present and future contribution of farmers in conserving, improving and making available plant genetic resources, particularly those in the centres of origin/diversity'.

The Conference further assigned the International Community as trustees for present and future generation of farmers for the purpose of ensuring their full benefits. To supplement such efforts, when the Convention of Biological Diversity was adopted in 1992, it recognized the sovereign rights of the states on the biological resources within the jurisdiction. Article 8(j) of the Convention further provided for community rights of indigenous people and fair and equitable benefit sharing arising out of the utilization of such resources. This benefit-sharing component constituted an important element in farmers' rights legislations that were to follow.

We have discussed about the basic aspects of the ITPGRFA in the previous chapter. Article 9.1 of the Treaty ensures recognition of contribution of farmers. The main components of farmers rights were considered to be:

1. Right to fair and equitable sharing of benefits arising out of the utilization of plant genetic resources for food and agriculture
2. Right to participate in national decision-making process in connection to plant genetic resources;
3. Protection of traditional knowledge; and
4. Right to save, use, exchange and sell farm-saved seeds and other propagating materials

5.4 PVP vis-a-vis Patents: What Developing Countries Stand to Gain

The primary driving force behind adoption of *sui generis* system over plant patents has been the seemingly draconian effects, the latter is to have over agriculture and food security in developing countries. As stated earlier, most of the developing countries are hot spots for biodiversity in plant genetic resources. They are also bestowed with extensive community knowledge of the farmers who have developed their innovations over generations.

Adoption of plant patents would authorise the patentee to enforce prohibition over re-use of the seeds that would invariably result in increased cost for the farmers as they would be forced to depend on the large seed companies for supply of seeds which could be used only once. We shall discuss about the plight of formal seed sector with reference to Monsanto seeds in a later chapter. Secondly, breeding of protected varieties would be banned under law while such protection would not sustain the innovations that usually takes place on the farm. Thirdly, patenting could encourage the rights to focus upon specific genetic traits such as disease-resistant varieties, high yielding variety, higher oil content variety, drought-resistant variety, thereby promoting monopoly rights for such varieties. Fourthly, patenting coupled with restricted on-farm breeding would lead to standardization of varieties making our agricultural fields uniform with monoculture thereby eroding the vast genetic diversity of the countries. Fifthly, it would move the seed sector towards greater degree of formalization, causing significant impact to small and marginal farmers who constitute the majority in developing countries.

Adoption of *sui generis* plant variety protection as an option under TRIPS would circumvent almost all of the above bottlenecks and thus balance the rights and obligations in a more sustainable fashion. Thus, choice of PVP over patents has been found to have a major beneficial effects on developing countries. However, as we shall see later, the most widely publicised *sui generis* system under UPOV is also against the interests of the developing countries in view of some of its biased provisions.[1,2] This has led to many countries adopting their own non-UPOV provisions [4].

5.5 PVP in South Asian Countries

Among the South Asian countries discussed here, all have opted for *sui generis* protection of plant varieties. Nevertheless, none of them have subscribed to UPOV. Further, all are parties to the ITPGRFA (with Sri Lanka opting into the system very late; while others being a party since early days).

5.5.1 India

India has by far the most comprehensive and extensively developed plant variety protection laws in the region. The Indian legislation is covered under the Protection of Plant Varieties and Farmers Rights Act (2001) that is in compliance to the TRIPS requirement. The law in India stands out uniquely as it has provided a comprehensive coverage to protection of both plant varieties as well as the rights of farmers [5].

5.5.1.1 Protection of Plant Varieties and Farmers Rights Act, 2001

The Act covers all categories of plants except micro-organisms. The salient features of the Indian legislation are as follows: [6]

1. An authority called the Protection of Plant Varieties and Farmers' Rights Authority would execute and implement the provisions of the Act and shall

---

[1] Registration of new plant varieties: New varieties of plants can be registered provided they conform to the NDUS criteria, i.e. novelty, distintness, uniformity and stability. A variety is considered novel if on the date of filing, it has not been sold or disposed of anywhere; it is considered as distinct if it is distinguishable by at least one essential characteristic from any other variety; it is considered as uniform if it is sufficiently uniform in its essential characteristics subject to variation that might be expected and is considered as stable if its essential characteristics remain unchanged after repeated propagation.

[2] Essentially derived variety: A plant variety is considered to be essentially derived variety when it is (i) predominantly derived from the initial variety while retaining expression of the characteristics of genotype or combination of genotype of such initial variety, (ii) clearly distinguishable from such initial variety, (iii) conformed to the initial variety in expression of essential characteristics that result from genotype or combination of genotype of initial variety except variation in such characteristics resulting from the process of derivation.

consist of representatives from all stakeholders including those of indigenous communities.

2. For a variety to be eligible for registration, it needs to satisfy the criteria on novelty, distinctiveness, uniformity and stability. The variety would be considered as novel if the concerned propagating material of the variety has not been sold or disposed within India earlier than one year or outside India earlier than six years. It shall be considered as distinct if it is distinguishable by at least one essential characteristic from any other variety whose existence is known in any country at the time of filing. It shall be considered as uniform if it is sufficiently uniform with respect of its essential characteristics, subject to variation of that may be expected from specific features of its propagation. Finally, it shall be considered as stable if these essential characteristics remain unchanged after repeated propagation.
3. The period of protection under the Indian law is nine years for trees and vines and six years for other crops that may be reviewed and renewed on payment of fees.
4. The Act provides for exclusive rights to the breeder or his successor or licensee to produce, sell, market, distribute, import or export the variety against the certificate of registration. The breeder of essentially derived variety shall have the same rights as that of the plant breeder of other new varieties.
5. Researchers have been provided access to protected varieties for bonafide research purposes.
6. The farmers have been provided the right to protect varieties developed or conserved by them and have the freedom to save, use, sow, resow, exchange, share and sell farm produce of a protected variety except sale under commercial marketing arrangement (branded seeds). The farmers have also been made immune to innocent infringement if he is not aware of existence of breeders right at the time of such infringement.
7. Communities have been recognised and appropriate compensation for their contribution have slated to be determined by the PPVFRA.
8. The Act confers the PPVFRA right to grant compulsory license in case of complaints about availability of seeds of any registered variety to public at a reasonable price. The license can be granted to any person for production, distribution or sale of the seed after three years from date of registration.
9. There is a provision for sharing benefits accrued to the breeder from a variety that has been developed from indigenously derived plant resource.
10. A National Gene Fund has been instituted under the Act.
11. Institutional mechanisms related to dispute resolution, notification of crop species, storage of reference samples and other provisions have also been provided.

An important aspect of the Indian law is worth mentioning. The legislation has very deftly balanced and dovetailed the informal and formal systems of agriculture. Farmers are recognised as breeders. At the same time, breeders have been granted exclusive rights on varieties. Taken together, the law on one side incentivizes the breeding community (including professional breeders), at the same time provides safeguard to the farming community.

5.5.2 Bangladesh

Bangladesh is a signatory of the TRIPS and being an LDC has the option of achieving compliance by 2021. The country is also signatory of the CBD, Cartagena Protocol and ITPGRFA. Thus in the plant variety protection front, the country envisages an IPR regime that like India balances the rights and obligations of breeders and farmers alike. Bangladesh is yet to have a full-fledged legislation but has set up a series of policies and draft guidelines in this respect. Incidentally, provisions of PVP in Bangladesh exist under the Draft Patent Act (2013), Draft Bangladesh Biodiversity Act (2012) and the Draft Plant Variety and Farmers Rights Protection Act (2014) [7–9].

5.5.2.1 PVP Provisions Under Draft Patent Act

The draft legislation on patents in Bangladesh endeavours to accord protection to farmers' rights, traditional knowledge, bio-safety and food security. In this regard, inventions based on traditional knowledge are disqualified from being protected. The legislation requires disclosure on the source and use of traditional genetic resources and misappropriation is liable to forfeiture of the protection. The Government is empowered to provide compulsory licensing during conditions of nutritional exigencies, health exigencies, etc., and also parallel imports.

5.5.2.2 Provisions Under Draft PVP and Farmers' Rights Act

Bangladesh has opted for a *sui generis* system in relation to PVP. The draft legislation for PVP and farmers' rights has provisions for prior informed consent and requirement for equitable sharing of benefits in case of using farmers traditional varieties and farmers traditional knowledge of breeding in line with requirements under CBD and ITPGRFA. Moreover, Bangladesh has recognised sharecroppers as farmers and has accorded protection to traditional farming practices. The farmers are entitled to saving, sowing, resowing, exchanging and selling farm-saved seeds and use of terminator variety of seeds is prohibited. In some unique exceptions, Bangladesh has resorted to the definition of distinctiveness, uniformity and stability in line with UPOV and has not accepted farmers as breeders.

5.5.2.3 PVP Provisions Under Draft Biodiversity Act

The draft Bangladesh Biodiversity Act also has provisions for prior informed consent of the community, access to equitable benefit sharing for using traditional genetic resources, guarantees of rights in traditional practices and provisions for in situ and ex situ conservation.

5.5.2.4 Challenges to Bangladesh PVP Regime

One of the main challenges of the PVP regime of Bangladesh is the inability of farmers to get recognition as breeders (something the Indian legislation has managed to ensure). Further, there is no provision to develop capacity among farmers to enable them to make use of existing plant genetic resources to develop new varieties and also a lack in adequate policy for promoting effective utilisation of germplasm.

Bangladesh farming community has a owner–client relationship. Under the circumstances and given the fact that there is an inadequate educational climate, it is difficult for the sharecroppers and legitimate cultivators of land to exercise their rights for ABS despite the same is being provided under law.

Thus, one of the chief challenges before the Bangladesh PVP is to ensure stronger farmers' rights in terms of their recognition as breeders,[3] their right to decision making, their exercising of rights to ABS and capacity building to make better use of available technology for improving plant yield and quality enhancement.

5.5.3 *Bhutan*

Bhutan has opted for a *sui generis* system for plant variety protection and the provisions with respect to the protection is provided under the Biodiversity Act of Bhutan (2003) [10].

The salient features for PVP under the Bhutan Biodiversity Act are as follows:

1. PVP is granted for plant varieties that are novel, distinct, uniform and stable.
2. Entitlement of rights is vested with the persons who have developed the variety and the rights holder shall be authorised to produce, reproduce, sell, export, import and stock.

---

[3]Breeders are usually referred to as individuals or organizations who develop new varieties of plants while farmers are considered as those who grow these varieties. However, as with most developing countries, where traditional farming is practised abundantly, a significant proportion of plant varieties are developed by the farmers themselves through crossing and selection. Such practices often form part of traditional and indigenous knowledge of farming communities. Thus, farmers of developing countries should rightfully be granted the status of breeders; a claim that is often deprived in provisions of many countries including Bangladesh.

3. The law provides exceptions to farmers to propagate seeds harvested and exchange the seeds for non-commercial purposes subject to discretion of the competent authority.
4. The rights shall remain effective for a period of 20 years from the date of grant and 25 years for trees and vines. Moreover, the exhaustion provision shall also ensure that the rights to breeders shall not hold for subsequent propagation of the protected variety.
5. The Government has also reserved the right to grant compulsory licensing under usual provisions for the same.

In addition to the Biodiversity Act, the Seeds Act of Bhutan (2000) is also worth its mention. This legislation regulates the quality of seeds and planting material and also regulates the import and export of quality seeds and seedling for agricultural use. Mandated to enhance rural livelihoods, the Seeds Act encourages private entrepreneurs and farmers organisations in the seed industry, promote farmers acceptance of improved seed varieties and promote export-oriented production of seeds.

5.5.3.1 Challenges to Bhutan PVP Regime

The Biodiversity Act of Bhutan is the single overarching legislation that incorporates the doctrines of biodiversity conservation, traditional knowledge conservation, plant variety protection and access to benefit sharing. However, the rules and regulations envisaged under the Act are yet to be finalised which is a major impediment for its implementation in the desired manner. It is important for any country to share and exchange biological resources with neighbouring countries under mutually agreed terms and conditions. Such materials transfer and sharing protocols are yet to be in place putting the endemic plant varieties at risk of either piracy or over-containment.

In addition to this, given the vast diversity of the plant genetic resources and the remoteness of the country, it is important to have a comprehensive documentation of the resources and sharing the same among users of the germplasm. Skill development, capacity building and access to facilitatory tools and technology are considered to be instrumental in achieving success of the PVP regimes in Bhutan [11, 12].

5.5.4 Nepal

Nepal being a member of the WTO is obliged to provide IPR protection to plant varieties as mandated under the TRIPS. However as an LDC, it had time till 2013 to develop an appropriate regime. The country has also ratified the ITPGRFA in 2007.

The country nevertheless till date is yet to come up with relevant legislations. As a predominantly agrarian country where agriculture comprise the mainstay for majority of population, protection of plant varieties vis-a-vis rights of farmers is of particular importance. In fact, Nepal has clearly mentioned in the Protocol of Accession to the WTO that it would devise a plant variety protection law that safeguards 'the rights of related stakeholders in accordance with the needs of the country'. As with most developing countries, Nepal faces special challenges due to lack of technical, financial and human resources for developing supportive IPR policies [13].

Seed development, certification, registration and release of seeds are regulated in Nepal through the Seeds Act (1988) which requires the seeds to conform with the criteria of distinctness, uniformity and stability. It is thus imperative for Nepal to evolve a workable system by utilising the flexibilities and options available under the TRIPS. It is nevertheless recognised by most scholars that UPOV is not the *sui generis* system that suits Nepal's needs. Adoption of a *sui generis* mechanism similar to those of India and Bangladesh could prove effective in this regard.

Nepal's legislation pertaining to Access to Genetic Resources for Fair and Equitable Sharing of Benefits (discussed in more details in the relevant chapter) is also in draft form, that is envisaged to provide crucial legislative framework for documentation and registration of plant varieties and devise a mechanism of regulating its access. The same is essential in implementing necessary farmers rights to indigenous varieties of seeds and traditional farming practices.

Nepalese farmers have over the years developed many plant varieties that are inseparable components of agricultural biodiversity of the country. The new legislation in this area should thus ensure that the farmers gain legal ownership of their varieties and knowledge therein. The *sui generis* system is thus expected to implement the following farmers rights:

1. Right to grant prior informed consent for use of their varieties and knowledge to develop new plant varieties
2. Right to regulate access to their variety and also access to the associated community knowledge
3. Right to know the primary, secondary and any other use of their variety.

5.5.4.1 Challenges to Nepal PVP Regime

Nepalese farmers have been traditionally used to mixed farming, i.e. there was high interdependence of agricultural production, livestock rearing and use of tree-based resources. Traditional knowledge was extensively used.

Saving seeds, farmer-to-farmer exchange, are hallmarks of Nepal's agriculture with more than 90% seed supply being provided by the informal sector. Thus, institutionalization of the agriculture sector, meeting obligations to formal seed companies while safeguarding the rights of farmers with concomitant preservation of traditional practices and diversity are the chief challenges before the PVP regime in Nepal [13].

5.5.5 Myanmar

Myanmar's predominant agrarian economy and its recent thrust towards economic growth has placed agriculture in the forefront of its development agenda. Quality seed production and access to seeds has been thus accorded priority. Myanmar's seed sector is managed mostly by the public sector. However, it is felt that rejuvenation of the country's agricultural production would largely depend on its farmers access to improved seeds and improved plant varieties particularly rice. In this regard, Myanmar has not been uncomfortable in opening its seed sector to multinational seed corporations using formalised seeds [14, 15].

The country has acceded to the WTO in 1995 and the CBD in 1994 and is as such under obligation to implement the provisions contained in these treaties. It has yet to adopt a comprehensive plan of protecting plant varieties although the bias is more towards the UPOV. It has thus participated in the UPOV Workshop in 2004, conducted the DUS test for its plant varieties in 2006 conducted a number of PVP workshops during the period 2003–2014 with an aim of developing a system acceptable to a cross section of stakeholders.

5.5.5.1 Challenges to Myanmar PVP Regime

Myanmar is typified by a highly skewed distribution of land and productive assets that has translated into high levels of rural inequality. Agricultural productivity is low and is subjected to high volatility. One of the primary reasons for this is access to low-quality seeds and inefficient weed and pest control mechanisms. The transition to democracy has opened new opportunities for the country and government has focused on agriculture as a principal vehicle to address food security and promote inclusive development. However, the implementation of enabling policies and sustaining the endogenous farming practices remains a major challenge [16].

Although Myanmar has opted for a non-UPOV *sui generis* system, its provisions are significantly tilted towards UPOV. Thus, the country needs to address the needs and concerns of the farmers while it develops and opens its seed sector to the formal breeders. The country also needs to address its weak and obsolete farmland laws so as to harmonize them with the newer legislations.

5.5.6 Thailand

Agriculture remains a major economic activity for a large portion of the population of Thailand. Thus, introduction of IPR in the sector through a plant variety protection regime is considered to be important. Thailand's plant protection regime is regulated by the Plant Variety Protection Act (1999) that was an outcome of the country's

5.3 Privilege for the Farmers

joining the WTO and becoming signatory to the TRIPS. The Thai PVP represents a *sui generis* system that is different from UPOV.

Introduction of an acceptable PVP regime in Thailand is complex. This is owing to the fact that although farming community occupies a significant portion of the population and farmers produce around 20 percent of the seeds required for agriculture, majority of the seed marketing is controlled by seed corporations such as Chia Tai or Monsanto. Thus, the main challenge is to protect the farming community while nurturing innovations for developing better germplasm. Thai PVP has in this regard divided plant varieties into two, namely the new plant varieties and extant plant varieties [17–19].

5.5.6.1 Plant Variety Protection Act of Thailand

The journey for drafting a relevant legislation for PVP began in 1994, when two bills were introduced for consideration. Both the bills (having small differences between themselves) were based on the UPOV Convention 1991 and were done in accordance with its principles. Thus, the proposed Thai legislation did not take into account the needs and rights of farmers to propagate their germplasm and to reuse seeds, vesting most of the privileges with the transnational seed corporations. Needless to say, it was met with great skepticism and resentment of stakeholders. This led to the scrapping of the entire process with a new proposal that combined both the legislations that took into consideration the rights of farmers to a substantial extent. Thailand's Plant Variety Protection Act was finally adopted in 1999, which was essentially a *sui generis* version although heavily drawn from UPOV.

Some of the salient features of the Thai PVP Act are as follows:

1. The PVP law defines a breeder as a person who has created a new plant variety. Thus, while an individual farmer can be a breeder, the legal definition precludes a community of farmers from right to protection of a variety that they have created. This is very much the same line as followed under UPOV.
2. The breeders rights provide protection to newly created varieties that conform to the criteria of novelty, distinctiveness, uniformity and stability.
3. Duration of protection varies. It is for a term ranging from 12–17 years for plant varieties and 27 years for trees.
4. Breeders enjoy exclusive rights over their varieties. However, it grants exceptions under inadvertent use or propagation; use in research and education; cultivation or propagation by farmers; non-commercial use.
5. There is provision for compulsory licensing of new varieties.

5.5.6.2 Major Concerns and Challenges of Thai PVP Law

Legal protection of Thai PVP Act is accorded to extant plant varieties and providing a differential treatment in favour of farmers and local farming communities. Extant varieties are divided into three classes, e.g. local domestic plant varieties, general domestic plants and wild plant varieties.

There is a controversy surrounding local domestic plant varieties. The protection accorded to this category is to grant exclusive rights to farmers and local farming communities over local domestic varieties occurring in the territory of Thailand. However, interestingly, nowhere in the Thai legislation is the term 'farmers rights' or 'right of local indigenous communities' mentioned explicitly. However, despite its existence, since its inception seldom has a farmer been able to register a variety as local domestic variety. This is primarily owing to the fact that these varieties are usually more heterogenous and also unstable, thereby failing to satisfy the DUS criteria required for registration. The other important flip side is the rigid definition of local domestic variety as one that occurs only in one location in Thailand.

It is nowadays sometimes felt that there are no local domestic varieties in Thailand. In contrast, the general domestic and wild varieties predominate. Further, under the PVP Act, rights for local domestic varieties rest with the local communities or indigenous groups. Local community is defined as a 'group of people residing commonly inheriting and passing over culture continuously', without any categorical mention of indigenous people.

It is important thus that the Thai PVP probably needs to be tweaked. Although it has made an attempt to evolve a mechanism beyond the ambit of UPOV, it is questionable whether the legislation has actually been able to provide the outcome that it has intended.

Benefit sharing from plant variety protection is another area of concern.

5.5.7 Sri Lanka

Sri Lanka is not a member of UPOV and acceded to the ITPGRFA only in 2013. However, it is a member of the WTO and signatory of the TRIPS that make it obligatory on its part to provide adequate protection to plant varieties under Article 27.3(b). Nevertheless, there is no legislation for enabling this provision, except for an effort to have a draft Plant Variety Protection Act in 2001 that went into stakeholder consultation but was never adopted owing to several inconsistencies.

Sri Lanka also does not have an appropriate legislation to protect biodiversity; and as such, there is no safeguard against misappropriation of genetic and biological resources.

5.5.7.1 Challenges to Sri Lanka PVP Regime

As stated above, Sri Lanka is yet to implement a suitable system for plant variety protection, protection of farmers rights and also safeguard misappropriation of genetic and biological resources. This despite the fact that under the WTO, Sri Lanka was supposed to have the mechanism in place by 2005. The main challenge before

Sri Lanka is thus to have the legislation in the first place. It could be justifiable to have a *sui generis* system but it has to decide on whether it shall be the UPOV or a variant. Farmers community knowledge and a vast diversity of plant genetic resource typify the biodiversity landscape of the country that makes devising an acceptable option of particular relevance.

5.6 Conclusion

In view of the predominance of agriculture in the economy and the existence of large plant diversity, plant variety protection has assumed particular importance in the countries of South Asia. Making use of options available under the TRIPS, all the countries have adopted *sui generis* systems for protection of plant varieties that is distinct from the UPOV. Nevertheless, as we have seen the regime is far from uniform and complete. Most of the countries (except India) have failed to develop a workable framework although most of them are in the process of developing one. It is also interesting to note that although farmers innovations have played a significant role in agriculture in all the countries, relatively few of them have made provisions under the national law to protect farmers rights and recognize farmers as breeders. It is important therefore to tweak the systems as they evolve in order to make them more inclusive and align them to the developmental needs of the region.

References

1. Plant Patent Act 1930. Government of United States of America (1930)
2. Dewan M (2011) IPR in agriculture: an overview. J Intellect Prop Rights 16:131–138
3. Bilkis A, Rafah A (2016) Protection of traditional agricultural knowledge and food security in developing countries - a critical analysis. IOSR J Hum Soc Sci 21(5):27–35
4. Singh A, Manchikanti P (2011) Sui generis IPR laws vis-a-vis farmers rights in South Asian countries - implications under WTO. J Intellect Prop Rights 16:107–116
5. Swaminathan MS (2002) The Protection of Plant Varieties and Farmers Rights Act: from legislation to implementation. J Intellect Prop Rights 7:324–329
6. The Protection of Plant Varieties and Farmers Rights Act 2001. Gazette of India, Government of India No 64 (2001)
7. Draft Bangladesh Biodiversity Act, 2012. Government of Bangladesh (2012)
8. Draft Patent Act, 2013. Government of Bangladesh (2013)
9. Draft Plant Variety and Farmers Rights Protection Act, 2014. Government of Bangladesh (2014)
10. The Biodiversity Act of Bhutan, Water Sheep Year 2003. Ministry of Agriculture, Royal Government of Bhutan (2003)
11. Ghimiray M (2005) Conservation and utilization of Bhutanese rice genetic resources, Vol 5747, pp 1753–1765
12. Review and Compendium of Environmental Policies and Laws in Bhutan. Asian Development Bank (2014)
13. Adhikari K (2008) Legal mechanisms to protect Farmers Rights in Nepal. PRO-PUBLIC and South Asia Watch on Trade, Technology and Environment (SAWTEE)

14. Kyi T (2015) Overview of agricultural policy in Myanmar, In Agriculture in Brief. Ministry of Agriculture and Irrigation, Government of Myanmar
15. Nwe KM (2006) Current situation of new plant variety protection system in Myanmar
16. Myanmar in transition: Opportunities and challenges (2012) Asian Development Bank, Manila
17. Lertdhantewe P (2014) Thailand's sui generis system of plant variety protection. QUNO Brief Pap 3:1–5
18. Lertdhantewe P (2014) Protection of plant varieties in Thailand. J World Intellect Prop 17:142–159
19. Lertdhantewe P (2015) Reinventing Thailand's plant protection regime. J Intellect Prop Rights 20:320–329

Chapter 6
Protection of Traditional Knowledge and Indigenous Knowledge

6.1 Background

Traditional knowledge is defined as a cumulative body of knowledge and beliefs that is handed down through generations by cultural transmission. It concerns the relationship among living beings (including humans) between themselves and with the environment. In this context, traditional knowledge (TK) is very intimately embedded into the fabric of society and cultural ethos. The term indigenous knowledge (IK) is also in use and many times interchangeably with TK. Despite similarities, TK and IK are also sometimes differentiated although across a thin line.

According to the World Bank [1], indigenous knowledge is characterized by the following:

1. It is local knowledge.
2. It is culturally unique.
3. It is the basis of local-level decision-making in agriculture, health care, natural resource management, education and so on.
4. It is usually held by communities rather than individuals and enables problem-solving among communities.
5. It is tacit knowledge and therefore difficult to codify.

Both traditional and indigenous knowledge play a crucial role in development paradigms.[1] Protection of TK and IK under intellectual property rights has received particular impetus after the adoption of CBD in 1992.

Although TK and IK are present all over the world, they seem to have played a more dominant role in the non-industrial and technologically less advanced societies,

---

[1]The difference between traditional knowledge and indigenous knowledge is subtle. Indigenous knowledge is usually referred to such traditional knowledge that is held by an indigenous community; in contrast, traditional knowledge is more generic. Thus, while all indigenous knowledge is traditional knowledge, all traditional knowledge is not necessarily indigenous knowledge.

i.e. in developing and least developed countries. It has been found also that much of the holders of TK and IK are indigenous or tribal communities.

6.2 Protection of Traditional Knowledge

The importance of traditional knowledge has placed a special onus on its protection and its recognition as a sovereign right of the state harbouring the same. Intellectual property protection of traditional knowledge can occur through two forms, namely:

1. Positive Protection: This gives the TK holders right to seek remedies in event of its misappropriation and to secure protective legal rights over the TK. This is achieved either through existing laws or through appropriate *sui generis* laws.
2. Defensive Protection: This provides for safeguarding against illegitimate use or misappropriation of TK and prevents others from using the TK. This is usually done through documentation, disclosure, etc, as a tool to stop granting of IPRs to the concerned traditional knowledge [2].

6.3 Misappropriation of Traditional Knowledge

The importance and versatility of TK and IK make it prone to misappropriation. In a separate chapter, we have discussed the case of piracy of ayahuasca vine from the Amazon forests. Many a times, it is found that there is a breach of contractual agreement on access and use of TK that adversely affect the holder of TK. Misappropriation not only involves removal of the concerned life form, plant or animal but also illegal removal of the associated cultural knowledge.

Such misappropriations often lead to grant of wrong patents that are neither novel nor inventive, being based on the TK that has been existing and being used for centuries.

6.3.1 Examples of Misappropriation of TK in India

Misappropriation of TK has been witnessed in all parts of the world. Some examples from India include the following [2]:

1. **Turmeric** (*Curcuma longa*): Although known for healing wounds and being in use in India for centuries, it was granted US patent in 1995.
2. **Neem** (*Azadirachta indica*): The tree is widely used and mentioned in Indian texts for over 2000 years for its insect repellent and pest control properties, use in human and veterinary medicine, cosmetics and so on. In 1994, it was granted a patent by EPO for its anti-fungal properties.

3. **Nap Hal**: This was a wheat land race variety in India that was granted a patent by EPO in 2003. On basis of a petition filed with the EPO that the patent in question was granted to an Indian land race Nap Hal, the patent was revoked in 2004.
4. **Amla** (*Phyllanthus emblica*): This tree that is widely grown in India produces ingredients for a traditional medicinal formulation used for centuries. USPTO had granted five patents on amla based on claims on therapeutic values of its extracts.

Many such examples abound in patent literature that substantiates a concern of misappropriation of Indian traditional knowledge. Need is thus felt to develop mechanisms of protecting such knowledge as part of a secure intellectual property regime [3, 4].

6.4 International Instruments for Protecting Traditional Knowledge

CBD and TRIPS represent the chief instruments for protecting traditional knowledge and preventing its misappropriation. As we have discussed before, CBD provides states with sovereign rights over its natural and cultural resources. This serves as an effective mechanism of safeguard against inappropriate use of TK. TRIPS also provides important handles for providing IPR protection through patents and *sui generis* systems for protecting TK.

6.5 Protection of TK/IK in South Asian Countries

South Asia shows extensive demographic diversity and has a history of ancient civilizations. The countries discussed here are thus endowed with a rich trove of TK and IK.

6.5.1 India

India has adopted strong and proactive measures for safeguarding traditional knowledge under the provisions of TRIPS and CBD. Although there is no separate and specific legislation for protecting TK, provisions are available for the same under multitude of legislations. Some of these include the following.

6.5.1.1 Biological Diversity Act, 2002

The Act has been passed in 2003 to set forth the obligations under CBD to provide for conservation of biological diversity, sustainable use of its components and fair and equitable sharing of benefits arising out of its utilization. Thus, protection of traditional knowledge under this Act is restricted to providing informed access and ensuring equitable sharing of benefits arising out of its utilization as a check to misappropriation [5].

6.5.1.2 Plant Varieties and Farmers' Rights Act, 2002

As we have discussed earlier, 60% of India's agricultural produce originates from farmers cultivation and the seeds in use are farmers varieties. Farmers seeds and indigenous farming practices in India comprise one of the rich source of traditional and indigenous knowledge in the country. The Plant Variety and Farmers' Rights Act provides adequate means of protecting farmers varieties of crops and protects farmers knowledge in propagating land races and these varieties. As the farmers are recognized as breeders under the provisions of the Act, it is a means of conserving farmers knowledge; and to be used in developing further agricultural innovations [6].

6.5.1.3 Access and Benefit-Sharing Mechanisms

Providing access to traditional knowledge through prior informed consent and evolving mechanisms for a fair and equitable benefit sharing as a result of its utilization is one of the major ways for implementing protection [7].

6.5.1.4 Documentation of Traditional Knowledge: Traditional Knowledge Digital Library (TKDL)

The newer versions of the patent law in India have provisions for mandatory disclosure of source and geographical origin of any biological material for applying for patent in India. Wrongful disclosure and non-disclosure constitute reasons for opposition and revocation of patents, if granted. It is further stated that existing local, community or indigenous knowledge (even oral transmission) are grounds for anticipation and thus denial of grant of patent.

In the context of above, and in order to achieve an international safeguard against patenting of products based on traditional knowledge, India has resorted to the approach of extensive and comprehensive documentation of TK/IK as a process of incorporating the said knowledge as part of prior art [8].

TKDL, an initiative of the Council of Scientific and Industrial Research (CSIR) of India, is a database/knowledge repository of traditional knowledge available in the country in languages and formats that is understandable to examiners in international patent offices. This is of particular importance as most of the information on TK exist in languages and forms that are non-comprehensible to patent offices. TKDL actually envisages to bridge this divide. TKDL nevertheless covers essentially knowledge related to traditional medicines covering the domains of Ayurveda, Siddha, Unani and Yoga in digitized format.[2] The TKDL has also led to development of a traditional knowledge resource classification (TKRC) for the purpose of systematic dissemination of information contained in the library and its retrieval.

The TKDL offers unique benefits to the country. Once a TK is recorded in TKDL, it legally becomes part of public domain knowledge and thus a part of prior art. This offers ample opportunity to track patent applications that use such knowledge and enables its rejection. In 2006, Government of India approved providing access of TKDL to international patent offices through non-disclosure agreement between respective IPOs and CSIR. A very large number (close to 100) applications have been rejected as a result of this initiative.

6.5.1.5 Other Resources for Documenting Traditional Knowledge in India

As stated above, the TKDL encompass traditional knowledge related to medicine. Many other resources exist in India that document other forms of traditional knowledge. Some of these include:

1. Community Biodiversity Registers (CBRs): A village-wise resource that has been initiated by certain states for documenting knowledge, innovation and practices of communities.
2. People's Biodiversity Registers (PBRs): This is a documentation of local knowledge on biodiversity undertaken at state level.
3. Plant Biodiversity Register: Initiated by Indian Institute of Science, the initiative documents 75 registers in 10 states of India.
4. Society for Research and Initiatives for Sustainable Technologies and Institutions (SRISTI): This is a documentation of innovation developed by individuals at village level. The initiative is known as HoneyBee Network.

---

[2] Ayurveda, Siddha, Unani and Yoga constitute indigenous systems of medicine practiced in India. The doctrine of Ayurveda aims to keep structural and functional entities of the human body in a functional state of equilibrium, which signifies good health. It is based on the five element theory. Siddha system of medicine contends that medical treatment for human is oriented not merely to the disease, but also to the ecosystem of the individual thus taking into account the patient, environment, age, habits and physical condition. Unani System of medicine is based on established knowledge and practices relating to promotion of positive health and prevention of diseases. It originated in Greece and moved eastwards being greatly enriched by the Arabs before reaching India during the medieval periods. Yoga is a way of life to improve the physical and mental well-being of individuals through influence of behavioural patterns. (Reference: Arthapedia, www.arthapedia.in)

6.5.2 Bangladesh

Similar to India, Bangladesh is in possession of rich traditional and indigenous knowledge that it has sought to protect. Being member of both CBD and TRIPS, it also uses the international instruments to enable protection of its natural resources in form of TK and IK among others [9].

6.5.2.1 Draft Biodiversity and Community Knowledge Protection Act, 1998

This legislation although in draft form seeks to provide a holistic approach towards protecting traditional knowledge including the cultural aspects related to knowledge of biodiversity. Interestingly, Article-4 of the said legislation very explicitly mentions community knowledge as an object of protection as:

'any alteration, modification, improvement of collective and cumulative knowledge or technology ...... in the composition of biological extracts used by the communities'

The Bangladesh legislation does not provide patenting of life forms in any way [10].

6.5.2.2 Draft Plant Varieties and Farmers' Rights Act of Bangladesh, 2006

The instruments for providing protection to traditional knowledge related to plant varieties are rather deficient in Bangladesh. The registration of a plant variety in Bangladesh follows the UPOV criteria that favours commercial plant breeders and monoculture of crops. Although there are provisions for farmers' rights, there is no clear elaboration about the ways in which farmers' rights can be executed. Unlike India, farmers are not considered as breeders in Bangladesh, and as such there is no provision of registering farmers varieties of seeds, although many such varieties stem from traditional knowledge and traditional farming practices [11].

6.5.3 Bhutan

Although the Kingdom of Bhutan is endowed with a rich array of traditional knowledge and indigenous cultural practices, the country has a relatively weak legislative and policy framework with respect to TK. The Biodiversity Act of Bhutan (2003) is the only available instrument in this regard. Nevertheless, the subject is dealt with only cursorily in Chapter - 4 of the Act. The legislation provides that TK in Bhutan is a subject of protection in so far as its holders are also the holders of the rights.

The rights exist whether it be in material or other form and continue to be enjoyed in perpetuity and are inalienable. It is also stated that anybody aspiring to use TK in Bhutan has to obtain prior informed consent from the owner of the knowledge (i.e. in most cases the concerned local community) who would have the right to accept or reject the application. Bhutan also is obliged under the Act to maintain an inventory of traditional knowledge within the country [12].

No detailed framework or procedural elaborations exist for enforcing the protection of TK.

6.5.4 Myanmar

Myanmar has no known and existing provisions for protection of traditional knowledge.

6.5.5 Nepal

After ratification of the ITPGRFA, Nepal is committed to put in place legislative frameworks for protecting farmers' rights over genetic resources and associated traditional knowledge. Nevertheless, none of the above commitments is very explicitly reflected by any legislation in Nepal. Being a country with large ethnic population harbouring significant traditional and indigenous knowledge, it is important for all the legislative frameworks to acknowledge the fact that indigenous local communities are the true owners and custodians of genetic resources (GR) and associated traditional knowledge (ATK). Nepal maintains a Community Biodiversity Register (CBR) and has envisaged a community-based biodiversity management approach (CBM). The CBM is envisaged to empower farmers, farming communities and local institutions through a participatory mechanism so that the available biodiversity is managed in a sustainable manner. It is also to ensure that the benefits (both economic and social) percolate to the local communities.

The Community Biodiversity Register documents ATK, one of the methods to facilitate its protection by law. CBM also forms the basis of ABS, with requirements of prior informed consent for accessing genetic resources. Participatory plant breeding has been practised in Nepal, and farmers are given the right of breeders, but the mechanisms of providing ownership of new varieties to breeder farmers are not present. These gaps have emerged as major impediments in protecting TK associated with plant varieties and biodiversity in Nepal. CBM laws are also used as instruments for implementing ABS although with constraints that might be expected from such a scenario [13].

6.5.6 Sri Lanka

Sri Lanka's rural population harbours large knowledge on biodiversity and sustainable practices in agriculture and health. Collective farming practices, family-based craftsmanship and healing methods have served as important livelihood options for a number of communities. The knowledge and information have been passed across generations mostly through oral transmissions [14].

Notwithstanding the above aspect, traditional and indigenous knowledge in Sri Lanka is not recorded properly. Moreover, existing legal provisions of IPR do not cover traditional knowledge. This leads to chances of severe misappropriation and also misuse.

6.5.6.1 Code of Intellectual Property Act No 59 of Sri Lanka

This is the only existing law of IPR which has no provision on traditional knowledge.

6.5.6.2 Biodiversity Conservation Action Plan

The Biodiversity Conservation Action Plan (BCAP) addresses the issue of collecting, using and protecting traditional knowledge in connection with biodiversity. BCAP has recommended archiving of information concerning TK and also recommended evolving legislations for indigenous knowledge protection. None of these recommendations have fructified.

6.5.7 Thailand

Thailand does not have a *sui generis* system for protection of traditional and indigenous knowledge in the country. Traditional medicinal intelligence, which is considered a type of TK, is defined by the Act on the Protection and Promotion of Thai Traditional Medicinal Intelligence, B.E. 2542 (1999)[3] [15]. A Community Forest Act is also being drafted by the government.

Thailand is endowed with large body of traditional cultural expressions which is not protected and thus subjected to piracy. During 2002, in an initiative involving the Sanphol Co Ltd, and the Thai Gems and Jewellery Traders' Association, a patent application was filed for the traditional method of heating stones, a process that was

---

[3]Traditional Medical Intelligence: Traditional Thai medicinal Intelligence means the basic knowledge and capability concerned with traditional Thai medicine which encompass medicinal procedures concerned with examination, diagnosis, therapy, treatment or prevention, promotion and rehabilitation of the health of humans or animals. The knowledge also covers production of traditional Thai drugs and devices that has been passed down along generations.

considered to be a part of TK for processing gemstones in the country. The matter was mutually settled with intervention of the government as it was felt that traditional gem-burners would become potential infringer of the patent, if granted.

6.5.7.1 Act on the Protection and Promotion of Thai Traditional Medicinal Intelligence, B.E. 2542 (1999)

This Act provides protection for Thai Traditional Medical Intelligence as a traditional knowledge and is the only legislative framework in Thailand on the subject. The objective of the legislation is to provide a framework for collecting, documenting and recording Thai medical intelligence and compile the same in form of a reference database. It is thus envisaged to be a mechanism for recording knowledge.

Two major sections of the legislation are pertinent in mentioning. Section-21 of the Act requires a person to be a Thai national to be eligible for registering for protection. Furthermore, such an applicant needs to invent, develop or inherit the formula on Thai traditional medicine and/or its associated text. Section-34 provides the right holder exclusive rights over ownership for production and over research, improvement or further development of the formulae. The legislation, however, grants exemptions to research and production of medicine for household applications.

In this context, it is worth mentioning that among the several shortcomings of TK protection in Thailand, some of the major are the lack of a proactive mechanism to promote TK, develop a mechanism to enable appropriate benefit sharing with indigenous communities for exploitation of TK and to prevent its misuse.

6.5.8 Challenges to TK/IK Protection in South Asian Countries

The protection of TK in various South Asian countries is subjected to several challenges. One of the common problems for all is the inability of codification and documentation that impedes the protection of intellectual property rights. Secondly, there are no laws that are exclusively devoted to protection of TK. In case some, legislation is available, and they form part of other laws, e.g. biodiversity law. It is important to define and delineate the contours of TK that requires protection. It is seen that in a majority of cases, protection of TK covers medicinal formulations drawn from natural sources. Extension of the provisions to landraces in agriculture and farming practices remains elusive. Further, seldom do we find TK/IK provisions adequately address the conservation of traditional cultural expressions.

The other important aspect of TK is the threat imposed on its sustenance because of continuous erosion of tribal culture and tribal habitat. Communities are being increasingly formalized and subjected to modern practices; habitat is fragmented and lost to developmental projects. Along with such onslaught vanishes the traditional knowledge being held over generations. The challenge before the respective governments is to ensure inclusive growth of the communities on one hand while sustaining the traditional knowledge on the other.

6.6 Traditional Cultural Expressions

While TK and IK have received reasonable patronage through various legislative frameworks in different countries, protection of traditional cultural expressions (TCE) has not been that forthcoming. In fact, defining and identifying TCE is more complex. Traditional cultural expressions are defined as expressions of folklore that include music, art, design, signs, symbols, narratives, architectural forms, handicrafts. They are integral part of indigenous communities and are used to transmit the core values and beliefs of the community to society. TCEs are invariably linked with creativity and that makes their protection a vehicle for conservation of cultural diversity [16].

6.6.1 Protection of TCEs: Initiatives of WIPO

WIPO-UNESCO Regional Consultation on Protection of Expression of Folklore for Countries of Asia and Pacific during April 1999 recognized that the countries of Asia and Pacific were endowed with rich cultural heritage. The group went on to note that:
   'the heritage was suffering from widespread unfair exploitation for commercial and business interests. Important elements of traditional knowledge and folklore were being lost and would continue being lost in absence of a proper legal mechanism to protect them at national and international levels. However, existing intellectual property rights regimes were inadequate to address these issues and therefore effective protection of folklore required sui generis legislation [17].'

6.6.2 Using Certification Marks and Labels of Authenticity to Protect TCEs

WIPO during 2001 advocated improved certification marks to protect TCEs. Such a certification was to guarantee geographical origin of the TCE and material, mode of manufacturing and quality of the product. The method was found to be effective for protecting craftwork and artwork of indigenous communities; certify their origin; and also devise appropriate benefit-sharing mechanisms. The process accorded good protection to *Toi iho* (Maori Art of New Zealand) and was sought to be used in South and Southeast Asia for protection of their cultural attributes.

6.6.3 Success Story of 'One Tambon One Product' Project in Thailand

The project was started by the Thai government in 2001 to improve income of village communities. The main strength was the ability of local artisans to commercialize unique products and handicrafts made from locally available raw materials and using indigenous skills and knowledge that were handed down across generations. Articles comprised of cotton and silk garments, artistry items, pottery, fashion accessories, household gifts and decorative items. Products were quality screened for export potential, and once selected, the products were fixed with specially designed authentication labels (OTOP Labels). The scheme which was implemented in more than 50000 tambons across Thailand faced major hurdles in terms of dissemination of information and capacity building initiatives of local artisans. Though not directly connected with protection of TCE, the initiative provided a model of how TCEs can be incentivized and protected [17].

6.7 Conclusion

The rich traditional and indigenous knowledge of the countries discussed here has made the region susceptible to misappropriation. As such, devising frameworks for protection have assumed particular importance. Despite the fact, the countries do not have legislation specifically to guard traditional knowledge although mechanisms are built into other legislations. Bangladesh is the sole exception to have drafted a bill for conservation of community knowledge although the same is yet to be passed. Thailand too has an instrument in this respect. A second approach for protection of traditional knowledge is the one adopted by India wherein information is documented and passed on to the IP offices across the world so as to prevent others from patenting traditional medicinal formulations. It is nevertheless felt that more needs to be done to formalize institutional mechanisms and develop coherent instruments for protecting traditional knowledge.

References

1. Indigenous knowledge. World Bank. http://www.worldbank.org/afr/ik/. Accessed 25 Sept 2017
2. Hirwade M, Hirwade A (2012) Traditional knolwedge protection: an Indian perspective. DESIDOC J Libr Inf Technol 32:240–248
3. Chaudhury A, Singh N (2012) IPR and patents in the perspective of ayurveda. Int Q J Res Ayurveda 33:20–26
4. James T (2016) IPR issues related to medicinal and aromatic plants (herbs and their allied products). J Tradit Folk Pract 2,3,4:7–17
5. The Biological Diversity Act 2002. Government of India (2002)

6. The Protection of Plant Varieties and Farmers Rights Act 2001. Gazette of India, Government of India No 64 (2001)
7. Afreen S (2008) Biopiracy and protection of traditional knowledge: intellectual property rights and beyond. Indian Institute of Management Calcutta Working Paper 629
8. Gupta V (2005) Traditional knowledge digital library. In: Sub-regional experts meeting in Asia on intangible cultural heritage: safeguarding and inventory making methodologies, Bangkok
9. Rahaman MR (2015) Protection of traditional knowledge and traditional cultural expressions in Bangladesh. J Intellect Prop Rights 20:164–171
10. Draft Biodiversity and Community Knowledge Protection Act, 1998. Government of Bangladesh (1998)
11. Draft Plant Variety and Farmers Rights Protection Act, 2014. Government of Bangladesh (2014)
12. The Biodiversity Act of Bhutan, Water Sheep Year 2003. Ministry of Agriculture, Royal Government of Bhutan (2003)
13. Poudel B et al (2010) Implementing ABS regime in Nepal through community based biodiversity management framework. J Agric Environ 11:143–157
14. Watson M, Gamage G (1998) Status and trends in access to genetic resources and traditional knowledge in Sri Lanka. In: South and South East Asia regional workshop on access to genetic resources and traditional knowledge, IUCN Regional Biodiversity Programme, Chennai
15. Act on the protection and promotion of Thai traditional medicinal intelligence, B.E. 2542. WIPO (1999). http://www.wipo.int/edocs/lexdocs/laws/en/th/th019en.pdf. Accessed 25 Sept 2017
16. Traditional Cultural Expressions. WIPO. http://www.wipo.int/tk/folklore. Accessed 25 Sept 2017
17. Zografos D (2007) Legal protection of traditional cultural expressions in east and southeast Asia: An unexplored territory. Aust Intellect Prop J 18:167–178

Chapter 7
Geographical Indications and Appellation of Origin

7.1 Background

Sovereign rights of nations over their natural resources and enhanced international trade have necessitated clear delineation of country or region of origin for the concerned product. A large spectrum of natural products owe their property to the geographical characteristics of their location. The TRIPS Agreement during 1994 has provided for protection of origin of a product at a given geographical location as an intellectual property right known as geographical indication (GI).

As per Article 22.1 of the TRIPS Agreement [1],

Geographical indications are indications which identify a good as originating in the territory of a Member, or a region or locality in that territory, where a given quality, reputation or other characteristic of the good is essentially attributable to its geographical origin.

This provision of protection of GI drew heavily from existing international legislation and treaty, the most prominent of them being the ones highlighting appellation of origin.

Geographical indications are somewhat distinct from other forms of IPRs and have a primary role to play from the development perspective [2]. This makes them particularly useful to developing countries in their endeavour to secure national wealth and knowledgebase [3]. Two characteristics of GIs are that unlike other forms of IPRs they are not 'created' but are 'recognised' at a given point of time. Secondly, they are usually owned by a community rather than an individual or an organization [4].

Although GIs originated in France, as we shall see they have assumed pivotal significance in Asia where it goes much beyond trade and commerce with natural products. GIs have begun to play a crucial role in protecting indigenous cultures and traditional cultural expressions of the countries and have provided great impetus in enhancing livelihood of communities and in providing economic thrust to the qualifying regions. Typical examples of geographical indications in Asia include Darjeeling Tea (India), Mysore Silk (India), Bhutanese Red Rice (Bhutan), Jamdani Silk (Bangladesh), Padma Hilsha (Bangladesh), Ceylon Tea (Sri Lanka), Mongolian Cashmere (Mongolia), etc. [5].

7.2 Origins of the Concept of Appellation of Origin

The concept of appellation of origin was derived from the Paris Convention in 1883 where indications of source were listed as an object of protection. It provided protection against false indications of source of goods, although the appellation of geographic origin became territorial links only, with no implication on characteristics or quality of the product. This was followed by the Madrid Agreement in 1891 and the Lisbon Agreement in 1958. Till the TRIPS Agreement, the protection of geographical indications was either enforced through trademarks or through appellation of origin under the Lisbon Agreement.

7.2.1 The Madrid Agreement for Repression of False or Deceptive Indications of Source of Goods, 1891

This was the first agreement to provide rules for false or deceptive indication of source. Not much different from the Paris Convention, it required the indication to be protected by domestic laws. As per Article 1.1 of the Madrid Agreement, 'all goods bearing a false or deceptive indication by which one of the countries to which this Agreement applies, or a place situated therein, is directly or indirectly indicated as being the country or place of origin shall be seized on importation into any of the said countries'. Another limitation of the Madrid Agreement [6] is that it does not protect generic appellations and allows the courts of each country to decide whether the GI constitutes an indication of source or a generic name.

7.2.2 The Lisbon Agreement for the Protection of Appellations of Origin and their Registration, 1958

The Lisbon Agreement [7] provides a higher standard of protection to appellation of origin. Article 2.1 of the Agreement has defined the concept of appellations of origin as follows:

Geographical name of a country, region, or locality, which serves to designate a product originating therein, the quality and characteristics of which are exclusively or essentially due to the geographical environment, including natural and human factors

The Agreement makes it mandatory that the product is identified by the geographical names, and any other names indicating the products does not qualify protection as an appellation of origin. The Agreement also affords protection against usurpation and imitation. Under the interpretation of the Lisbon Agreement, indication of origin or an appellation denoted through translation of the original name constitutes imitation. Furthermore, usage of words like kind, type, make, imitation is also forbidden. Nevertheless, the Lisbon Agreement is seriously handicapped when it comes to international protection as there are only a very limited number of countries that are signatories to this Agreement. As per 2015 statistics, the Lisbon Agreement is signed by only 33 countries of the world [8].

7.3 The TRIPS and TRIPS Plus Provisions for Geographical Indications

The TRIPS Agreement is the most significant of all multilateral agreements for protecting geographical indications, that provide two-level protection. Firstly, it provides minimum standard protection for all WTO member states under Article 22 as follows [1]:

"the use of any means in the designation or presentation of a good that indicates or suggests that the good in question originates in a geographical area other than the true place of origin in a manner which misleads the public as to the geographical origin of the good"

Secondly, it provides additional protection to wines and spirits under Article 23 as follows:

"interested parties to prevent use of a geographical indication identifying wines for wines not originating in the place indicated by the geographical indication in question or identifying spirits for spirits not originating in the place indicated by the geographical indication in question, even where the true origin of goods is indicated or the geographical indication is used in translation or accompanied by expressions such as kind, type, style, imitation or the like."

7.3.1 Limitations Under TRIPS

Despite TRIPS being the only comprehensive instrument for according protection to GI, there are several limitations associated with the provisions. A major limitation is the lack of providing appropriate guidance for determining GIs that qualify protection, the reduced scope of protection of many of them and methods to protect GIs from non-wine, non-spirit products.[1] The requirement of Article 22.1 for indications which identify a good as originating in a territory or a country or a region is problematic. There is no definitive test to determine the connection between a good and its geographical source. Further, Article 22.1 does not have any provision to protect non-agricultural products as it permits only 'raw material characteristics' to be evaluated. Thus, human intellectual expressions such as traditional cultural expressions remain out of the ambit of protection under Article 22.1. Apart from this, the lack of an international GI registry and prohibitive evidentiary costs also impedes the protection of GIs under TRIPS [3, 4].

Recognizing the limitations above, the Doha Round has attempted to introduce TRIPS reforms under Article 22.1 although the same has failed till date in view of lack of consensus in the WTO Council.

7.3.2 Alternative Bilateral and Multilateral GI Protection

Failure of the TRIPS to provide appropriate and adequate protection levels to all categories of products has led WTO Member States to expand international GI protection through a variety of bilateral and multilateral agreements. Regional and bilateral free trade agreements (FTAs) have become the preferred choice for willing nations to evolve the so-called TRIPS Plus provisions. Initiative in India has been noteworthy, with TRIPS Plus provisions in the GI Act incorporating robust provisions of protecting both agricultural and non-agricultural items. FTAs have promoted international GI protection between India and the European Union. ASEAN countries have also resorted to such provisions to protect GIs under intra-ASEAN FTAs.

7.4 Geographical Indications and Equitable Development

GIs have the potential to significantly contribute to human development of a country or a community and also play an important role in accelerating economic development. One of the primary characteristic of GI that it is held by a community rather than an individual or organization is particularly useful in making it a social enabler. Owners of GIs have the opportunity to exercise their legitimate rights and make productive use of them. As such, it contributes to empowerment and contributes to equitable reach of its benefits. As GIs mostly cover low-income agricultural and

---

[1] *Why we need TRIPS Plus provisions for GIs in Developing Countries*: The TRIPS provides for protection of GIs through two tiers, namely base protection under Article 22 and additional protection for wines and spirits through Article 23. A very significant proportion of items sought to be protected through GI in developing countries belong to the non-agricultural categories, e.g. textiles, or fall in the category of traditional cultural expressions, e.g. handicrafts. Such items fail to qualify both under Article 22 or Article 23. Hence, it is imperative for TRIPS Plus provisions to accord protection to such items.

artisanal societies, it leads to a conservation of knowledgebase harboured in such communities [9]. They also facilitate sustaining traditional methods and know-how to maintain equity across generations. Incentives associated with GIs (covering both economic and legal angles) also create a positive impact on the community as a whole. GIs significantly differ from other forms of IPRs. Ninety percent patents for example are held by industrialized countries and 80% of these are held in the jurisdiction of developing countries. Thus, the benefits flowing out of the patents benefit the developed world making use of the markets of the developing world. In contrast, GI distribution is far more equitable. Trade advantages drawn from their use are thus generally pro-poor and thus more tuned towards developing countries [2].

7.5 Protection of Geographical Indications in South Asian Countries

Predominance of agricultural economy and rich cultural heritage makes Asia one of the hot spots of GI. Nevertheless, the notion of protecting GI as an intellectual property right is new. Most countries do not have separate legislations for protecting GI (*sui generis* systems) and they are incorporated within trademark laws or under laws of unfair competition. Trademark laws protect GIs either through collective marks (registered by a group of enterprises) or certification marks (registered by a supervisory entity) [10]. These are weak provisions compared to *sui generis* systems of GI protection. Entry into the WTO has led to some of the South Asian countries such as India and Bangladesh to put in place strong GI instruments.

7.5.1 India

India has implemented one of the most robust GI legislative and enforcement systems in the developing world through the Geographical Indications of Goods (Registration and Protection) Act (1999) and the Geographical Indications of Goods (Registration and Protection) Rules (2002). India's enactment of these laws and its growing role as one of the strongest international TRIPS Plus GI proponents has resulted from previous and ongoing foreign IP threats to its sensitive natural products and traditional goods [11]. The plight with the Basmati patent has possibly been the major accelerator of the enactment of such laws.

7.5.1.1 The Battle of the Basmati

During the 1990s, an US company was granted a US patent for varieties of Basmati rice (*Oryza sativa*) very similar to the ones traditionally grown in the Himalayan slopes of northern India. The company earned the right to label the patented variety of rice as "Basmati" both in the USA and other foreign markets.

Basmati rice was cultivated in northern India for centuries and constituted a major source of export revenue. More than 80% of the produce was exported and the revenue during the time was close to USD 2.2 Billion. The labelling right granted to the US company was thus considered as piracy of a traditional Indian rice variety and also an attempt to wreck the export market. Heavy negotiations from India led to the USPTO rejecting 13 of the 20 claims for the patent in view of lack of originality and also the company withdrew the claim of labelling the variety as Basmati.

The case nevertheless highlighted the inherent weakness of the institutional systems in India for protecting traditional varieties of agricultural crops whose quality owes to the specific geographical characteristics of the region in which it is produced. Similar issues were also witnessed (although to a lesser extent) for varieties of tea grown in Kenya, Nepal or Sri Lanka as Darjeeling Tea. This paved the way for formulating international instruments to safeguard such knowledgebase.

7.5.1.2 Geographical Indications of Goods (Registration and Protection) Act (1999)

In the GI Act of India [12], indication includes any name, geographical or figurative representation or combination thereof conveying or suggesting geographical origin of the goods to which it applies. Under the ambit of the Act, goods mean any agricultural, naturally occurring or manufactured goods or any goods of handicrafts or of industry and include foodstuff.

1. The Act provides very comprehensive definition of what constitute agriculture, naturally occurring or manufactured goods. Agricultural goods are derived from land through agricultural practice and include cultivation operations in the field. It excludes breeding and rearing of livestock, dairy farming, poultry farming and so on. Thus, the Act makes provisions for according protection to traditional farming practices by communities. Natural goods on the other hand are those that occur spontaneously in nature. Manufactured goods are those that are made commercially from basic raw materials through application of physical labour and mechanical processes. Interestingly, the Act considers sugar and tea as both agricultural as well as manufactured product.
2. The Act provides for a Registrar of GI, who is also the Controller General of Patents, Designs and Trademarks. The Registrar maintains a GI Registry and a Register of Geographical Indications.
3. The Indian law provides for a GI to be registered in respect of any or all of the goods, and the classification conforms to the international classification of goods.
4. Registration of certain GIs is prohibited, e.g. those that are likely to cause confusion or deception; those that are against public morality; those that are religiously susceptible. Indications that are determined to be generic names and ceased to be

protected in the country of origin or which have fallen into disuse in that country are also prohibited to be protected under the Indian GI law.
5. The law also provides registration of homonymous GIs provided the Registrar is satisfied that they would practically remain differentiated and not cause any confusion.
6. Registration of a GI would be for a period of 10 years and may be renewed from time to time for a further period of 10 years. Non-renewal would lead to the GI to be removed from the records.

The Indian GI Act is different from the TRIPS and conforms to the TRIPS Plus status with provisions to protect apart from agricultural products also natural products (e.g. coal and bauxite), manufactured goods such as sarees and shawls and also traditional cultural expressions (e.g. handicrafts).

7.5.2 Bangladesh

Bangladesh has evolved a *sui generis* system for protection of geographical indications similar to that of India. The GI Act of Bangladesh and GI Rules was adopted in 2013 and incorporates provisions of TRIPS Plus.

7.5.2.1 Bangladesh Geographical Indications Act, 2013:

The GI Act of Bangladesh [13] provides for the protection of geographical indications within the territory of Bangladesh. The Act has however been slashed to some extent with certain provisions being shifted to the Geographical Indications Rules 2015. The Act provides for the Registrar of Department of Patents, Designs and Trademarks as the competent authority for GI and allows registration of GI goods from any person or a group who are into producing he products. The Act also provides the registered authorized GI user to use the GI for a period of five years, with provision for renewal. An important flip side in the Act is the omission of granting Appellation of Origin for products.

7.5.3 Bhutan

Bhutan is yet to evolve a legal instrument to protect geographical indications. The country nevertheless has a very large number of traditional crops, vegetables, mushrooms and unique produce that are specific to the place and depend on the geographical location and climate. The products range from agro-produce such as cheese and fruit products to various forms of local handicrafts and weaving patterns.

7.5.4 Myanmar

Myanmar does not have any *sui generis* legislation or policy instrument related to geographical indications although the country harbours significant amount of agricultural, natural and cultural resources that warrants protection through appropriate GIs. Since 2013 when the champagne was officially given the first GI in Myanmar, the Ministry of Science and Technology worked to develop a Trademark Law that would also incorporate the provisions of geographical indications.

7.5.5 Nepal

Nepal is a relatively new entrant to the WTO and being a least developed country is yet to put in place an instrument to protect geographical indications. The country only has an Action Plan in order to fulfil TRIPS obligations. Nepal traditionally has a strong basis in crafts and similar products, at the same time indigenous practices in agro-based products. Geographical indication also serves as a major enabler for rural producers to exploit niche markets. This in turn impacts the standard of living of the communities through attainment of economic well-being.

7.5.6 Sri Lanka

The economy of Sri Lanka depends overwhelmingly upon one of the most famous GIs of the world namely Ceylon Tea. With an export earnings of more than USD 700 million, Ceylon Tea generates livelihood of one-tenth of Sri Lanka's population. The new IP Act adopted in 2003 provides for protection of GIs (Chap. 33 of Part IX) as a *sui generis* provision that deviates from the TRIPS. Interestingly, the GI law of Sri Lanka does not provide for registration and thus is subjected to vulnerability in enforcement similar to that experienced under copyright laws. GI protection is also provided through trademarks [14].

Except for the provisions going stronger than TRIPS in protecting agricultural products at part with Article 23 for protection of wines and spirits, the Sri Lankan law is substantially weak than that of neighbouring India or Bangladesh. For example, the Sri Lankan law does not cover handicrafts or fish products, both of which are important economic activities in the country.

7.5.7 Thailand

Thailand has a *sui generis* law for protection of GI that comprise of the GI Protection Act, 2003 and Ministerial Regulations, 2004.

7.5.7.1 Geographical Indications Protection Act 2003

The Act [15] is essentially meant to prevent the public from being confused or misled regarding geographical origin of goods and further to fulfil the obligations under Articles 22–25 of the TRIPS Agreement. As per the Act, name symbol or any other mark representing geographical origin, and details of particular quality, reputation or characteristic attributable to the specific location qualifies to be protected. Agricultural products, industrial products and handicrafts are eligible for GI. The Thai legislation allows producers and traders domiciled in the region of origin and also consumers to apply for the registration of GI.

7.5.7.2 Ministerial Regulation, 2004

The Ministerial Regulation contains rules and procedures related to the application for registration, publication, submission of opposition, registration, appeal, correction or revocation of a GI registration. It also fixes rates and fees and designates types of specific goods, e.g. rice, silk, wine and spirits.

7.5.8 Challenges to Protection of Geographical Indication in South Asian Countries

Agricultural countries advocate stronger enforcement of GIs as majority of GIs are based on agro-products. A chief challenge to the countries is to prevent deceptive use of GIs and imitations that often characterize GI products. Moreover, contiguity of the countries that are endowed with similar geographical characteristics makes it difficult to distinguish one product with another in the endeavour to provide protection. Dealing with the two tier protection system under the WTO – base protection and additional protection for wines and spirits are also important aspects to be addressed by the countries.

7.6 Conclusion

The abundance of endemic products originating from the various countries of South Asia makes the region particularly important for geographical indications. In addition to agricultural products, a number of handicrafts from the region are also protected by GI. The countries have advocated TRIPS Plus provision in order to subsume non-agricultural components into the protection regime.

References

1. Trade Related Aspects of Intellectual Property Rights, World Trade Organisation, Geneva (1992). http://www.wto.int/TRIPS. Accessed 25 Sept 2017
2. SAWTEE (2004) Geographical indications under TRIPS: protection regimes and development in Asia. SAWTEE Policy Briefs No 8
3. Rangnekar D (2002) Geographical indications: a review of proposals at the trips council. ICTSD and UNCTAD, p 7
4. Marie-Vivien D, Bienabe E (2012) The strength of the link to the origin as a criterion: geographical indications for agriculture and handicraft goods. Perspective Standards, No 17, CIRAD
5. Saha T, Bharti N (2006) Beyond wines and spirits: developing countries GI products and their potential in WTO regimes with special reference to India. J Intellect Prop Rights 11:89–97
6. The Madrid Agreement for Repression of False or Deceptive Indications of Source of Goods (1891) WIPO. http://www.wipo.int/treaties/en/ip/madrid. Accessed 25 Sept 2017
7. The Lisbon Agreement for the Protection of Appellations of Origin and their Registration (1958) WIPO. http://www.wipo.int/treaties/en/registration/lisbon/. Accessed 25 Sept 2017
8. WIPO (2017). http://www.wipo.int. Accessed 25 Sept 2017
9. Traditional knowledge and geographical indications (2002) Report on Commission on Intellectual Property Rights, London
10. Jain S (2009) Effects of extension of geographical indications: the South Asia perspective. Asia Pac Dev J 16:65–86
11. Ravi V (2003) Protection of GI in India, In WIPO Asia Pacific Symposium on GI, New Delhi
12. Geographical Indications of Goods (Registration and Protection) Act 1999 (1999). Gazette of India, Government of India
13. Bangladesh Geographical Indications Act 2013 (2013). Gazette of Bangladesh, Government of Bangladesh No, p 64
14. DeSilva LM (2015) Geographical indications: need of a registration system for Sri Lanka in 3rd International Research Conference, KDU
15. Geographical indications protection act 2003 (2003). Government of Thailand

Chapter 8
Genetically Modified Crops, Agriculture and Biosafety

8.1 Background

Biotechnology has resulted in massive strides in agriculture with respect to increasing the production, improving the quality and enhancing the value of crop plants. Higher productivity is the key to alleviation of poverty in developing countries particularly in rural areas. In terms of agricultural production, productivity gains encompass factors such as higher crop yields, lower pesticide and fertilizer application, improved crop quality, better storage and easier processing conditions, and easier production techniques. Genetically modified crops carrying specific genetic traits have been developed and released for commercial application. These crops range from high-yielding varieties, disease- and pest-resistant varieties and so on. There are traits of biofortification, phytoremediation, production of bio-pharmaceuticals, etc.

Almost 150 million hectares of crop acreage around the world have been planted with GM crops [1]. Although the Americas constitute the largest acreage, Asian fields are replete with various GM varieties particularly cotton, soyabean, maize, potato. Almost 22 developing and developed countries have commercial cultivation of GM crops with Argentina, Brazil, China and India among the developing countries that produce largest quantity of transgenic crops.

The increasing cultivation of GM crops has raised a wide range of concerns with respect to food safety, environmental effects and socio-economic issues. The chief issue is the threat of introgression of the transgene into natural gene pool, impact on the germplasm, evolution of mutants and importantly a loss of biodiversity. Socio-economic issues include concerns for access to genetic resources, loss of traditions (e.g. saving, resowing seeds) and monopoly by firms leading to formalisation of seed sector leading to resource constraints for the farmers.

8.2 The Cartagena Protocol on Biosafety

The Cartagena Protocol on Biosafety came into force in 2003 and by 2011 was adopted by 161 countries of the world. The objective of the Protocol as stated

"is to contribute to ensuring an adequate level of protection in the field of the safe transfer, handling and use of living modified organisms resulting from modern biotechnology that may have adverse effects on the conservation and sustainable use of biological diversity, taking also into account risks to human health, and specifically focusing on trans-boundary movements" [2, 3].

8.2.1 Salient Features of the Protocol

The Cartagena Protocol promotes biosafety through establishment of rules and procedures for safe transfer and handling of live modified organisms (LMOs) and their trans-boundary movement. There are two sets of procedures. One covers those that are intentionally set to be introduced into the environment. The other covers those LMOs that are intended to be used as food or feed or for processing. Regulations covering transboundary movements involve creation of detailed documentation concerning the LMO including its identity and contact point for further information. This feature enables importing countries to have information regarding the concerned LMO and also the procedures to handle the same in a safe manner.

In order to create a mechanism for facilitating exchange of information among parties that include capacity building, financial procedures, compliance procedures and public engagement, the Cartagena Protocol provides for establishment of a Biosafety Clearing House.

8.2.1.1 Procedure for Advanced Informed Agreement (AIA)

The Advanced Informed Agreement (AIA) is applicable for LMOs to be intentionally introduced into the environment. It applies only for the first trans-boundary movement and extends across seeds, live animals and other organisms that has the ability to pass on the modified genes to succeeding generations. The AIA provides the importing country to assess the risk associated with the LMO. There are four components in the procedure namely notification by exporter, acknowledgement by the importer, decision procedures and review of decisions.

8.2.1.2 Procedures for LMOs Intended for Use as Food or Feed for Processing

This category of LMO is not intended for growing new crops but intended for direct use as food or feed. It represents a very large category of agricultural commodities. For such applications, the Protocol requires governments of user countries to approve these commodities for domestic use and communicate the decision to the international community through the Biosafety Clearing House within a fortnight of its decision. Detailed information about the product and the decision should accompany the communication.

8.2.1.3 Risk Assessment and Risk Management

The Protocol empowers governments to undertake risk assessments that aim to identify the potential adverse effects of the LMO on environment. There is also provision to have this study financed by the exporter.

As an obligation, onus of management and control of any risks associated with release of LMOs to environment rests with the corresponding country. Furthermore, the key elements of this management and control comprise of monitoring, research, capacity strengthening and domestic stakeholder coordination.

8.2.1.4 Other Miscellaneous Provisions

The Cartagena Protocol provides detailed framework for handling, transport, packaging and identification of LMOs and also laid down procedures in the event of unintentional trans-boundary movement. The Protocol also provides for capacity building for countries that trade LMOs, a provision of financial assistance under the Global Environment Facility, and initiatives for raising public awareness and participation in all aspects of biosafety. Setting up of institutional mechanisms at national level is also an important provision under the protocol.

8.3 The Nagoya-Kuala Lumpur Supplementary Protocol on Liability and Redress

The Nagoya–Kuala Lumpur Supplementary Protocol was adopted in 2010 during a session on Cartagena Protocol in Nagoya. The Supplementary Protocol was signed till 2014 by 51 countries of the world. It is intended to supplement the Cartagena Protocol on Biosafety by providing international rules and procedures on liability and redress for damage to biodiversity resulting from LMOs. The focus of the Supplementary Protocol is on the procedures of remedial measures that countries should adopt in the event of damage to biodiversity by LMOs and GMOs.

The Supplementary Protocol also provides flexibility in regulatory approaches by allowing parties to use their existing laws or new laws to protect the damage caused through LMO/GMOs. Thus, there is a context for safe use of biotechnology without jeopardising the concerns of biosafety [2].

8.4 The Global Concerns on Use of Genetically Modified Organisms in Food and Agriculture

The growing population has led to a continuous increase in the global demand for food. Nevertheless, there is a concomitant reduction in arable land that has put a special challenge on the world's food and agricultural systems. Moreover, there is an enhanced consumer demand for improved food quality, ability of food to enhance health and also demand for such food that conforms to desired safety standards. Over the years, biotechnology has emerged as a major enabling tool in improvement of food quality and quantity by increasing food production that are derived from genetically modified crops. Important characteristics of such food include higher yield, need for less quantity of agricultural chemicals, improved nutritional content, imparting special properties to the food, increasing their shelf life and so on [4].

The global debate on genetically modified crops (GM crops) and genetically modified food and food ingredient (GM food) has currently shifted its focus from whether it should be used or not to how it can be used safely. As GM crops are developed and released for field trials and more of them being approved for commercial cultivation, there is an increasing concern on their impact and potential risk to human health and particularly to the environment. There is an imminent risk of cross-fertilization resulting in contamination of the natural germplasm, and thus a risk to the biodiversity. There is also a risk of the GM variety subjugating a number of land races due to their improved characters. Apart from these concerns, it is the concern related to the economics of agricultural production. This range from the farmers' ability to save and resow seeds; the access of farmers to improved seeds and the various facets of IPR protection [5].

8.5 GM Crops and Biosafety in South Asian Countries

South Asia represents a hot spot for biodiversity and also has the highest acreage of genetically modified crops outside the Americas. Rules and protocols governing biosafety are thus of particular relevance to the region. Among the countries that form part of our discussion, all the countries are parties to the Cartagena Protocol and have acceded to the obligation of fair and safe use of genetic material. Among them, India has the largest arable area under GM cultivation, essentially cotton.

8.5.1 India

India ratified the Cartagena Protocol in 2003 and has put in place a structured legislative and institutional mechanism for safeguarding biosafety.

8.5.1.1 Rules for GMOs

The Ministry of Environment and Forests notified the rules and procedures for manufacture, use, import, research and release of GMOs as well as products made by use of such organisms in 1989 known as Rules 1989. They fall under the Environment Protection Act, 1986. The Rules 1989 provide for constitution of six statutory competent authorities for regulating use of GMOs. These are the Recombinant DNA Advisory Committee (RDAC), Institutional Biosafety Committee (IBSC), Review Committee on Genetic Manipulation (RCGM), Genetic Engineering Approval Committee (GEAC), State Biosafety Coordination Committee (SBCC) and District Level Committee (DLC). Tasked with defined functions, these authorities provide overall approvals, monitoring, guidelines and implementation of GM technology application in agricultural and other uses [6].

8.5.1.2 Guidelines for Research in Transgenic Plants, 1998

This was brought out by the Department of Biotechnology that guide research into transgenic plants including allergenicity and toxicity of transgenic seeds, plants and parts thereof.

8.5.1.3 Seed Policy, 2002

The Seed Policy 2002 has a specific section (No 6) on transgenic plant varieties. This section warrants that environmental safety and biosafety of all genetically modified crops/varieties are to be tested prior to commercial release. Further, it provides for all transgenic seeds to be imported only through the designated nodal agency namely the National Bureau of Plant Genetic Resources. Interestingly, the policy states that transgenic varieties can be protected under the Plant Varieties Protection and Farmers Rights Act in the same way as non-transgenic varieties after their release for commercial cultivation.

8.5.1.4 Plant Quarantine Order, 2003

The provisions of Plant Quarantine (Regulation of Import into India) Order, 2003, are applicable for import of transgenic seeds. It requires issuance of import permit for which the designated competent authority is the National Bureau of Plant Genetic Resources. As per the Order, import permit and phyto-sanitary certificate from originating country has to be mandatorily obtained by all plant breeders and researchers prior to import of seed or planting materials.

8.5.1.5 Regulation for Import of GM Products Under Foreign Trade Policy, 2006

This set of regulations inserted into Schedule I (Imports) of the Foreign Trade Policy notifies the relevant provisions for import of genetically modified food, feed, organisms and live modified organisms into the country.

8.5.1.6 National Environment Policy, 2006

This policy provides for reviewing the regulatory processes for genetically modified organisms and also the National Biosafety guidelines and Biosafety Operation Manual.

8.5.2 Bangladesh

As a signatory to the Cartagena Protocol, Bangladesh framed its Biosafety Guidelines in 2005 and the NBF was developed in 2006. The Biosafety Rules were reviewed in 2012. Bangladesh has approved limited farm cultivation of Bt brinjal (eggplant) and trials are being conducted for golden rice and blight-resistant potato, both of GM varieties [7].

8.5.2.1 Biosafety Guidelines, 2005

It is applicable for all biotechnological research and development activities covering all categories of institutions, e.g. universities, research laboratories, industries and also on all aspects of field trial, trans-boundary movement, handling, risk assessment, safe transit and so on.

8.5.2.2 National Biosafety Framework, 2006

This provides the framework for management of biotechnology products in Bangladesh. The NBF has two fold objectives—an oversight into existing regulations; and an identification for the future needs for effective legislation and administrative procedures in biotechnology application. The NBF is important in context of biosafety as it would form the umbrella regulation for use of all forms of GMO in Bangladesh.

8.5.2.3 Biosafety Rules of Bangladesh, 2012

The Rules provide for regulation of development, import, export, use, and movement of all GMO products and empowers the state to adopt punitive measures against misuse of GMO products. The operating document comprises of the Biosafety Guidelines of Bangladesh that is legally binding under the Biosafety Rules with the Ministry of Environment and Forests being the nodal authority for implementation of the rules in Bangladesh.

8.5.3 Bhutan

Bhutan ratified the Cartagena Protocol in 2002. However, it neither grows GM crops nor does it import GM crops or food. The National Biosafety Framework was ratified in 2006 and implemented in 2010 [8].

8.5.3.1 Food Act, 2005; Food Rules and Regulation, 2006

This is the universal legislation that cover all aspects of food safety including those from GM food. The Rules and Regulations of 2006 aim at preventing introduction of feed-borne hazards into food items, regulate production, processing, transport and distribution of food.

8.5.3.2 National Biosafety Framework, 2007 and Draft Biosafety Bill, 2013

The NBF has been prepared in accordance with the prescriptions of National Environment Commission of Bhutan. The country is currently finalizing the Biosafety Bill. This Bill that envisages mitigation of adverse effects of genetically modified organisms on conservation and sustainable use of natural resources. In this context, the legislation is slated to regulate the transit, trans-boundary movement, safe handling and use of all genetically modified organisms. An important element of the legislation is the establishment of BAFRA, National Biosafety Commission, and Regulatory guidelines for reporting and monitoring, guidelines for risk assessment and database for GMOs and products.

In addition to the above, the Plant Quarantine Act (1993), the Seed Act (2000), Environment Assessment Act (2000), Biodiversity Act (2003) have various provisions having implications on biosafety aspects of genetically modified crops.

8.5.4 Myanmar

Myanmar acceded to the Cartagena Protocol in 2001 and ratified the same in 2008; while the National Biosafety Framework was implemented in 2006. The legislation in the country is however still in the draft stage. Only one GM crop, namely insect resistant Bt cotton is under commercial cultivation in Myanmar [9].

8.5.4.1 Myanmar National Biosafety Framework, 2006

The NBF provides policy, regulatory regime and mechanisms of handling safe transfer of GMOs/LMOs. It also envisages establishing a system for enforcement and monitoring of biosafety regulations and also to undertake training and capacity building exercises.

8.5.4.2 Draft Biosafety Law of Myanmar, 2006

The Law that is still in a draft stage is applicable to development, contained use, field test, intentional introduction into the environment, and import and export of GMO that is envisaged to have an adverse effect on environment particularly those on conservation and sustainable use of biological resources. Adverse effects and risks to human health are also considered. The law also intends to provide a standard operating procedure for handling GMOs including decision making connected threto. Measures to deal with non-compliance, enforcement, liabilities and penalties are also elaborated in this law.

In addition to the above regulations, other existing laws such as the Forest Law (1992), Plant Quarantine Law (1993) and the Seeds Law (2011, enforced in 2013) also have certain provisions for dealing with biosafety-related issues.

8.5.5 Nepal

Nepal's biosafety legislations and policy frameworks are still in a nascent stage. There is only a rudimentary level research in GM crops with no variety either grown, registered or commercialized in the country. Nepal has signed the Cartagena Protocol in 2001 but is yet to ratify it and its National Biosafety Framework is still in the draft stage [10].

8.5.5.1 Draft National Biosafety Framework, 2007

Similar to other countries, in consonance with the mandate, the NBF applies to production, development and contained use, field test, intentional release into the environment, import/export of GMOs that might have adverse effect on the environment and risks to human health. Research, development, safety in transport and public participation form important areas of focus under the NBF.

8.5.5.2 Draft Biosafety Bill, 2007

The Biosafety Bill applies to the development, production, contained use, field test, intentional introduction into the environment, and import and export of GMO that may have an adverse effect on the conservation and sustainable use of biological diversity and environment, taking also into account the risks to human health.

The Plant Protection Act (2002) and the Seeds Act (2010) are other legislations that have certain provisions for regulation of biosafety.

8.5.6 Sri Lanka

Sri Lanka has signed the Cartagena Protocol in 2000 and ratified it in 2004 and has in place a National Biosafety Framework since 2005. Nevertheless, the research into GMOs for food, feed or processing is yet to go out of the confines of the laboratories. Field testing and trials are still being awaited pending passage of the proposed Biosafety Bill. Current regulatory instruments and legislations related to biosafety are thus mostly those integrated into other related legislations [11].

8.5.6.1 Plant Protection Act, 1999

The Act prohibits introduction into Sri Lanka and spreading therein any organisms or seeds that would be prejudicial to the country's environment.

8.5.6.2 National Biosafety Framework, 2005

Sri Lanka's NBF is based on a conservative approach, wherein it is envisaged to minimize the negative impact of biotechnology in form of damage to environment and biodiversity that might be caused through intentional introduction of GMOs.

8.5.6.3 Draft National Guidelines for Import and Planned Release of GMOs and Products Thereof, 2005

Although yet to be finalized, the guidelines envisage regulating trans-boundary movement of GMOs.

8.5.7 Thailand

No GM crops are presently grown in Thailand on a commercial scale, although field trials have been conducted for Flavr Savr tomatoes, Bt corn, Bt cotton and papaya. Field trials have been suspended since 2003 as a result for concern for health and environment. Thailand signed the Cartagena Protocol in 2006.

8.5.7.1 Plant Quarantine Act 2008

According to the Act, GM plants are prohibited in Thailand and their importation would require case by case approval in terms of regulations, notifications and relevant orders when such imports are necessary for the purpose of research or experimentation alone. Notifications issued under the Act by the Department of Agriculture give a comprehensive documentation of conditions and guidelines required to be adhered to and also a list of prohibited GM materials for the benefit of stakeholders.

8.5.7.2 National Biosafety Framework, 2006

Thailand's National Biosafety Framework is arranged across five key sub-frameworks, together which govern the regulation and control of biosafety in the country. The sub-frameworks include National Biosafety Policy Framework, National Biosafety Legal and Regulatory Framework, National Biosafety Institutional Framework, National Biosafety Handling Framework, and National Biosafety Technical Guidelines Framework. The NBF thus integrates various scattered legislations and regulatory instruments into a harmonious system for biosafety.

8.5.7.3 Draft Act on Biosafety, 2012

The principle of the draft Act on the Biosafety B.E. is to control and monitor the utilization of living modified organisms (LMOs), including its safe direct use LMOs for food or feed or processing, both from abroad or domestically, in appropriate manner and in accordance with international implementation, for protection and conservation of biological diversity, taking into account of human and animal health and also consumer protection.

The Act has 73 articles spread over 8 chapters. Operational provisions on import, export, transit and contained use of LMOs (including field trial and intentional release into environment) are also covered in the Act. Additionally, there are provisions that guide procedures of packaging and identification and also liability and redress during eventualities.

8.6 Conclusion

The region discussed here exhibits the largest spread of GM crops in the world outside the Americas. Despite environmental concerns associated with GM technologies, we have seen a progressive growth of governance and legislative frameworks for biosafety, safe movement and containment of GMOs and also effective systems for liability and redress. As evident from above, it is important to strengthen the latter substantially if GM crops are to be adopted further to enhance agricultural production.

References

1. ISAAA (2016) Global status of commercialized biotech/GM crops. ISAAA Brief 52
2. Convention for Biological Diversity, Statute of Convention of Biological Diversity, Annex I (1992). http://www.cbd.int. Accessed 25 Sept 2017
3. Cartagena Protocol on Biosafety, Annex to the Convention of Biological Diversity (2006). http://www.cbd.int/cartagena. Accessed 25 Sept 2017
4. Kerr WA, Smyth S (2014) PPMP conflicting rules for the international trade of GM products: Does international law provide a solution? AgroBioForum 17:105–122
5. APO (2016) Use and regulation of genetically modified organisms: Report of the APO study meeting on the use and regulation of GMO, China
6. Ahuja V, Jotwani G (2006) The Regulation of Genetically Modified Organisms in India. Department of Biotechnology, Government of India
7. Biosafety Guidelines of Bangladesh (2005). Gazette of Bangladesh, Government of Bangladesh
8. Yangzom T (2013) Biosafety regulation of GE/GM plants in Bhutan, South Asia Biosafety Conference, New Delhi
9. National Biosafety Framework of Myanmar (2006). Government of Myanmar
10. Thapa M (2013) Regulatory frameworks for GMO and hybrid seeds in Nepal. Agron J Nepal 3:128–137
11. Perera A (2016) Biosafety regulations in Sri Lanka, ILSI Research Foundation

Chapter 9
Access to Genetic Resources and Sharing of Benefits

9.1 Background

As stated in a previous chapter, developing countries comprise of more than 90% of the biological diversity in the world. This range from forest wealth, marine and freshwater resources, large expanse of endemic germplasm of agricultural, economically important and medicinal plants, and finally a large tacit knowledge of endogenous communities that are primarily drawn from these natural resources. While it is of seminal importance to conserve such resources, it is also important to promote their judicious exploitation as most of these natural resources are unequivocal sources of livelihood for the communities that harbour them. This has led to the concept of wise use of the world's biodiversity in order to balance needs with obligations. The underlying challenge is therefore regulation of access to such resources and equitable sharing of benefits arising from their use. The latter objective is particularly pertinent to developing countries which are usually denied of the expected share of the benefits [1].

9.2 The Issue of Access and Benefit Sharing

Article 15 of the Convention of Biological Diversity defines the terms and conditions for access to genetic resources and benefit sharing. The hallmark of the Article is the recognition of sovereign rights of the State over its natural resources and thus makes it obligatory on part of the user of such resource to take prior informed consent of the owner of the resource. It further provides that the conditions of access shall be regulated by mutual agreed upon terms between the Contracting Parties [2, 3].

9.3 The Case of Ayahuasca Patent Revocation: Why Do We Need a Harmonious ABS Regime

In 1986, Loren Miller obtained an US patent on a strain of ayahuasca vine. Ayahuasca vine (that is native to the Amazon rainforest) is known for its use throughout the Amazon region for its healing properties since centuries. It has been used to treat sickness, contact spirits and foresee the future. The plant is considered sacred by the local community. The local community provided Miller with a sample of ayahuasca in 1974, which he cultivated in the Hawaii and developed a stable variety that was eligible for being patented. The plant patent on ayahuasca was called Da Vine, where Miller claimed it represented a new and unique variety that was distinct from other known forms primarily because of the colour of its flower petals [4].

Several years after grant of the patent, tribal leaders came to learn of the protection and claimed that this was a part of their traditional knowledge that was pirated out by foreigners. Application for the revocation was made to the US Patent and Trademark Office in 1999, by the Coordinating Body of Indigenous Organizations of the Amazon Basin (COICA). They filed a request of re-examination based on the following points:

1. Da Vine was not in fact distinct or new as claimed but was a part of prior art. It thus did not satisfy the novelty criterion of the Patent Act. The description of ayahuasca in Millers patent was already illustrated in the scientific literature and known to the indigenous Amazonian people.
2. The vine is found in an uncultivated state and thus its patenting violates provisions of the Plant Patent Act.
3. The ayahuasca plant was sacred to the indigenous people. As such, granting patent to the same that was acquired surreptitiously was a violation of public policy and morality thereby contravening with the utility criteria of the Patent Act.

Examination indicated that Da Vine was identical to the other specimens of ayahuasca found in the US herbarium collections. It was found that the same plant was described in herbarium data of Chicago's Field Museum at least one year prior to Miller's application. Based on this finding, the Patent and Trademark Office allowed the re-examination request and after reviewing the facts ordered rejection of Miller's patent entirely.

The ayahuasca patent revocation case has set forth few major issues regarding the US patent system in relation to life forms. These are as follows:

1. Biotechnology and use of biodiversity for industrial applications have resulted in a complete redefinition of the morality factor. Inventions based on traditional knowledge, community knowledge, etc., made without informed consent of the concerned community; exploitation of natural resources causing loss of biodiversity; generation of products that result in environmental contamination, etc., constitute immoral activities under the present understanding that should result in refusal in grant of patent. The provision of Article-27.2 of the TRIPS which states that patent protection would be barred in commercial exploitation of an invention would harm public policy or morality, somewhat addresses this issue.

2. Recognition of Foreign Prior Use: The US patent law does not recognize foreign prior use in the form of traditional knowledge as a prior art for a patent. This exclusion provided by the law has been strongly criticized in recent times, particularly in the wake of increased international communication, travel and trade. In the ayahuasca case, Miller travelled to Ecuador where the indigenous people gave him sample of the vine. As the source of information was outside the United States, subsequent patent applications did not require him to acknowledge the traditional knowledge. It is felt that due to increased ease of traveling to foreign countries, information gathered there, whether previously published or not should be credited as prior art under the Patent Act.
3. Morality component in the utility requirement: Elucidation of utility is one of the fundamental requirement under patent laws. There is sufficient ground to advocate that a component of morality should be introduced into the requirement of utility in patent applications. In the past, utility of an invention was sufficient to make it patentable and rejection of patents on the basis of immorality was limited to its use to defraud buyers or for use in gambling or similar activities.

9.4 Evolution of International Protocols for ABS

Immediately after the CBD came into effect, groups of megadiverse countries primarily from South America, Africa and Asia pushed for adoption of an international regime based on the argument that the obligations of user countries were instrumental in enforcing ABS in the countries of origin. The claim received high support in view of large number of cases of misappropriations that had occurred in the past. Apart from the Ayahuasca case of Brazil, Ethiopia had also experienced a somewhat similar case for its teff crop with a Dutch company. In this case, although the company signed up for sharing benefit with teff farmers, the terms could not be effectively negotiated due of lack of a clear governance framework.

This call was finally adopted by the World Summit for Sustainable Development at Johannesburg in 2002, which put in place the Johannesburg Plan of Implementation. This led to the Bonn Guidelines for Access to Genetic Resources and Fair and Equitable Sharing of Benefits Arising out of their Utilization.

9.4.1 The Bonn Guidelines

The Convention of Biological Diversity was adopted in 1992. However, it was not before 1999 that work began to develop appropriate instruments to implement its provisions. An inter-governmental meeting in October 2001 resulted in formulation of the Bonn Guidelines on Access to Genetic Resources and the Fair and Equitable Sharing of Benefits Arising out of their Utilization. The Guidelines were adopted in 2002.

The scope of the Bonn Guidelines extends across all genetic resources and associated traditional knowledge and community practices.

The Bonn Guidelines are non-binding guidelines, envisaged to be adopted on a voluntary basis. It was felt that there was need to evolve an international regime for ABS and devise effective instruments of implementation of the provisions enshrined under Article 15 and Article 8(j) of the CBD. In course of the COP7, the Ad Hoc Working Group in ABS was mandated with this task of negotiating and elaborating an acceptable system, which was continued during subsequent COPs. The negotiations ended in the Nagoya Protocol.

9.4.2 The Nagoya Protocol

The Nagoya Protocol is the chief operating instrument for harmonising ABS regimes in member countries. The primary objective of the protocol is fair and equitable sharing of benefits arising out of utilization of genetic resources. Incidentally, the protocol also envisages to provide appropriate access to resources and also appropriate transfer of relevant technologies. It thus aims at conservation of biodiversity along with sustainable use of natural resources. The scope of the Nagoya Protocol applies to Article 15 of the Convention of Biological Diversity and also to traditional knowledge applied to genetic resources [5].

As with most of the similar instruments, the Nagoya Protocol is a minimum standard agreement; i.e. it sets the minimum standard and leaves room to the contracting parties to evolve more stringent measures of access and benefit sharing. The Protocol also does not overlap with or contradicts other instruments provided that they are not prejudicial to the tenets of the Convention of Biological Diveristy or the Protocol itself; i.e. their exercise would cause damage to biodiversity and safeguard of genetic resource and their appropriation.

Some of the salient features of the Nagoya Protocol are listed as follows:

1. Benefits arising from utilization of genetic resources and also their subsequent application and commercialization shall be shared in a fair and equitable way with the party providing the resources, i.e. the country of origin. The benefits can include both monetary as well as non-monetary benefits.
2. Administrative, legislative and policy measures shall be adopted to ensure that the actual holder of the resource, i.e. indigenous or local community get share of the benefit through domestically laid down laws as per mutually agreed terms.
3. In exercise of sovereign rights over the natural resources, access to such resources shall be based upon prior informed consent of the concerned party. Such consent shall also be subject to the involvement and consent of the local and indigenous community harbouring the resource concerned.
4. The parties shall develop and put in place a comprehensive institutional mechanism for implementing the requirement of prior informed consent. This would include a clear compilation of rules and procedures and also appropriate provisions for dispute resolution.

9.4 Evolution of International Protocols for ABS

5. It would be ensured that the parties develop domestic measures to ensure that the traditional knowledge associated with genetic resources that are held by local communities and/or indigenous communities are adequately safeguarded. Access to such resources should be through prior informed consent of the concerned community.
6. The indigenous communities who are holders of traditional knowledge shall inform the users of such knowledge about their obligations. Local and indigenous communities would also be included into the decision-making process.
7. There are certain special considerations laid down in the protocol. These include promotion of research into conservation and sustainable use of biodiversity through simplified access conditions; provision for expeditious access during conditions of emergencies and natural calamities; and provide for special access to genetic resources associated with food and agriculture with reference to food security.
8. In addition to the above, the protocol provides for creation of an ABS Clearing House and Information Sharing mechanism; a mechanism of trans-boundary movement; global multilateral benefit-sharing system; national focal points and competent national authorities; systems for monitoring utilization of genetic resources; and compliant domestic legislations for implementing the provisions of the protocol.
9. Raising of global and local awareness on access and benefit-sharing and building capacity of stakeholders is also important provisions of the protocol.

9.5 ABS in South Asian Countries

The countries under discussion are all signatories to the CBD and have since then ratified the Nagoya Protocol. This obligation coupled with other collateral protocols/treaties has led to a proactive attempt by the countries to evolve their own laws to enforce the ABS.

9.5.1 India

India is one of the hot spots of genetic resources, plant resources, forest resources, community resources and those derived from traditional knowledge. Two major legal frameworks in India are instrumental in enforcing the obligations enshrined in the ABS. These are:

1. National Biodiversity Act (2002)
2. Protection of Plant Varieties and Farmers Rights Act (2001)

While all the legislation have several facets, we shall discuss here only those that have direct implication on ABS.

9.5.1.1 National Biodiversity Act 2002

National Biodiversity Act (2002) warrants safeguard to benefit sharing on a case by case basis. The Article 21 (1) of the NBA states:

'...benefit sharing to be carried out in accordance with mutually agreed terms and conditions between persons applying for such approval, local bodies concerned and the benefit claimers'

The Indian NBA envisages enforcement of ABS in one or more of the following ways:

1. Joint ownership of IPRs
2. Transfer of technology
3. Location of production units to improve standard of living
4. Establish venture capital funding
5. Payment of monetary and non-monetary benefits

Let us consider examples of some benefits arising out of the above provision of the NBA. Bio India Biologicals, a plant product-based agro-company-sourced neem leaf *(Azadirechta indica)* from cultivators in Andhra Pradesh and exported the same outside the country for developing pharmacutical valued added products. During 2012, NBA received a royalty of around USD 72,000, part of which was transferred to the local group for re-planting neem trees.

9.5.1.2 Protection of Plant Varieties and Farmers Rights Act 2001

The Plant Varieties and Farmers Rights Act also serves as an important instrument in India for regulating ABS. The Act is discussed in greater details in the relevant chapter. With regard to ABS, the Indian PVP Act provides for the applicant of registration to provide in details passport data of the parent line, i.e. the source and origin of the germplasm. Information of any specific indigenous or local community or tribe or village involved in developing the breed is also required to be provided under the same clause. Under the Act, the Plant Variety Regulatory Authority is empowered and mandated to determine the benefit-sharing norms for any developed variety. Thus, the provisions of the Act play a crucial role in regulating the access to any indigenous resource while developing a given plant variety and also provide a framework for a workable benefit-sharing model.

9.5.1.3 Challenges for ABS Regimes in India

Despite existence of a number of frameworks, India is still far from evolving a strong ABS regime. One of the major challenges is to establish institutional structures to detect access to biological resources. Apart from certain regions of Northeast India, rarely there exist any movement restriction in regions that comprise biological hot spots.

To make matters worse, there is also very scanty documentation of local knowledge and little effort on creation of databases (except the creation and maintenance of Traditional Knowledge Digital Library by CSIR, as discussed in a different chapter), and also guidelines for ABS implementation in the country. It is also important to enhance technological capabilities for validation of local knowledge. Indian companies (especially pharmaceutical companies) often source a number of materials from the country's biological resources. It would be important for the companies to share benefit with the local communities. Although there exist a number of gaps in implementation of a seamless ABS regime in India, the country also has a major success story in ABS that can be evolved as a model practice for the country and outside, as we shall see in the following section.

9.5.1.4 The Kani Tribal Model: Success Story in ABS Implementation

Although there are gaps in achieving a harmonious ABS regime in India, the country nonetheless has also witnessed one successful model of ABS that can be cited as an example [6]. An indigenous tribe in Kerala called the Kani have long recognised the use of arogyapacha in enhancing stamina. After this discovery (or rediscovery) the active principle in arogyapacha was developed as a drug called Jeevani by an organisation called Arya Vaidya Shala in association with the Tropical Botanical Garden Research Institute (a government research laboratory). Post commercialisation, 50% of the royalty is shared with the Kanis and more than 70% of the tribal members receive the benefits. The interesting part of the story is that this unique and successful benefit-sharing and informed access model pre-dates the CBD.

9.5.2 Bangladesh

Bangladesh signed and ratified the Convention of Biological Diversity in 1992 and 1994, respectively, making it among the first group of countries to enter into a rule-based regime for protection of environment and natural resources. However, it signed the Nagoya Protocol in 2011 which it is yet to ratify, along with the supplementary protocol of the Nagoya–Kuala Lumpur convention. This delay in ratification has been attributed chiefly due to lacuna in capacity building for prudent handling of the protocol [2].

Very similar to India, access to genetic resources and benefit-sharing aspects in Bangladesh has been usually dealt with under two legal provisions namely:

1. Protection of Plant Varieties and Farmers Rights Act (2014)
2. Bangladesh Biodiversity Act (2012)

Both of the above legislation are in advanced stages of adoption.

9.5.2.1 Bangladesh Plant Variety Protection and Farmers Rights Act 2014

The Plant Variety Protection and Farmers Rights Act (2014) has provisions for prior informed consent and benefit sharing in case of using traditional farmers' varieties of seeds. ABS provisions are also envisaged under use of traditional breeding practices and the associated community knowledge.

9.5.2.2 Bangladesh Biodiversity Act 2012

The Bangladesh Biodiversity Act in 2012 seeks to regulate access to biological resources in the country, protect knowledge of the local communities, provide for conservation and sustainable utilization of biodiversity and to ensure the benefits from utilization of knowledge are appropriately shared with the local communities who have actually held and conserved the knowledge over generations.

As mentioned above, Bangladesh has maintained a strict position with respect to capacity building issues as a prerequisite of ratification of the Nagoya Protocol. It has pushed for raising public education and mass awareness on ABS, community empowerment and translation of dissemination materials into local languages. Apart from this, it has stressed on developing negotiation skills on Mutually Agreed Terms (MAT) and Prior Informed Consent (PIC) procedures. Apart from the above, Bangladesh has stressed upon creation of a detailed inventory and repository of biological resources.

9.5.2.3 Challenges for ABS Regimes in Bangladesh

Implementation of the Nagoya Protocol for Bangladesh is being delayed owing to issues concerning capacity builing on legal and institutional aspects towards ensuring effective handling of the process. Development and fine-tuning of this support system is a key challenge for the country to evolve a functional ABS regime. Apart from this, similar institutional support would also be important in implementing the provisions of the Biological Diversity Act of Bangladesh that includes among others community empowerment, developing negotiation skills on mutually agreed terms (MAT) and prior informed consent (PIC). The country also needs to prepare a biodiversity register that provides a detailed inventory of all the biodiversity resources that needs protection [7].

9.5.3 Bhutan

Bhutan as a signatory to the CBD had acceded to the Nagoya Protocol, although it is yet to evolve a definitive legislative provision for enforcing its application.

Constitutionally, Bhutan has expressed its commitment for wise use of its genetic and biological resource to achieve economic, social and spiritual development of its people. The same is also enshrined in *Bhutan 2020: A Vision for Peace, Prosperity and Happiness.*

Article 1.2 of the Bhutan Constitution states that 'the rights over mineral resources, rivers, lakes and forests shall vest in the State and are the properties of the State, which shall be regulated by law' [8, 9].

9.5.3.1 Bhutan Biodiversity Act 2002

The Biodiversity Act of Bhutan 2003 was enacted to provide wide ranging coverage to all forms of natural wealth of Bhutan including regulation of access to genetic resources and associated traditional knowledge prior to the adoption of the Nagoya Protocol. However, experience with this Act since 2003 and the adoption of the Nagoya Protocol in 2010 has underpinned need for a more comprehensive and encompassing ABS policy for Bhutan that would suffice in implementing various provisions of the international regime.

9.5.3.2 Challenges and Status of Implementation of ABS

Although the Biodiversity Act of Bhutan is yet to evolve a comprehensive mechanism of implementing access and benefit-sharing protocol, the country has in place various policy frameworks to facilitate the same. The ABS policy is based on some basic principles. Firstly, it is accepted that there is an intimate link between Bhutan's biological and genetic resources and its unique traditional and cultural ethos. It is thus felt that the legislative framework should adequately address the intertwined existence of both these aspects. Secondly, fair and equitable sharing of benefits arising out of utilisation of Bhutan's natural resources with the local communities who are their custodians would be in alignment with Article-5 of the Constitution of Bhutan that mandates conservation and sustainable use of its natural resources.

With regard to facilitating ABS, the Biodiversity Action Plan of 1998, 2002 and 2009 lays down a broad ambit for bioprospecting, sustainable use and commercial and research exploitation of the natural resources of Bhutan. Some enabling provisions are also provided under the Forest and Nature Conservation Act of Bhutan.

The fundamental challenge before Bhutan is to develop a harmonious version of the legislative framework that balances its obligations under the CBD and Nagoya Protocol with those that exist in the constitution and other collateral instruments of the country [7, 10].

9.5.4 Myanmar

Myanmar does not have any legislation or policy instrument related to ABS. It is felt important that the Environment Conservation Law (2012), the Seed Law (2011) and Wildlife Law (2011) may be appropriately tweaked to incorporate ABS provisions.

9.5.5 Nepal

Similar to Bhutan, although Nepal is signatory to the CBD and is committed to provide a comprehensive ABS regime under the Nagoya protocol, its legislative frameworks have failed to reflect these commitments [11, 12].

9.5.5.1 Draft Access to Genetic Resources and Benefit-Sharing Bill

Nepal has drafted an Access to Genetic Resources and Benefit-Sharing Bill (called the ABS Bill) that mandates to provide sovereign rights over the country's genetic resources and traditional knowledge, facilitate access to such resource and work out a modality for equitable sharing of benefits to local communities. Traditional knowledge has been accorded priority in the legislation and a National Genetic Resource Council has been tasked with negotiating the procedures. The legislation if implemented would vest the rights of genetic resources with the local communities and will also allow governments, local bodies and other organizations to document biodiversity and associated components that warrant protection.

9.5.5.2 Nepal Biodiversity Strategy 2002 and Nepal Biodiversity Strategy and Implementation Plan 2014

The National Biodiversity Strategy (NBS) of Nepal was designed to provide a strategic policy framework for 20 years to shape up the country's framework in line with the obligations of the CBD. Although vague in some aspects, the NBS provides liberal access to the country's genetic resources with proposals to protect the rights of farmers and local communities. While it provides for identification of priority areas for bioprospecting, the strategy does not define the process of prior informed consent (PIC) and on the mutually agreed terms (MAT) for utilisation.

The Biodiversity Strategy and Implementation Plan (BSIP) provides for a 35-year vision. It calls for expanding the community-based management of plant genetic resources, ex situ conservation programmes, promoting indigenous knowledge, skills and practices for a sustainable management of biodivesity. The Plan has also attempted to identify institutional mechanisms in implementation.

9.5.5.3 Challenges in Implementation of ABS

Nepal is yet to formalise its ABS legislation and enter into a regime warranted under the CBD. The draft ABS Bill, although reasonably comprehensive does contain certain vagaries. For instance, it has not acknowledged the specialities and issues associated with agricultural genetic resources. The Bill is deficient in disclosure requirement for IPR and provisions for documentation of agro-genetic resources and technology transfer are weakly elaborated [12, 13].

9.5.6 Sri Lanka

Despite accession and ratification to the CBD, Sri Lanka does not have an explicit legislative or policy framework for regulating access to genetic resources. Access to biological and natural resources in Sri Lanka is large governed by two legislation namely the Import and Export Control Act and the Flora and Fauna Protection Ordinance. Both these instruments are primarily aimed at regulating movement of animals and plants or parts thereof across the country border as a part of trade.

Sri Lankan law does not recognize the sovereign rights of the State over its biological resources. Similarly, there is no clear provision of access to genetic resources through mutually agreed terms and prior informed consent. As such, the frameworks fail to conform with the minimal standards warranted under Articles 15, 16 and 19 of the CBD.

Sri Lanka is also not a party to the Nagoya Protocol. Nevertheless, the Biodiversity Conservation Action Plan (BCAP) envisages to have an overhaul of the existing scenario so as to incorporate provisions of ABS. The Ministry of Environment that is tasked with implementing CBD has in 2000 worked on evolving a draft legislation to govern ABS.

The draft legislation primarily covers genetic resources and derivatives both from in situ as well as ex situ sources. It encompass all species indigenous to the territory of Sri Lanka, migratory species naturally occurring within the territory of Sri Lanka, and non-indigenous species in the territory of Sri Lanka. The draft leaves out traditional uses of the resources.

9.5.7 Thailand

Thailand acceded to the Nagoya Protocol in 2012. However, the following legislative frameworks that existed in the country have emerged as the enabling provisions in terms of access and benefit sharing.

9.5.7.1 Plant Varieties Protection Act 1999

This Act provides for protection of higher plants (however including mushrooms and seaweeds). The access to the genetic materials of domesticated and wild plant varieties and sharing of the benefits arising from their utilization is specified in Section 52A and Section 53 of the Act. The first section requires any person who collects or procures any domesticated or wild plant varieties for the purpose of variety development, education, research or commercialization to obtain permission from the competent authority and make a profit-sharing agreement prior to beginning the work. The accrued income is remitted to the Plant Variety Protection Fund. The second section requires the above user to comply by regulations prescribed by the Commission.

9.5.7.2 Protection and Promotion of Thai Traditional Medical Knowledge Act, 1999

This Act provides protection for knowledge related to Thai traditional medicine as well as plant varieties utilized for traditional treatment and illness prevention purposes. At present, the access to such knowledge and the herbal varieties and sharing of the benefits arising from their utilization is specified by Section 19 of the aforesaid law. Under the provisions, whoever intends to use traditional Thai medical knowledge needs to register and obtain license from the competent authority, comply with relevant guidelines and pay the requisite fees for the purpose.

9.5.7.3 National Committee on Conservation and Utilization of Biological Diversity Regulation on the Criteria and Methods of Access to Biological Resources and Sharing of Benefits Arising from Biological Resources, 2011

Thailand had during the negotiations to enter the Nagoya Protocol constituted National Committee for implementing ABS. The Committee provides for the protection for biological resources that have not been protected by legislation existing, include animal resources, micro-organism resources and parts of living organism, to be not contradict or be in conflict with legislation existing.

9.5.7.4 Challenges in Implementation of ABS

The legislations and frameworks present in Thailand pre-dates the Nagoya Protocol and therefore does not conform with all the provisions contained therein. It is thus important to align the provisions in a way so as to achieve harmonization with the Protocol and thus with the other countries. Thailand is yet to evolve a comprehensive legislative and regulatory framework for ABS.

9.6 Conclusion

The extensively biodiversity rich countries of the BIMSTEC are hot spots for ABS although most of them lack an adequate legislative and policy framework for its protection. As such, misappropriations are common in all these countries. Evolution of regional frameworks holds a particularly bright prospect in view of the commonality in environmental and community settings.

References

1. Access and benefit sharing policy of Bhutan. Ministry of Agriculture, Royal Government of Bhutan (2012)
2. Halewood M et al (2013) Implementing mutually supportive access and benefit sharing mechanisms under the plant variety treaty, CBD and Nagoya protocol. Law Environ Dev J 9(1):68–96
3. Bijoy CR (2007) Access and benefit sharing from the indigenous peoples' perspective: the TBGRI-Kani model. 3/1 Law, Env Dev J. http://www.leadjournalorg/content/07001pdf1
4. Convention for Biological Diversity, Statute of Convention of Biological Diversity Annex I (1992). http://www.cbd.int. Accessed 25 Sept 2017
5. Facteau L (2007) The ayahuasca patent revocation case: raising questions about the current US patent policy. http://www.bc.edu/schools/law/lawreviews. Accessed 01 June 2007
6. Ghimiray M (2005) Conservation and utilization of Bhutanese rice genetic resources. Vol 5747, pp 1753–1765
7. Nazeen M (2015) Access and benefit sharing under CBD and Nagoya protocol: Bangladesh perspective. Government of the Peoples Republic of Bangladesh, Ministry of Environment and Forests
8. National Agro Biodiversity Policy of Nepal (2004), www.farmersrights.org/pdf/asia/nepal. Accessed 25 Sept 2017
9. National Biodiversity Strategy and Action Plan for Bangladesh. Ministry of Environment and Forests, Government of the Peoples Republic of Bangladesh (2004)
10. Nepal Biodiversity Strategy 2002. Ministry of Forests and Soil conservation, Government of Nepal (2002)
11. Norbu N (1999) Timber genetic resources conservation and sustainable utilisation in Bhutan
12. Pandel B (2010) Implementing ABS regime in Nepal through community based biodiversity management framework. J Agric Env 11:143–157
13. Ranjan P (2009) International regime on access and benefit sharing: negotiation dynamics and South Asian issues. SAWTEE Policy Brief 17

Chapter 10
Cross Country Comparisons

10.1 Introduction

Majority of countries in our discussion are signatories to the TRIPS and also are bound by multiple bilateral and multilateral trading agreements and are members of free trade associations. Bangladesh, Nepal and Myanmar being members in the LDC category have time till 2020 to comply with provisions of the TRIPS. BIMSTEC binds the seven countries through multilateral trade agreements in multiple sectors as described in previous chapters. In this context, the relationship between various treaties and conflicts of compliance to one or more of them is an issue that warrants attention [1, 2].

10.2 Economic Profiles of the BIMSTEC Countries

The years following the economic meltdown during 2008–2009 saw the South Asian countries maintaining a robust annual GDP growth rate that was typically 2–3 times higher than the OECD average. A comparative picture is provided in Table 10.1. India exhibits the highest growth among the group, followed close behind by Bangladesh, Myanmar and Bhutan. Nepal exhibits the lowest growth within the group [2, 3]. Taken together, the average percentage annual growth of GDP for the BIMSTEC is close to 5% (for the year 2016) (Fig 10.1).

Considering macroeconomic profiles, BIMSTEC is a rapidly growing economic space compared to many regions of the world. One of the important features of regional economic health is intra-regional trade. This is showing an upward trend and is rapidly catching up with important regions such as MERCOSUR, Andean, SAARC and so on. On one hand, the sectors such as raw materials or finished goods perform well. On the other hand, traditional sectors such as textiles also predominate in world trade [2].

Table 10.1 Comparative data of annual GDP growth percentage[a]

Country	2006	2007	2008	2009	2010	2011	2012	2013	2014	2015	2016
Bangladesh	6.67	7.06	6.01	5.05	5.57	6.46	6.52	6.01	6.06	6.55	7.11
Bhutan	6.85	17.93	4.77	6.66	11.73	7.89	5.07	2.14	5.75	6.49	6.17
Brazil	3.96	6.07	5.09	−0.13	7.53	3.97	1.92	3.00	0.50	−3.77	−3.59
China	12.72	14.23	9.65	9.40	10.64	9.54	7.86	7.76	7.30	6.90	6.70
India	9.26	9.80	3.89	8.48	10.26	6.64	5.46	6.39	7.51	8.01	7.11
Myanmar	13.08	11.99	10.26	10.55	9.63	5.59	7.33	8.43	7.99	7.29	6.50
Nepal	3.36	3.41	6.10	4.53	4.82	3.42	4.78	4.13	5.99	2.73	0.56
OECD	2.96	2.53	0.18	−3.54	2.89	1.80	1.24	1.41	1.95	2.25	1.73
Sri Lanka	7.67	6.80	5.95	3.54	8.02	8.40	9.14	3.40	4.96	4.84	4.38
Thailand	4.97	5.44	1.73	−0.69	7.51	0.84	7.24	2.73	0.91	2.94	3.23–

[a]Source: World Development Indicators 2017, World Bank. Inclusion of countries Brazil, China and OECD group are for illustrating a comparative picture with the BIMSTEC

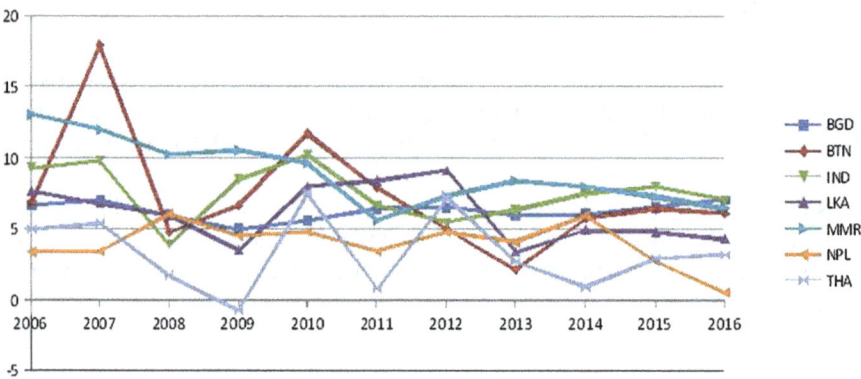

Fig. 10.1 GDP annual growth rate (*World Development Indicators, 2017*)

BIMSTEC is partly linked to SAARC [4] and partly to ASEAN [5]. As such, the overall economic performance of the region is also dependent upon its relationship with these two blocs. In relation to global value chain, its relationship with SAARC is growing at a very fast rate although in absolute terms it continues to remain low. With ASEAN, it is strong and also undergoing robust growth. In terms of trade deficit, BIMSTEC is net trade deficient with the ASEAN but net trade surplus with SAARC [2]. Under such considerations, BIMSTEC has large opportunities with SAARC and ASEAN to expand regional economic activities. This is a major impetus for strengthening regional IPR regimes so as to achieve a seamless system of trade and economic well-being.

10.3 Status of Accession to International Treaties

We have taken a look at some of the major international treaties that have shaped the global intellectual property regimes. We have also noted that the CBD [6] and TRIPS [7] have been the primary instruments while other instruments have contributed to providing frameworks based on which domestic regimes could be devised.

Considering the seven South Asian countries that comprise the BIMSTEC (all of which are members of the WTO except Bhutan which has observer status), all are signatories to the CBD and thus obliged to enforce provisions for protecting natural wealth and traditional knowledge through IPRs. As members of the TRIPS (except Bhutan), they are subject to the provisions of Article 27.3(b) for protection of life forms and plant varieties. Further, when it comes to plant variety protection, all the countries have sought to enforce the same through *sui generis* systems rather than plant patents. Bhutan being non-member has to devise relevant protection regimes under the ambit of its own constitution [8].

UPOV and the ITPGRFA are the two treaties that are available to shape the *sui generis* regimes. While none of the countries have opted for the UPOV, countries except Thailand have either ratified or acceded to the ITPGRFA [9]. Thailand has signed the treaty but is yet to ratify it.

The above pattern of membership has endowed the bloc with a few characteristics. As ITPGRFA is more tilted towards promotion of farmers' rights and privileges, the countries have evolved provisions along this line. Nevertheless as we have seen, much of the *sui generis* systems in countries like Bangladesh or Thailand are akin to the UPOV.

Table 10.2 provides the comparative status of accession to international treaties[1] among the BIMSTEC countries.

The issues of biosafety and ABS are governed through the Cartagena Protocol and Nagoya Protocol, respectively. Cartagena Protocol has been ratified or acceded to by all countries except Nepal and thus provide necessary guidelines on GM crops and trans-boundary movement of GMOs. As we shall discuss in a subsequent chapter, this difference in accession by contiguous countries (e.g. India and Nepal or Nepal and Bhutan) often pose a threat to regulation of biosafety. With respect to the Nagoya Protocol, Bhutan and India have ratified the same, while Myanmar has acceded to it and thus all these three countries are party to the Protocol. Bangladesh and Thailand have signed the protocol but is yet to ratify the same, while Nepal and Sri Lanka are non-signatories to the Nagoya Protocol [6, 10, 11].

---

[1]*Accession and Ratification of Treaties*: Any country which either ratifies or accedes to a Treaty becomes a party to it and is legally bound by the instrument. Merely signing a treaty does not make it a party. States which sign a treaty or protocol when it is open for signature can ratify it at a later stage to be considered as a party. If a state does not sign when a treaty is open for signature, it can only accede to the same at a later date to be considered as a party.

Table 10.2 Status of treaties/protocols[a]

Treaty/protocol	Country						
	Bangladesh	Bhutan	India	Myanmar	Nepal	Sri Lanka	Thailand
WTO	Member	Observer	Member	Member	Member	Member	Member
TRIPS	Member (1995)	×	Member (1995)	Member (1995)	Member (2004)	Member (1995)	Signed (1995)
CBD	Ratified (1994)	Ratified (1995)	Ratified (1994)	Ratified (1994)	Ratified (1993)	Ratified (1994)	Signed (2003)
NP	Signed (2011)	Ratified (2013)	Ratified (2012)	Acceded (2014)	×	×	Signed (2012)
CP	Ratified (2004)	Acceded (2002)	Ratified (2003)	Ratified (2008)	×	Ratified (2004)	Acceded (2005)
NKLSP	Ratified (1994)	×	×	Ratified (2014)	×	×	Signed (2012)
ITPGRFA	Ratified (2003)	Ratified (2003)	Ratified (2002)	Acceded (2002)	Acceded (2009)	Acceded (2013)	Signed (2002)
UPOV	×	×	×	×	×	×	×

[a]Source: List of Parties compiled from WTO (www.wto.org), CBD (www.cbd.org), WIPO (www.wipo.int), Accessed on 17.10.2017. WTO: World Trade Organization; TRIPS: Trade-Related Aspects of Intellectual Property Rights; CBD: Convention on Biological Diversity; NP: Nagoya Protocol; CP: Cartagena Protocol; NKLSP: Nagoya–Kuala Lumpur Supplementary Protocol; ITPGRFA: International Treaty on Plant Genetic Resources in Food and Agriculture; UPOV: International Union for Protection of New Plant Varieties

10.4 Comparison of the Natural Wealth Protection Frameworks at National Levels

In the present section, we take up a comparative exploration of the various existing frameworks for protection of natural wealth.

10.4.1 Plant Variety Protection and Farmers' Rights

Plant genetic resources are the foundation for food security in any developing country. Further, endemic plant resources are a source of other commercial and trade values such as development of fibre, feed, medicines, phytochemicals and various other industrial products. The CBD had been instrumental in highlighting the importance of according IPR protection to such resources, before which they were designated as common heritage of mankind. Consequently, countries have embarked upon evolving several governance frameworks that have sought to address the concerns and rights of owners, users, breeders and farmers.

10.4 Comparison of the Natural Wealth Protection Frameworks at National Levels

Table 10.3 Cross country comparison of protection regimes for PVP

Parameters	Bangladesh	Bhutan	India	Myanmar	Nepal	Sri Lanka	Thailand
Specific legislation	Yes(draft)	No	Yes	No	No	Yes	–
Disclosure of source	Yes	Silent	Yes	–	–	–	–
Protection of methods based on TK	Yes	–	Yes	–	No	Yes	-
Farmers as breeders	No	–	Yes	–	–	–	No
Category of protection	Sui generis	Sui generis	Sui generis	Sui generis (but UPOV like)	Sui generis (but UPOV like)	Sui generis	–

When it comes to the South Asian countries about which we have discussed at length in the preceding chapters, the frameworks are far from uniform. India alone has evolved a very comprehensive legislation and mechanisms that are specifically tailored to safeguard the rights associated with plant varieties and those of farmers. Thailand also has a complete law as far as PVP is concerned but this fails to address the rights of farmers while providing exclusive rights to the breeders. The laws of Bangladesh are envisaged to be closely resembling those of India although they are still in draft form. Myanmar, Nepal and Sri Lanka do not have encouraging legislative provisions while Bhutan continues to be guided by the overarching Biodiversity Act that lacks adequate depth and coverage in terms of plant varieties. Table 10.3 gives a comparative picture of the PVP regimes in the countries grouped under some identified parameters.

The following aspects of the comparative picture need further elaboration.

Predominance of Sui Generis Systems

All the countries have opted for a *sui generis* system of PVP thereby making use of the provisions of sovereign rights under TRIPS. Countries such as Nepal and Bhutan in view of their geographical characteristics have massive biodiversity in their plant genetic resources. They have also relied on centuries-old farming practices. Thus, adoption of the *sui generis* system of protection is likely to prevent the harmonization of agricultural fields with formal seed sector.

Rights of Farmers

An important corollary of the concept of PVP is the extent of protection of farmers' rights. By accepting farmers as breeders in countries like India, the matter has been settled once and for all. In Bangladesh and Thailand, farmers are not considered as breeders and thus the rights flowing from such a recognition does not exist. Sri Lanka, Nepal and Myanmar have no legislation while Bhutan's law is silent as far as farmers rights are concerned.

Notwithstanding the state of provisions above, farmers occupy the pivotal position in maintaining and propagating the plant genetic resources in all the countries. The primary challenge and requirement of the countries thus are to ensure that farmers' rights are appropriately addressed and safeguarded [12, 13].

Protection of Community Rights

As stated before, most of the farmer's knowledge and knowledge of various farming practices in these countries are held by communities. It is thus imperative to ensure that in the process of protection of rights, the protection is accorded to the community concerned. Except for countries such as India, the laws are silent in terms of provisions that ensure flowing of the privileges to communities.

10.4.2 Traditional and Indigenous Knowledge

The countries of South Asia being discussed here are abodes of ancient civilizations and as such have a major repository of traditional knowledge, indigenous knowledge and traditional cultural practices. TK and IK as we have seen comprise community knowledgebase and thus legislative frameworks aimed at protecting such knowledge should be effectively directed towards communities. Interestingly, except Bangladesh, no other countries have a legislation that specifically protects traditional knowledge. Protection is accorded through associated legislation (wherever it exists) under the overall ambit provided under TRIPS and the CBD.

Bangladesh stands out among the group by enacting the Community Knowledge Protection Act, specifically tailored to protect TK. In India, the approach is to regulate access to such knowledge through devising appropriate ABS regimes and also to undertake large-scale systematic documentation of such knowledge through vehicles such as the TKDL. Nepal on the other hand makes use of its all-encompassing Community-based Biodiversity Management (CBM) to provide protection. Bhutan, Myanmar and Sri Lanka have no existing provisions although Bhutan has sought to protect traditional knowledge to some extent through the Biodiversity Act by regulating access to the resources (similar to India).

Table 10.4 provides a summary of the comparative status based on certain identified parameters.

Although legislative and regulatory frameworks have sought to protect traditional knowledge and indigenous knowledge, the provisions do not specifically highlight the protection of traditional cultural expressions. However, as we shall see, traditional cultural expressions are often subject of protection through geographical indications.

10.4 Comparison of the Natural Wealth Protection Frameworks at National Levels 113

Table 10.4 Cross country comparison of protection regimes for TK/IK

Parameters	Bangladesh	Bhutan	India	Myanmar	Nepal	Sri Lanka	Thailand
Specific legislation	Yes	No	No	No	No	No	–
Collateral legislation	–	Yes	Yes	No	No	No	No
Linked to access	Yes	Yes	Yes	No	No	No	–
Systematic documentation	No	No	Yes	No	No	No	No
Community-based approach	Yes	Yes	No	No	Yes	No	–

10.4.3 Geographical Indications

Geographical indications are instrumental in institutionalizing the locational origin of products by ensuring protection to geographical names. South Asian countries (particularly the ones discussed in this book) are hot spots for geographical indications.

As we have seen in the relevant chapter, GI protection is often undertaken through tweaking of the Trademark Laws covering registration and certification marks. Alternatively, using the provisions under the TRIPS, a *sui generis* system is evolved with specific legislation. India, Bangladesh and Thailand have evolved *sui generis* GI legislations in line with obligations under TRIPS. India's GI Act provides for the most comprehensive framework with provisions for protecting natural, agricultural as well as manufactured products, and also products such as tea that represent a mix of agricultural and manufactured product. Bangladesh and Thailand have their respective legislation (very similar to that of India) with TRIPS Plus provisions.

Bhutan and Nepal have no frameworks or legislation for protecting GI, whereas Myanmar in the absence of a *sui generis* system has sought to accord protection to GI under its Trademark Law. Sri Lanka represents an unique example within the group because while it does not have a specific legislation for protecting GI (the same is sought to be a part of the IP Act), there is no provision for registration of GI. Thus, the situation is somewhat akin to the copyright laws and is open to the same types of vulnerability.

Table 10.5 summarizes the comparative picture of the GI protection regimes.

In this context, it may be mentioned that both Nepal and Bhutan have a substantial potential for protecting its Himalayan water sources through GI. The term 'natural mineral water' is used to refer to water sourced from mountains that is purified naturally by passage through a series of aquifers. Such sources are abundant in the Himalayas and have vast economic value to the region of origin. Protection

Table 10.5 Cross country comparison of protection of GI

Parameters	Bangladesh	Bhutan	India	Myanmar	Nepal	Sri Lanka	Thailand
Specific legislation	Yes	No	Yes	No	No	No	Yes
Collateral legislation	–	–	No	Yes	No	Yes	–
Provision for registration	Yes	–	Yes	–	No	Yes	–
Certification through trademark law	No	No	No	Yes	No	No	–
Potential for GI	High	Very high	High	High	Very high	Very high	High–

of appellation of origin for such water sources can provide major gains to mountain communities by exploiting this Himalayan GI. It is imperative therefore for countries such as Bhutan and Nepal to evolve comprehensive legislative frameworks to make use of this opportunity.

10.4.4 Genetically Modified Crops

Genetically modified crops are important offshoots of biotechnology and have a definitive role in enhancing agricultural yield and promoting food security. The South Asian countries discussed here as we have seen are among the most populous regions of the world and face a major conflict between food and forest. Recourse to GM crops is often seen as an effective means of increasing crop yield without compromising on forest land, and also achieving food and nutritional security for the burgeoning population. On the other side, GMOs are also viewed as major threats to biodiversity and naturally occurring varieties of plants.

Except India, other countries of the region have a relatively small acreage of land under GM crops. Bhutan for instance does not grow or import GM crops. Myanmar and Bangladesh have only a very limited cultivation of GM crops (Bt cotton in Myanmar) and there is no GM crops grown in Thailand [14].

In terms of legislative frameworks, India has evolved a Biosafety Guidelines and Rules for GMOs in accordance with the Cartagena Protocol. It has also evolved a Seed Policy on transgenic plant varieties. Bangladesh has framed and adopted its own biosafety guidelines although the provisions have allowed only limited farm cultivation of Bt brinjal and trials for golden rice (Vitamin-A enriched rice). Myanmar has evolved only a policy and regulatory framework with its legislation still under review. Bhutan has neither any framework or any legislation, while Nepal has a very

10.4 Comparison of the Natural Wealth Protection Frameworks at National Levels

Table 10.6 Cross country comparison of GM crops and biosafety guidelines

Parameters	Bangladesh	Bhutan	India	Myanmar	Nepal	Sri Lanka	Thailand
Specific legislation	Yes	No	Yes	No	No	No	Yes
Collateral legislation	–	–	No	Yes	No	Yes	–
Provision for registration	Yes	–	Yes	–	No	Yes	–

rudimentary version of legislative and policy framework. Legislative instruments for biosafety are integrated with other instruments in Sri Lanka while Thailand has sought to create an unified National Biosafety Framework by incorporating relevant provisions from various instruments.

Table 10.6 summarizes the comparative picture of the GM crops' governance in the different countries.

10.4.5 Access to Genetic Resource and Sharing of Benefits

The provisions under the instrument for access to genetic resources and equitable sharing of benefits arising out of their exploitation probably constitute the overarching framework for implementing all the other instruments stated above. This is because safeguards provided under PVP or TK or GI need to be regulated and enforced through controlled access along with mechanisms that enable effective flow of benefits to the owner communities.

Unfortunately, although the instrument for ABS is weak in all of the countries discussed here, a serious impediment for evolution of a regime that adequately safeguards knowledge and IPR of the concerned countries. Sri Lanka and Nepal are exceptions in not being a signatory to the Nagoya Protocol although parties to the CBD.

None of the countries have a specific legislative framework for implementing ABS. It is sought to be enforced through provisions in various other collateral legislations and instruments. India for instance has attempted to build in provisions for enforcing its obligations under Nagoya Protocol through the Plant Varieties Protection and Farmers Rights Act and the Biodiversity Act. Both these legislation nevertheless are in place and enacted. Bangladesh is yet to ratify the Nagoya Protocol, and very similar to India has sought to incorporate ABS provisions under its Plant Variety Protection Act and Bangladesh Biodiversity Act. None of the legislation have however been adopted till date.

Bhutan and Nepal have not yet enacted provisions for implementing ABS. Myanmar does not have any legislative instrument for ABS.

Table 10.7 Cross country comparison of ABS regimes

Parameters	Bangladesh	Bhutan	India	Myanmar	Nepal	Sri Lanka	Thailand
Specific legislation	No	No	No	No	No	No	No
Collateral legislation	Yes	No	Yes	No	No	–	Yes

Thailand has acceded to Nagoya Protocol but has sought to incorporate provisions for ABS in its existing legislative frameworks.

A summary of the comparative picture is provided in Table 10.7. What is important to emphasize is the fact that although all the countries have weak ABS regimes, all of them comprise extraordinary hot spots of biodiversity and traditional/indigenous knowledge. Large size, remoteness in location and vast diversity of natural and cultural resources make stringent access mechanisms imperative if the knowledgebase has to be conserved.

10.5 Conclusion

Despite the growing importance and international significance of the BIMSTEC bloc, the region is far from homogeneous with respect to legislation and policies for protection of natural wealth. Majority of countries are yet to evolve frameworks on crucial aspects such as access and benefit sharing, or specific legislative provisions for protecting traditional and indigenous knowledge.

References

1. Dhar B (2003) The Convention on Biological Diversity and the TRIPS Agreement: Compatibility or conflict. In: Bellmann C, Dutfield G, Melendez-Ortiz R (eds) Trading in knowledge: Development Perspectives on TRIPS, Trade and Sustainability. ICTSD, London, pp 77–87
2. RIS (2016) BIMSTEC: the road ahead. Research Information Systems, New Delhi
3. World Development Indicators (2017) World Bank. http://wdi.worldbank.org/tables. Accessed 25 Sept 2017
4. South Asian Association for Regional Cooperation, SAARC (2017) http://www.saarc.org. Accessed 25 Sept 2017
5. Association for South East Asian Nations, ASEAN (2017) http://www.asean.org. Accessed 25 Sept 2017
6. Convention for Biological Diversity, Statute of Convention of Biological Diversity, Annex I (1992). http://www.cbd.int. Accessed 25 Sept 2017
7. Trade related aspects of intellectual property rights, World Trade Organisation, Geneva (1992). http://www.wto.org/TRIPS. Accessed 25 Sept 2017

8. Gamel A, Ahsan I (2014) Review and compendium of environmental policies and laws in Bhutan: Input to the Asian Judges' Network on environment. Asian Development Bank, Mandaluyong City, Phillipines
9. International Treaty on Plant Genetic Resources for Food and Agriculture, Food and Agricultural Organization, Rome (2017). http://www.fao.org. Accessed 25 Sept 2017
10. Singh A, Manchikanti P (2011) Sui generis IPR laws vis-a-vis farmers rights in South Asian countries - Implications under WTO. J Intellect Prop Rights 16:107–116
11. WIPO (2013) Summaries of conventions, treaties agreements administered by WIPO. World Intellectual Property Organization, Geneva
12. Khan Z (2016) Protection of biodiversity in India and Bangladesh: A legal perspective. ILI Law Rev Summer 2016:223–235
13. Ravi S (2004) Manual on Farmers Rights. M.S. Swaminathan Research Foundation
14. ISAAA (2016) Global status of commercialized biotech/GM crops. ISAAA Brief 52

Chapter 11
IPR and Development in South Asia: Issues and Implications

11.1 Introduction

The emerging world order calls for a comprehensive development policy that balances rights and obligations. Developing countries, including the ones discussed in this work, are at the crossroad wherein they have to make important decisions regarding their stand on globalization and conservation. While trade and markets need to be opened up with developed economies, adopting necessary safeguards to its own natural wealth through appropriate protections and policies is imperative.

As discussed in the initial chapters of this book, contrary to popular beliefs, intellectual property rights-based protection seems to be more beneficial to developing countries when it comes to natural wealth protection.

11.2 Imminent Threats to Conservation

The part of South Asia that is being discussed here represents one of the most populous regions of the world, with imminent challenges of land use, environment degradation, food security and climate change. Notwithstanding the significant success of non-agricultural activities and services, agriculture accounts for one-fourth of the region's GDP and 55–65% of livelihoods to the majority of population. For example in India, agriculture supports livelihood of half its population contributing 15% of GDP of the country. This large dependence on agriculture puts serious pressure on forest and other natural vegetation belts of almost all the countries. Rapidly declining forest cover not only erodes biodiversity, it also drives out indigenous population and local communities that depend on it for livelihood. This in turn often results in loss of community knowledgebase. Conservation efforts are thus required to be built around holistic frameworks that factor in demographic, environmental, livelihood and institutional parameters.

Highly populated South Asia experiences major challenges in conservation. A closer examination of the major threats to conservation highlights a number of broad facets. While all of these should be appropriately addressed for achieving sustainable development, some of them can be achieved through intellectual property protection policies and practices. The following points give an illustrative list of some of the major parameters to be kept in mind while devising policy options.

11.2.1 Patterns of Land Use

South Asia has limited land resources in terms of quality and quantity that is vastly skewed. India for instance supports 17% of the global population with only 2.4% of land area. Agricultural land also takes up majority of areas in all the countries except Bhutan. However, ever-increasing demographic pressure on land has resulted in severe erosion of forest cover along with concomitant loss of biodiversity, traditional knowledge and community-based natural heritage. It is imperative therefore to evolve land use policies that would ensure health of the ecosystem, promote rural development, protect forest resources, improve watershed management and strengthen local capacities [1].

11.2.2 Depleting Water Resources

Phenomenal population growth, urbanization and large agricultural land-use have resulted in the South Asian region being transformed from a water-affluent to water-scarce region. Except Nepal and Bhutan, the availability of water in the region is significantly less than the world average. Some of the chief contributory factors for this include unsustainable agricultural use of water, poor governance and storage, and wasteful irrigation methods.

11.2.3 Unsustainable Livelihood Practices

High levels of poverty coupled with weak economies have resulted in major sections of the population to follow unsustainable livelihood practices. It is seen that either they are ecologically unfriendly, thereby causing environmental pollution and/or degradation, or they cause substantial health and occupational hazards. Interestingly, many such practices have been closely embedded into traditional cultures and thus difficult to uproot. An example of such a practice is shifting cultivation or 'jhoom' that is practised by the endemic population of certain parts of Northeast India and has been instrumental in denudation of forest cover in the region.

11.2.4 Loss of Biodiversity

South Asia has an extraordinary biodiversity. Sri Lanka, Nepal (Eastern Himalayan region), Bhutan (Eastern Himalayan region) and India (north-eastern region, Sundarbans, Eastern Ghats and Western Ghats) are recognized biodiversity hot spots. Incidentally, the Himalayan region alone houses more than 25,000 plant and animal species. Despite this incredible feature, the entire South Asian region is subjected to a number of anthropogenic threats—mostly population growth, uncontrolled urbanization and ruthless exploitation of natural resources. For example, ten per cent of India's flora and fauna comprise threatened species. The progressive loss of biodiversity is alarming because it causes not only depletion of natural wealth but also concomitant loss of livelihood and community knowledge associated with its use.

11.2.5 Climate Change

Climate change through anthropogenic and non-anthropogenic causes has a severe effect on conservation. Vanishing habitats and ecosystems deplete plant, animal and microbial populations and also put communities at risk of survival. Associated increase in diseases exerts a multiplier effect on the outcome.

11.3 Imperatives of Regional Cooperation

The countries focused here have a large portion of shared borders and most of them share the same zoo-geographical and agro-climatic zone. Thus, threats to natural wealth discussed above would readily move across political borders. It is thus imperative to arrest and control these threats through regionally evolved cooperative mechanisms rather than those adopted at individual country levels. Thus, it is currently accepted that the major objectives of poverty eradication, sustainable development and food, energy and water security in South Asia are unachievable without cooperation at regional level. Such need for regional cooperation in environmental and conservation issues has fuelled the South Asia Environmental Cooperation Programme in 1982. Intergovernmental organizations in the domain include the SAARC, the South Asian Environmental Cooperation Programme (SACEP) and South Asia Regional Seas Programme, all of which are mandated to develop regional cooperation in environment and conservation.

The countries comprising BIMSTEC as a bloc are yet to evolve a structured programme in line with the above. However, its multisectoral focus makes the bloc far more amenable to such an initiative. The regional cooperation paradigms need to cover apart from core environmental issues other aspects such as protection of plant varieties, landraces and indigenous agricultural products, traditional knowledge and traditional cultural expressions among others [2]. Evolution of protocols for the access to genetic resources and application of biotechnology are among the other priorities that the BIMSTEC countries need to address at regional level.

11.4 Key Issues for IPR-Based Development in South Asia

Development paradigms in South Asia are a complex system. Discussion of the various externalities and mechanisms is not subject of discussion in this book. We take into account a very narrow view of how sustainable development of the region could be accelerated by securing food security, biodiversity conservation and cultural preservation through IPRs. In this context, a few key issues can be highlighted that seem to be pivotal in achieving this goal.

11.4.1 The Transition from Common Heritage to Secured Wealth

Till the 1990s, the natural resources of the world were considered as common heritage of mankind, free to be utilized by one and all. The CBD instituted a radical change in this paradigm providing countries sovereign rights over their resources. For countries of South Asia, all of which comprise of developing states with relatively weak intellectual property regimes, this obligation under the CBD was difficult to realize [3]. Ironically, one of the most serious bottlenecks was to determine what should be protected and to what extent. Some of the other issues were devising appropriate legislations; putting in place adequate enforcement mechanisms; undertake capacity building for stakeholders; and finally harmonizing the regimes with other obligations so as to evolve a workable model. It is understandable therefore that all of the countries have failed to reach a consensus.

Provisions under the TRIPS have called for countries to evolve *sui generis* systems that suit their individual requirement [4]. Yet, many models of *sui generis* systems seem to be biased to the developed countries interests. For example, UPOV that is considered as a *sui generis* alternative for protecting plant varieties has not been found to be appropriate for many countries including India [5].

The difficulty in evolution and enforcement of appropriate policies and practices has led to countries taking inordinately long to reach a consensus. As we have seen in the last chapter, most countries (with exceptions of India and to some extent Thailand and Bangladesh) have failed to have a system of their own.

Access and benefit sharing (ABS) is probably the most important instrument to achieve security to the natural wealth. Yet, most of the countries have failed to develop specific legislative frameworks, let alone adequate enforcement of the provisions [6]. This has led to a continued draining of intellectual resources through various forms of biopiracy.

11.4.2 Legislation Versus Livelihood

An illustration of how legislation fails to implement the desired effect when livelihood is at stake; and the importance of coherent interplay of various institutional mechanisms can be best understood from India's plight with the Bt cotton cultivation in India [7]. During a time when the regulatory frameworks were at a formative stage and GM crops had not made inroads into the country, a few seeds for the transgenic cotton were surreptitiously transferred and planted to the fields. There was no way of identifying transgenic crops from normal ones, and the matter passed unnoticed till the major bollworm rampage of 2001. Large tracts of cotton devastated, while transgenic varieties (with the anti-bollworm Bt gene) stood strong. The biosafety watchdog in India, the Genetic Engineering Approval Committee (GEAC) under the Department of Biotechnology, was informed by the seed company that unapproved varieties of Bt cotton were planted on the field. GEAC enquiry substantiated the claim and afflicted states ordered to destroy the crops and the fields were to be sanitized. Interestingly, the orders were never implemented and it was later informed that given the extensive damage caused by bollworms that drove several farmers to the brink, the 'farmers interests would not be harmed'. Massive debates at state level and the central level as well as various farmers' association strongly advocated the farmers' rights to access improved seeds and denounced the delay in approval of Bt cotton.

The story above highlights a number of take-home lessons for the policy maker. Firstly, biosafety institutions are incapable of adequate surveillance of farming communities that can rapidly spread transgenic seeds. Secondly, even if there is a definite and known violation of Indian environmental laws and procedures, farmers cannot be prevented from growing, saving and distributing transgenic cotton. Thirdly, the incident underlies the inherent weakness of the regulatory institutional framework in implementing the biosafety procedures. Fourthly, in the attempt to enforce regulatory provisions, it is important to factor in the necessities of livelihood, i.e. to provide opportunity to the farmers to grow insect-resistant cotton and thereby enhance yield and returns on investment. Clearly, the conflict between legislation and livelihood has to be resolved at policy level [8].

11.4.3 Safeguarding Rights of Farmers

IPR is an effective tool to support agricultural development that rejuvenates the seed sector through incentives. However, the main contention is that such incentives should not jeopardize the rights and privileges of the farmers.

Farmers have played a pivotal role in achieving agricultural productivity for all the countries. Yet, formalization of the seed sector in order to introduce better quality seeds to improve yield and impart special properties such as disease resistance has more often than not ended up in marginalizing the farmers. The onus of production as well as the associated right is passed on to a new class of individuals called the breeders. One of the major challenges therefore is to evolve a framework that enables coexistence of both farmers and breeders, balance their rights and obligations, and ensure that the community knowledge of farmers developed over generations is adequately conserved [9].

The TRIPS makes no mention of the necessity to protect farmers' rights, although it does provide respective countries to evolve their own systems of protection of plant varieties. The ITPGRFA in contrast provides the onus on member states to protect farmers' rights, although not stating the same explicitly. Elements in the ITPGRFA that provide for the rights to farmers are protection of traditional knowledge, equitable sharing of benefits, and the rights of farmers in decision-making for the management of plant genetic resources [10].

Cullet [11] has argued that farmers' rights can be conceived in two forms—defensive and positive, a notion that can be extremely pivotal in shaping the protection regimes in South Asia. The defensive rights allow farmers and the government of respective countries to fight appropriation of knowledge and resource through available legal tools. For example, this approach determines whether traditional knowledge would be protected through trade secrets (i.e. non-disclosure of the knowledge to the public domain) or through documentation of the knowledge and release of the same into the public domain so as to anticipate patents being granted in other jurisdictions based on this knowledge. The positive rights in contrast recognize farmers' rights as property rights for the knowledge holders that give them control over the knowledge. Thus, it provides the farmers the ability to commercialize their own knowledge and practices on plant genetic resources. An important implication of the above is that strengthening of farmers' rights would mean restriction of other forms of IPRs on grounds of achieving food security or environmental conservation. Whether granting farmers' right equivalence to a class of property right would benefit them and agriculture is nevertheless a matter of debate and has not been substantiated. This is more apparent in developing countries where agricultural community largely dwells in the informal sector.

The issue of regionalism needs to be discussed at some length. In the same literature as mentioned above, Cullet argues on the element of 'non-exclusivity' in the farmers' rights [11]. The non-exclusivity implies that the rights to protect individuals and communities of their knowledge and resource at a given place do not exclude granting similar rights elsewhere. This provision enables communities at different locations to produce, protect and commercialize their own products. This element of non-exclusivity embedded into farmers' rights would be particularly important to the countries that we are discussing here. India, Bangladesh, Nepal, Bhutan and Myanmar are contiguous countries sharing common borders; in some cases, e.g., India and Bangladesh or Nepal and Bhutan occupy the same agro-climatic zones. Thus, it is common to expect occurrence of the same plant varieties, same community practices, etc., in some of them. Under such circumstances, non-exclusive farmers' rights play an enabling role in furthering food security and developmental concerns in such countries while balancing the obligations of the rights to the farming community.

Approaches of various countries to the issue have been diverse. India recognizes farmers as breeders and thus bestows them with significant proportion of rights. Many countries do not have a clearly defined mechanism. The issue assumes relevance for countries such as Bangladesh where farmers are not considered as breeders and Thailand that is the only country within the BIMSTEC group not a party to ITPGRFA. Some implications of these differences would be discussed later.

11.4.4 Loss of Plant Biodiversity

Notwithstanding the need to conserve forest cover as mentioned above, the imperative to feed the population and attain food security is a fact that cannot be denied.

Habitat transformation, over-exploitation, alien introduced species, pollution and climate change have resulted in a massive threat to plant biodiversity. Eighty to ninety percentage losses in several major crops over the last century have been reported [12]. Similar degradation has occurred for fruit trees and vegetables.

Such a rapid loss in plant diversity highlights a need to identify new plants and develop new varieties of extant plants. Harmonious policy prescriptions are required to achieving both ex situ and in situ conservation of plants and plant genetic resources for food and agriculture. The challenge lies in how countries devise conservation strategies while facilitating access and ensure that the benefits flow adequately to local, indigenous and farming communities [9].

A major environmental issue is whether IPR protection leads to spread of monoculture and thereby a loss of genetic diversity. It has been found in general that formalization of seed sector flows from centralized R&D that discourages traditional agro-ecological experimentation by local communities. Biotechnology invests and promotes few high-value crops and varieties that grow widely, thereby accelerating loss of landraces. Klauss Bosselman has argued that 'monopoly rights system encourages and seeks to solidify an agricultural system that is environmentally damaging and incompatible with the concepts of sustainable development' [8].

11.4.5 Achieving a Balance Between Conservation and Development

The key imperative for sustainability is the ability to strike a balance between conservation and development, a concept of 'wise use' of the natural resources. As we have discussed before, maintaining plant variety diversity is a prime determinant in conserving agricultural sustainability. The issue is particularly important because agriculture comprises the mainstay of the economy in the countries being considered. Thus, on the one hand while policies should focus upon enhancing agricultural yield and in turn the income of farmers, it should focus on the other hand to ensure that the vast endemic diversity of agricultural crop varieties is maintained and not replaced by monocultures.

One of the main purposes of PVP and PBR was their purported role in encouraging rights holder to develop and deliver improved varieties. To what extent has this doctrine been successful? As Biswajit Dhar [5] argues, impact of PVP in countries that have adopted it on variety development and flow of benefits has not been obvious [5]. Most studies do not show a positive correlation between PBRs and definite improvement in R&D by private breeders. Comprehensive studies on the area are, however, lacking that leaves this domain in a rather grey area with uncertain contours.

Farm subsidies have been a typical feature of most developing countries including those discussed here. The subsidies were meant to ameliorate cost to farmers and provide them access to improved seeds. The Agreement on Agriculture of the WTO has set a ceiling on subsidies and thus led to constriction in farmers access to seeds. This might lead to limit farmers access to quality seeds as a result of increased seed prices.

The result of such a scenario is multipronged. While on the one hand the pressure on farmers to enhance yield and protect their crops against disease is high primarily from their economic standpoint of view, on the other hand their access to such varieties is limited. Moreover, the inclination of farmers to sustain landraces is also low in view of their low economic returns. An outcome has been a preponderance of 'stealth seeds' that are GM varieties crossed with endemic counterparts, and eventually sowed, saved and replanted. Apart from mixing of traditional and transgenic lines, such activities violate biosafety and environmental guidelines that often prove prejudicial to the environment as a whole. In a number of cases, the movement of germplasm takes place across international borders and often involves countries that have very different governance frameworks for plant varieties and biosafety [7].

Cultivation of medicinal and aromatic plants is traditionally undertaken in India, Bangladesh, Nepal, Bhutan and Sri Lanka. Such plants represent major revenue earners and have got large export value. The Himalayan region (both the western and eastern sectors) and the Western/Eastern Ghats of India are hot spots for endemic occurrence of a vast number of species of medicinal and aromatic plants. Bioprospecting of such varieties often leads to massive destruction of biodiversity and raises major concerns of ABS and biopiracy [13].

11.4.6 Arresting Erosion in Traditional and Community Knowledge

All the countries being discussed here are powerhouses of traditional and community knowledge that has been developed and inherited across generations. However, the formalization of agriculture, recourse to modern medicine and similar trends have resulted in a continuous erosion of traditional knowledge. Traditional and community knowledge can be protected in two ways. The first is to recognize them as IPRs and accord positive protection both in terms of knowledge and in terms of its access by outsiders to the community. The second is to ensure patent applications are anticipated by existing traditional knowledge or community knowledge [14]. For either of the mechanisms to work effectively, it is important to achieve a comprehensive documentation of the traditional knowledge, a serious lacuna that exists in most of the countries discussed herein.

India has developed a reasonably elaborate Traditional Knowledge Digital Library. However, implementation inadequacies exist. In contrast, countries like Sri Lanka have no protection of traditional knowledge despite being a hot spot for the same.

Closely associated with protection of TK is the existence of appropriate provisions of ABS. This is yet another lacuna that exists in the legal and policy frameworks of most of the countries [15].

The result of this state of affairs is the progressive erosion of traditional and community knowledge with unwarranted access to the same through biopiracy.

11.4.7 The Farm–Forest Nexus

As discussed above, the burgeoning population puts a massive pressure on the land and other natural resources. The table below (Table 11.1) indicates the land forest ratio over decades which shows the expected declining trends. Bhutan is the only exception where more than 80% of the land area is occupied by forest, followed by Myanmar that has a figure of 48%. India and Bangladesh have the lowest forest to arable land ratio. The land area under pasture is also significantly low in countries like India, Bangladesh and Sri Lanka that limits availability of fodder for the livestock. One of the fundamental challenges before all the countries is to address this farm–forest conflict, which as evident is chiefly driven by anthropogenic mechanisms [16].

Table 11.1 Land use and sectoral composition of GDP in BIMSTEC countries

Country	Land Area (Sq km)	Arable Land (% total land)	Cropland (% total land)	Pasture Land (% total land)	Agriculture (% GDP)	Industry (% GDP)	Service (% GDP)
Bangladesh	130,170	59	6.5	4.6	14.2	29.2	56.5
Bhutan	38,394	2.6	0.3	10.7	15.7	42.6	41.7
India	2,973,193	52.8	4.2	3.5	16.8	28.9	46.6
Myanmar	653,508	16.5	2.2	0.5	24.8	35.4	39.9
Nepal	143,351	15.1	1.2	12.5	27	13.5	57.5
Sri Lanka	64,630	20.7	15.8	7	7.8	30.5	61.7
Thailand	510,890	30.8	8.8	1.6	8.2	36.2	55.6

Source: Computed from The CIA World Factbook, Central Intelligence Agency. The sectoral composition of GDP are estimated 2017 figures for all other countries; and 2016 figures for India

11.5 Effects of Harmonization of Intellectual Property Norms and Standards

The TRIPS Agreement has established a regime that has tended to harmonize intellectual property rules. Although TRIPS sets minimum standards, these standards are considered as relatively high that often compromise with development interests of the concerned parties [17]. Apart from aspects of life form protection (including plants and plant varieties) and traditional knowledge, there are other development concerns such as access to emergency and life-saving medicines, education, technology transfer and diffusion, foreign direct investment. During the initial years of establishment of WTO and TRIPS, there was a consensus that there would be a significant transfer of knowledge and IP from developing to developed countries.

Against the backdrop of development concerns, Okedeji [17] has reviewed the costs and benefits of harmonization of IPR regimes as shown in the table below (Table 11.2). The fundamental question is to evolve a mechanism as to how harmonization and development objectives are appropriately dovetailed and how developing countries evolve internal legislations to implement these harmonization principles.

The seven South Asian countries in our discussion are bound by multiple bilateral and multilateral trading agreements and are members of free trade associations. Bangladesh, Nepal and Myanmar being members in the LDC category have time till 2020 to comply with provisions of the TRIPS. BIMSTEC binds the seven countries through multilateral trade agreements in multiple sectors as described in previous chapters. In this context, the relationship between various treaties and conflicts of compliance to one or more of them is an issue that warrants attention. One of the most prominent examples is the relationship between TRIPS and the CBD.

11.6 Implications of the TRIPS Plus Standards

As we have discussed before, the absence of acceptable universally enforceable frameworks at global levels has often resulted in countries to include various IPR

Table 11.2 Costs and benefits of harmonization

Examples of benefits	Examples of costs
Achieves uniform standards and thus investor confidence	Less flexibility for customization of domestic IP policy to support local investors
Easier development of new global rights	Forced associated development of collateral non-IP areas such as education, public health.
Centralized monitoring and more efficient use of resources	Adverse effect on local employment and development of domestic IP policies
Uniform fees	Loss of domestic income

provisions into the bilateral and multilateral trading agreements between themselves. In many cases, provisions outlined in such agreement are at standards higher than those required under the TRIPS, i.e. a TRIPS Plus standard. This is very much common with geographical indications [18].

One of the major implications of having such TRIPS Plus provisions is that they are often tilted towards the interest of the developed partner and as such interests and safeguards of the developing country are seriously compromised. Let us revisit the clause highlighting objectives of the TRIPS. It states:

'The protection and enforcement of intellectual property rights should contribute to the promotion of technological innovation and to the transfer and dissemination of technology, to the mutual advantage of the producers and users of technological knowledge and in a manner conducive to social and economic welfare, and to a balance of rights and obligations'.

Three most significant phrases highlighted here, namely 'mutual advantage of producers and users', 'manner conducive to social and economic welfare', and 'balance of rights and obligations', are the major handles that developing countries have used to safeguard their interests. Thus, the impetus of TNCs to aggressively introduce breeders varieties of food crops (GM or otherwise), without adequate rights to farmers for saving, replanting and breeding, has been countered by the argument of non-compliance to social and economic welfare. The minimum standards approach warranted by TRIPS subsumes the aforesaid requirement of the developing countries. Further, the MFN status and national treatment to products once they cross the boundaries are also viewed as important ways in which developing countries can access the developed country markets. TRIPS Plus standards are usually incorporated through free trade agreements. Thus, once the developing countries agree to enter the FTA in order to tap larger markets, they are compelled to compromise on the basic tenets of the TRIPS in protecting national interests.

11.6.1 *Examples of the TRIPS Plus and the Doha Declaration*

At this juncture, we take a slight detour to understand the implications of TRIPS Plus. While the provisions are equally applicable in all areas that qualify for protection under intellectual property rights, the issue of public health and generics can be discussed as a model. Sweeping pandemics of HIV/AIDS in Africa had led to the governments there to resort to development of generics and also use the TRIPS flexibility such as parallel importation, compulsory licensing to make life-saving medicines available to the people at low cost. Thailand, for example, has pursued a successful strategy of treating HIV with generic drugs. USA has consistently insisted on TRIPS Plus standards that prohibits generic varieties of drugs as also compulsory licensing in these countries as preconditions in various FTAs.

Such international pressures led to the Doha Declaration. Among others, it documented the following:

Each Member has the right to determine what constitutes a national emergency or other circumstances of extreme urgency, it being understood that public health crises, including those relating to HIV/AIDS, tuberculosis, malaria and other epidemics, can represent a national emergency or other circumstance of extreme urgency'. Although the matter concerned public health, the same logic holds for plant varieties, agriculture and conservation related issues.

11.6.2 TRIPS Plus in Plant Varieties

TRIPS Plus standards in plant varieties include extension of standards of protection such as reference to UPOV, no possibility of making exception to patentability of life forms, and reference to the highest international standards.

Reference to UPOV

The TRIPS obligations make no reference to UPOV. In the endeavour to introduce TRIPS Plus, developing countries are often forced to align with and accept UPOV as the *sui generis* alternative of plant variety protection. Discrete bilateral FTAs with various developed countries have compelled Cambodia, Jordan, Morocco, Tunisia and Vietnam to join the UPOV. In the South Asian group, Bangladesh has managed to avert the compulsion with the introduction of a phrase *'make every effort'* into the FTA. Accession to the UPOV as discussed before is particularly not encouraging to most of the developing countries because of its biased stand towards the developed economies.

Reference to Highest International Standards

Many texts in FTAs call for the implementation of IPRs in developing countries *'in accordance with the highest international standards'*. These standards are not defined. However, this incorporation not only puts increased onus on the parties, it also makes them susceptible to new standards being generated by the developed countries.

TRIPS Plus implications are visible in plant protection regimes of Sri Lanka, Thailand and Bangladesh. Although they have framed their *sui generis* systems, these instruments seem to be significantly aligned with the UPOV. Additional protection to wines and spirits and appellation of origin for GIs is another example of the impact of TRIPS Plus provisions. As we shall discuss in the next chapter, regional instruments overriding bilateral FTAs are among the best choices for these countries to circumvent higher standards of protection.[1]

11.7 Multilateral and Bilateral Access and Benefit-Sharing Mechanisms: Implications of a Mutually Supportive System

As evident from the discussion of key issues above, ABS is one of the crucial focuses of evolving an acceptable natural resource protection regime. The ITPGRFA, CBD and the Nagoya Protocol are the three governance frameworks for ABS that support two very different (yet consistent) pathways namely a multilateral and bilateral system for access and benefit sharing.

11.7.1 The Multilateral System of ABS Under ITPGRFA

The ITPGRFA advocates a multilateral system involving 64 crops and forages used in food and agriculture. Deposition of PGR under the system allows contracting parties to get facilitated access to a huge reserve of pooled PGR from all over the world at very low cost. Access is provided by the standard material transfer agreement (SMTA) that specifies permitted use of resources, benefit sharing, prohibitions and so on.[2]

---

[1] *Cases when developing countries insist on TRIPS Plus standards:* There is often a wrong notion that TRIPS Plus provisions are always insisted upon by developed countries and that they are always detrimental to the interests of developing countries. There are many instances when developing countries also insist on TRIPS Plus provisions in order to champion their own interests. The best example is farmers' rights. TRIPS do not have any obligation to farmers' rights. Developing countries with relatively stronger IPR regimes like India have pushed for TRIPS Plus level protection of farmers' rights in their national legislation. Similar tendency is observed for the protection of certain forms of GI or AO and also certain aspects of traditional knowledge-based products. As such, TRIPS Plus is a negotiating instrument that could be judiciously and appropriately handled by international groups in order to serve the best interests of all the concerned parties

[2] According to the SMTA, providers of genetic resources would also make available non-confidential information about the resource (Article 5b). However, they are not allowed to claim IPR over materials in the multilateral system that would restrict access to the same resource by others. They would also have to choose between two mandatory benefit-sharing options. Further, it is important to note that SMTA is a private contract between individual provider and recipients that is relied upon as the main driver of the multilateral system.

11.7.2 The Bilateral System of ABS Under CBD and Nagoya Protocol

During sharing of PGRs that are not included in the crops and genera under the multilateral system, or under circumstances where the purpose of sharing is beyond the ambit set out by the SMTA, national implementation occurs within the bilateral system. Such national ABS norms are provided by CBD under its Article 15. Such access is subject to prior informed consent upon mutually agreed terms. Nagoya Protocol further warrants PIC to be obtained from indigenous and local communities prior to accessing resources built upon traditional knowledge, and to set forth monitoring mechanisms.

11.7.3 Challenges for the Mutually Supportive System

The above two mechanisms are quite different but nevertheless consistent and mutually supportive. For the BIMSTEC countries, obligations for a multilateral system exist for all countries except Thailand by virtue of their ratification of ITPGRFA. Moreover, all the countries being parties to CBD are also in tune with bilateral ABS systems, while India, Bhutan and Myanmar are obliged to provide standards in tune with the Nagoya Protocol. National policy makers in countries nonetheless are uncertain about the actual demarcation of multilateral system of ITPGRFA and national ABS systems under the CBD and Nagoya Protocol, and on how to manage the interface between the two [19]. This has worked as an implementation challenge for a seamless ABS regime.

11.7.4 A Middle Path Again Through Regional Protocols?

The aforesaid scenario and implementation challenge bring us to a situation again wherein a search for a middle path could yield encouraging results. Could there be a somewhat narrowed down multilateral system that subsumes countries of the region? Such a system could ideally circumvent the limitations of the bilateral and multilateral system while paying due regard to the sovereign rights of the countries. It would probably require consolidation of the best practices of national policies while ironing out the dissimilarities. ABS for the BIMSTEC countries is very akin to one another in view of close geographical proximity and shared demographic history. Hence, a regional protocol covering provisions of ITPGRFA, CBD and Nagoya Protocol could certainly be an option.

References

1. World Development Indicators, World Bank (2017). http://wdi.worldbank.org/tables. Accessed 25 Sept 2017
2. Yahya F (2005) BIMSTEC and emerging patterns of Asian regional and inter-regional cooperation. Aust J Polit Sci 40:391–410
3. Convention for Biological Diversity, Statute of Convention of Biological Diversity Annex I (1992). http://www.cbd.int. Accessed 25 Sept 2017
4. Trade Related Aspects of Intellectual Property Rights, World Trade Organisation, Geneva (1992). http://www.wto.int/TRIPS. Accessed 25 Sept 2017
5. Dhar B (2002) Sui generis systems of plant variety protection: Options under TRIPS, Quaker United Nations Office. http://www.quno.org/. Accessed 25 Sept 2017
6. Richerzhagen C (2014) The Nagoya Protocol: Fragmentation or consolidation? Resources 3:135–151
7. Herring R (2007) Stealth seeds: biosafety, biopiracy, biopolitics. J Dev Stud 43(1):130–157
8. Bosselmann K (1995) Plants and politics: the international legal regime concerning biotechnology and biodiversity. Colo J Int Environ Law Policy 7(1)
9. Adhikari K (2008) Protection of farmers rights over plant varieties in South East Asian countries. South East Asian Council on Food Security and Trade, Kuala Lumpur
10. International Treary on Plant Genetic Resources for Food and Agriculture, Food and Agricultural Organization, Rome (2017). http://www.fao.org. Accessed 25 Sept 2017
11. Cullet P (2003) Food security and intellectual property rights in developing countries. IELRC Working Paper 2003-3. http://www.ielrc.org/content/w0303.pdf
12. Andersen R (2007) Protecting farmers rights in the global IPR regime. SAWTEE Policy Brief No 15
13. Oli K, Dhakal T (2008) Traditional knowledge in the Himalayan region, International Centre for Integrated Mountain Development
14. Traditional knowledge and geographical indications, Report on Commission on Intellectual Property Rights, London (2002)
15. Ravi B (2012) Access and benefit sharing policy concerns for South Asian countries, SAWTEE Policy Brief 12
16. Kakakhel S (2012) Environmental challenges in South Asia. ISAS Insights No 189, Singapore
17. Okediji RL (2003) New treaty development and harmonization of intellectual property law. In: Bellmann C, Dutfield G, Melendez-Ortiz R (eds) Trading in Knowledge: Development perspectives on TRIPS, trade and sustainability. ICTSD, London, p 1–10
18. GRAIN/Kalpavriksh (2002) Traditional knowledge of biodiversity in Asia Pacific: Problems of piracy and protection. GRAIN and Kalpavriksh
19. Halewood M et al (2013) Implementing mutually supportive access and benefit sharing mechanisms under the plant variety treaty, CBD and Nagoya protocol. Law Environ Dev J 9(1):68–96

Chapter 12
The Road Ahead: Challenges and Opportunities

12.1 Introduction

BIMSTEC stands out among other free trade areas in that it is mandated for multi-sectoral cooperation. Among the 14 identified priority areas, at least six of them bear direct implication on natural resource-based development. These include agriculture, fisheries, environment, culture, people-to-people contact and climate change [1]. Growing importance of the bloc, its enhanced regional role, and its relative homogeneity in certain economic parameters make it particularly amenable to evolve regional protocols towards trade, environment and conservation. BIMSTEC is also endowed with a reasonably vibrant capacity and relatively stronger institutions when it comes to technological cooperation, which has been leveraged significantly in the recent years through FDI and technology transfers [2].

12.2 Trade and Regional Value Chains in the BIMSTEC

As per certain conservative estimates, 60% of world trade is covered by regional trading arrangements. South Asian countries nevertheless exhibit a weak regional trade regime because of a lack of integrated trading arrangement, making the region just marginally above sub-Saharan Africa. Considering the South Asian Free Trade Association (SAFTA), the intra-regional trade is close to 4% per annum [3]. The intra-BIMSTEC trade share as a percentage of total BIMSTEC trade is also low. However, it has been progressively rising from 2.2% in 1990 to 4.8% in 2010 to 5.8% in 2014. The share of intra-BIMSTEC trade is highest for Myanmar, Nepal and Sri Lanka. These figures are indicative of the fact that BIMSTEC is yet to emerge as a preferred trading destination for its own members; particularly with respect to larger economies such as India. BIMSTEC is also characterized by weak regional value chains (RVC); the stunted development patterns being one of the many contributing factors. One of the unique feature of the BIMSTEC is that all the countries are endowed with vast natural resource and harbour extraordinary natural, demographic and cultural diversity. Moreover, they are essentially agrarian economies and thus trade dimensions with respect to agricultural and nature derived products has a large potential in driving the regional value chain. Some studies show that BIMSTEC countries often out-compete one another in agro-product marketing at global level. Evolution of integrated mechanisms could be particularly beneficial in leveraging such trade. Potential areas could be rice (India, Thailand); jute (India, Bangladesh); tea (India, Bangladesh, Nepal and Sri Lanka), spices (India, Sri Lanka, Thailand) and marine products (India, Bangladesh, Myanmar, Sri Lanka, Thailand). Intellectual property rights, particularly those concerning PVP, GI and ABS, are likely to play a key role in stabilizing and insulating such regional integration.

12.3 Development Priorities

Amidst the backdrop of Agenda 21 for Sustainable Development, the newly evolved goal post for addressing the sustainable development goals (SDGs) by 2030 has been a major priority for the countries of South Asia. The region had faced major challenges in implementation of the erstwhile Millennium Development Goals (MDGs) primarily in view of high population and lower levels of human development indices. Regional industrial strategies to create productive capacities across the countries through regional value chains have been touted as important strategies to accelerate growth. Nevertheless, it has risked further degradation of environment and loss of endogenous culture.

The 2030 Agenda focuses on key environmental and resource dimensions and challenges. This includes sustainable management of natural resources, combating climate change, environmental degradation, loss of biodiversity and working towards attaining sustainable consumption and production patterns.

The countries of South Asia under discussion here can be grouped under three classes as per income groups. Bangladesh, Myanmar and Nepal belong to the low income group; Bhutan, India and Sri Lanka fall within the category of low-middle income group; while Thailand belong to the upper-middle income group as per World Bank estimates. Considering the human development indicators, except Sri Lanka and Thailand (that are categorized as high, the rest of the countries belong to the low-middle category [4]). This income and human development disparity among the countries has emerged as a major impediment in fulfilling the SDG targets. Thus, achieving faster, inclusive economic growth and through sustainable utilization of nature and natural resources happen to be the priority for the countries. A study by the UN-ESCAP shows that sharing development experiences among countries in the subregion would be particularly useful to meet the development challenges. This would be in addition to aligning subregional efforts to national strategies during the course of contextualizing the SDGs at subregional levels [2]. Thus while developmental approaches are all carried out through the respective national governments, the priority is for implementing a cross-country-coordinated approach to link up complementarity and leverage synergy among the various endeavours.

The Approach for Agriculture

Enhancing agricultural production is a key aspect for development in the countries. Yet, the priority is on increasing small holder agricultural productivity which comprise of the major share of agricultural producers. It has been increasingly appreciated that there is a need for collaborative regional approach to agricultural and food-related technologies in order to reduce pressure on land and enhance crop productivity. This can be best achieved through sharing good agricultural practices, plant varieties and germplasm.

The Approach for Environment

Achieving development without depleting forest cover or damaging environment is imperative in achieving sustainability. As such, countries like Bhutan have resolved in their national agenda for SDGs to restrict depletion of the country's forest cover to 60%. Combating climate change through low-carbon strategies has also played a crucial role in the agenda of conservation. Strengthening partnerships as a means of implementation of these strategies has been a key approach.

The Approach for Endemic Human Population

Conservation of the endemic human population (including indigenous population) and their practices is likely to play a major role in driving sustainable development for the countries.

In a nutshell, policies for transformative development should prioritize investment to foster structural transformation, especially towards more efficient, less resource-intensive industrial development without prejudice to the environment.

12.4 Achieving the Priorities: Activism Versus Rationality

One of the important aspects of conservation is the eternal conflict between the so-called development lobby with the protectionist lobby. Interestingly, it is a similar lobby originating in the USA that has led to the establishment of the WTO and formulation of the TRIPS. It had been claimed that the US industries were losing millions of dollars owing to the weak informal IPR regimes in the developing countries. The onslaught of such logic had permeated into the agricultural sector as well [5].

It is argued that biotechnology companies are investing large sums of money for R & D to create improved quality seeds and plant varieties that are being taken away by the farmers of developing countries. Such countries, it was emphasized, should stop farmers from saving, reusing and replanting seeds belonging to these formal varieties. Notwithstanding the claim above, as we have mentioned in the previous chapter, there is no major evidence that provision of PBRs has actually led breeders to deliver high-quality seeds [6].

The opposite bloc refuted claims of the developed countries and contended that American firms actually owe developing countries millions of dollars as a rent to the biodiversity that they have accessed over the years to source raw materials for proprietary medicines. It was stated that formalization of the seed sector would not only promote monoculture, it would also erase the vast genetic diversity of the agricultural resources of developing countries.

These protracted arguments and counter-arguments have led to growth of activism among the stakeholders. India for instance (mentioned in a previous chapter) has faced violent episodes during the cultivation of Bt cotton in the fields of Gujarat during 1999. Much of the episodes were fuelled by the belief that the terminator technology was used in the seeds that were surreptitiously grown in the fields by the farmers. The use of GM seeds by farmers is understandable. For years on, there was a severe onslaught of bollworm in the cotton fields and this led to a complete loss in investment because of destruction of crops. Access to pest-resistant cotton varieties was thus certainly a priority over biosafety concerns. Anti-GM activists on the other hand contended that use of GM crops in the fields of India would obliterate the vast genetic diversity and subject Indian agriculture to the seeds produced in the west [5]. Thus, it was claimed that even short-term gains would be offset by long-term losses in terms of loss of agricultural sovereignty of the farmers.

Clearly, there is need to evolve a regime based on rationality. It is important to recognize that livelihood needs of farmers and indigenous communities are to be safeguarded as intently as national biodiversity. Rational approaches based on the 'wise use' paradigm are instrumental in attaining the objective. The decision therefore is not on whether to allow GM or not; or whether to allow access to traditional knowledge of a community or not. It is rather a decision as to what extent GM crop cultivation is to be allowed without significantly damaging the environment or without contaminating the natural gene pool. Similarly, when traditional knowledge-based materials are used, the basic approach is to ensure a controlled and informed access to the resource; appropriate legal protection; and most importantly fair and equitable sharing of the benefits arising out of its exploitation.

While evolving a mechanism of balancing activism and rationality in terms of natural resources protection, a few points are worth mentioning as follows:

Who Owes Whom?

When the agenda for IPR was incorporated by the USA in the last round of GATT, they argued that weak intellectual property regimes in developing countries were responsible for loss of revenue to US firms in terms of royalty. It was claimed that the world owed them USD 20 billion. In a report published by the UNDP [7], it was counter-argued that if a 2% royalty was charged on biological diversity developed by indigenous communities, the developed countries owed almost USD 300 million on unpaid royalties for farmers' crop seeds alone. It was estimated that royalties for medicinal plants would amount to more than USD 5 billion.

Vulnerable Crops

When farmers cultivate rice, they actually plant various varieties of rice with characteristics that are adapted to the soil, water and other climatic condition of the place. There are more than 100,000 varieties of rice worldwide, the majority of which are farmers varieties. As a result of Green Revolution, they are encouraged to plant a few high-yielding varieties only that denude genetic diversity to an alarming extent. This often lead to such crop varieties being susceptible to pests and diseases [7].

12.5 The Importance of Regional Initiatives

If harmonization of IPR regimes has detrimental effect at the global level, a certain level of harmonization or synergy can nevertheless prove to be beneficial at the region level. In South Asia, prospects of such regional harmonization are large owing to the large extent of commonality among the countries despite their significant differences. Regional initiatives of protecting natural wealth of countries through cross-country frameworks are viable alternative for countries of South Asia [8]. We have also discussed in the previous chapter how a regional initiative might be useful to address the issue of ABS under multilateral and bilateral systems.

As we have discussed earlier, the south and Southeast Asian region possess a number of regional blocs, each advocating their own stand in advancing development paradigms.

The South Asian Association for Regional Cooperation (SAARC) states that

'there is a need to prevent piracy of traditional knowledge built around biodiversity and there should be harmonization of the TRIPS Agreements with the UN CBD so as to ensure appropriate returns to the traditional communities'

Despite such a statement, there has been little coordinated action among SAARC countries for achieving the goal of evolving a common regime [9].

Similarly, no comprehensive implementation framework exists for ASEAN although the bloc has developed a draft 'Framework Agreement on Access to Biological and Genetic Resources' [10].

The Group of Allied Mega Biodiverse Nations (having members from Southeast Asia) have also recently signed the Cancun Declaration pledging to evolve a cross-country framework of preservation and sustainable use of biodiversity.

One of the major impediments for evolution of a regional initiative is non-availability of a champion country to propel the move. For such a step, it is important to have at least some countries that have stronger institutions, stronger frameworks and a greater power of negotiation. As we shall see below, BIMSTEC has an advantage of having India to play this enabling role.

12.6 The Centrality of India's Role

India is the largest and the most dominant member of the BIMSTEC in terms of economic growth, trade volume and sectors of active cooperation. Being one of the founding members of the bloc, India plays a central role in the growth and sustenance of the group. Moreover, India arguably has the most well-developed system of IPR in the region with well-defined legislations in terms of PVP, GI and GMOs. There are clear policies towards governance of TK and ABS. Furthermore, India also harbours significant diversity of indigenous communities with associated traditional knowledge; the management norms of which can be effectively transferred to the neighbouring countries.

India is thus poised for a central role in driving the regional intellectual property regime. Some of the salient features of Indian legislation and frameworks that make it suited to being adopted as a model include the following.

The Inclusive Nature of PVP

India by far has one of the most versatile non-UPOV *sui generis* systems that not only conforms to the rights of breeders but also adequately addresses the rights of farmers. By accepting farmers as breeders and the provisions to register farmers varieties, the law ensures conservation of genetic diversity and landraces.

Successful Models of ABS

India also has a relatively strong ABS regime. Provisions ensure that communities are recognized as holders of the knowledge and are made part of the PIC and MAT. We have seen the successful Kani tribal model in implementing ABS. There has also been significant success in protecting GIs and appellation of origin such as the basmati, Darjeeling Tea, Mysore silk. Pochampalli ikat and so on.

Effective Documentation of Traditional Knowledge

Lack of documentation is the most important challenge in protecting traditional knowledge. India's unique initiative of the TKDL has helped circumvent this bottleneck in a big way.

The question therefore is that how could the Indian frameworks be suitably dovetailed with those of neighbouring countries in order to develop a comprehensive system of IPR-based conservation mechanism. Such systems would also need to be synergistic with global regimes with appropriate changes incorporated in the latter.

12.7 Reforms to the TRIPS

Ever since the Doha Round, WTO members have made unsuccessful attempts to introduce reforms to the TRIPS so as to make it more developing country friendly. In attempts to evolve consensus, it has been found that three conflicting views from three separate stakeholder groups have emerged. The first is the Euro-American group comprising mostly of developed countries that govern international trade. The second group is the government and industries of the developing country concerned. The third group consists of peoples' organizations and NGOs who are essentially representative of the communities.

Understandably, the first group is firm about the provisions of the TRIPS and its endeavours to promote a universally binding IPR regime across the world. It advocates for UPOV-based plant protection regimes; additional coverage for GIs and large-scale use of GMOs. Thus, this bloc is against any dilution to the TRIPS in favour of developing countries and is opposed to reforms. The second and third groups, that consist of governments/industries and non-government/community-based organizations both from developing countries, have divergent views among themselves. While the first group is intent to promoting a reformed TRIPS regime providing *sui generis* protection to plant varieties, GI and TK that recognize the rights of farmers and owners of TK, the second group is more conservative on this count. It refuses to let the control go to the governmental machinery and advocates communities to be the absolute owners of PVP and TK. It goes beyond just providing recognition to the farmers for new seed and plant varieties; in contrast it makes them owners of such varieties. Thus, while adoption of the second group option might enable governments to incorporate the provisions through FTAs and other multilateral treaties, exercise of the third alternative is likely to curtail the control of government over the genetic resources to a significant extent [11]. A summary of the position is illustrated in the following table (Table 12.1).

Let us discuss the pros and cons of the latter two options in a somewhat greater detail.

Table 12.1 What the different stakeholders want

Parameter	Developed countries	Developing country governments	Developing country NGOs
Plant variety protection	PBRs	Breeders' rights with privileges to farmers	Farmers' rights only
Sui generis systems	UPOV standards	No clear stand	No clear stand but not UPOV
Ownership of IPRs	Market controlled	State owned	Community owned
TRIPS review	No amendments to lower standards	Review to harmonize with CBD; Not challenging protection on biodiversity or TK	Biodiversity and TK to be kept out of protection
Access	Unregulated	State controlled	Community controlled
Benefit sharing	IPR	IPR	Community management and community IPR

Scenario of Control by Government

This scenario is more akin to the proposition under the CBD [12]. In fact, the governments of Asia Pacific and many places in Africa have actually advocated adoption of standards in line with CBD. Thus while ownership of the bioresources and genetic diversity would rest with the state, a significant share would permeate to the local communities. IPR would continue to remain the chief instrument of safeguarding the privileges. Advantages of such a system would be the following:

- Greater control by state
- Greater flexibility to balance rights and obligations, i.e. rights of communities versus economic necessities of trade
- Better enforcement as government has control of the institutional mechanisms
- Greater scope of negotiation at international level to devise systems in tune with national requirement
- Ability to dovetail provisions with other policies

Disadvantages of the system would include the following:

- Policies prone to priorities of government rather than needs of community
- Scope of higher international pressure to accept provisions
- Difficulty in implementation in case of countries with unstable or weak governments
- Disadvantage for small countries

Scenario of Control by Communities

This scenario assumes a more activist-type regime as stated above. Such a scenario is more zero-based as it advocates a comprehensive overhauling of TRIPS and related agreements; scrapping of control regimes and dominance of community sovereignty over state control. Advantages of such a system are as follows:

- Gives a greater control to local communities and actual holders of knowledge over their own resources
- Ability to harmonize protection of resources held by similar communities even if they are located in different countries (particularly pertinent in South Asia where countries have large shared borders and belong to same geographical zone).

Disadvantages of such as system are as follows:

- Most communities lack relevant capacity and institutional systems for enforcing such provisions
- There is greater scope of biopiracy and illegitimate control over resources
- In absence of state control, there is a much reduced power of international negotiations
- It might lead to serious compromise of trade interests among countries and thereby slow down economic progress

In the light of the above, it can be argued that the best way forward is to push for reforms to the TRIPS and address the issues of harmonizing TRIPS with CBD [13]. It is important to recognize the need of commercialization of products derived from natural resources and those drawn from traditional knowledge. What is important is to achieve a system of controlled access and equitable benefit sharing; a system of legislative and policy frameworks that provide a level playing field for all categories of stakeholders. Ironically, levelling a playing field that is already steeply skewed towards developed economies calls for actions to adjust the slope significantly in favour of the developing countries.

12.8 International Negotiations for TRIPS Reforms

The developing countries have constantly pushed for reforms to the TRIPS during the TRIPS Council sessions, particularly those with respect to Article 27.3(b). Two major demands have been raised in the reforms agenda. First is the demand for harmonization of TRIPS with the CBD. The key harmonization points include access agreements based on mutually agreed terms, transparent description of research objectives based on TK, proof of inventive step, disclosure of source and country of origin of resources and TK, and fair and equitable sharing of benefits with the communities holding the knowledge [14]. Second is the demand of including some provision for incorporating farmers' rights in the TRIPS Agreement.[1] It has been felt that incorporation of the above two provisions would enable developing countries to leverage their conservation requirements vis-a-vis commercial utilization of natural resources in a more equitable manner. Although such demands have found support in many countries, developed countries continue to remain adamant on any changes in the TRIPS.

South Asian BIMSTEC countries stand particularly to gain from any such reform as ABS and TK are seriously compromised in the region. Such a reform would also end the era of pressure from FTAs in advancing the interest of the developed country blocs and shaping governance frameworks that are detrimental to the region's interests.

---

[1] Many developing countries across the world are of the opinion that a footnote should be inserted after Article 27.3(b) of the TRIPS that clearly elaborates that any *sui generis* system of PVP would provide for protection of innovation of local farming communities consistent with CBD and ITPGRFA. Further, it is also advocated that the footnote should state that traditional farming practices including the right to save, exchange and sell seeds should be maintained; as also the prevention of ant-competitive practices that are prejudicial to the food sovereignty of developing countries. Some countries have also advocated permitting inclusion of certain exceptions to the PVP rights in the TRIPS Agreement. [Source: WTO (www.wto.org)]

12.9 Revisiting the ITPGRFA: Challenges of Evolving a Multilateral Conservation System

Article 1 of the ITPGRFA relies on the following objectives for achieving sustainable agricultural diversity and global food security:

1. Conservation of plant genetic resources for food and agriculture
2. Sustainable use of PGR
3. Equitable sharing of benefits arising from the use of PGR

As agricultural diversity has arisen through human management of wild plant varieties (i.e. it is a man-made biodiversity), all of them are farmer or breeder varieties. Significant portion of such diversity thus stems from traditional community knowledge that have passed across generations and across boundaries of countries.

As per estimates, depending upon the crop, breeders typically work with upto 60 different varieties originating from 20–30 countries (Fowler2003). It is thus difficult to track the origins of any given crop variety. Thus, in contrast to other merchandise items, it is often difficult to evolve an acceptable system of rules of origin. And more importantly how do we then evolve a workable access framework?

In the document of implementing a road map of access and benefit sharing [15], it has been stated that plant genetic resources (essentially agricultural crops) are different from other elements of biodiversity in that they are not depleted with over use; in fact, they need to be used continuously and widely in order to conserve them for the future. This very aspect of conservation of plant genetic resources brings us closer to one of the provisions of ITPGRFA, i.e. to promote ex situ conservation practices and the requirement having a plant genetic resource depository.

12.9.1 Interdependence of Countries on Crop Varieties

A simple evaluation of the crop varieties (especially the ones related to food crops) across the world gives us an interesting picture. Food crops grown in a given place in the world need not have historically originated in that place. This is understandable given the historical trends of free exchange of plant materials across the world that led to plant germplasm moving vast distances across the globe. For example, potatoes originated in the Andes and has moved to Europe to evolve into staple food there. Wheat and barley were domesticated in Near East and later imported into North America. Rice with rare exception originated in Southeast Asia and has continued to remain the staple food crop in this area and other regions of South Asia [17]. Most countries in the world therefore heavily depend on each other for maintaining crop diversity required for their agricultural development, and that no country in the world is self sufficient in terms of crop diversity.

According to studies by FAO, extent of dependence on food crops for a region on products originating at some other region is over 50%. Interestingly, India and

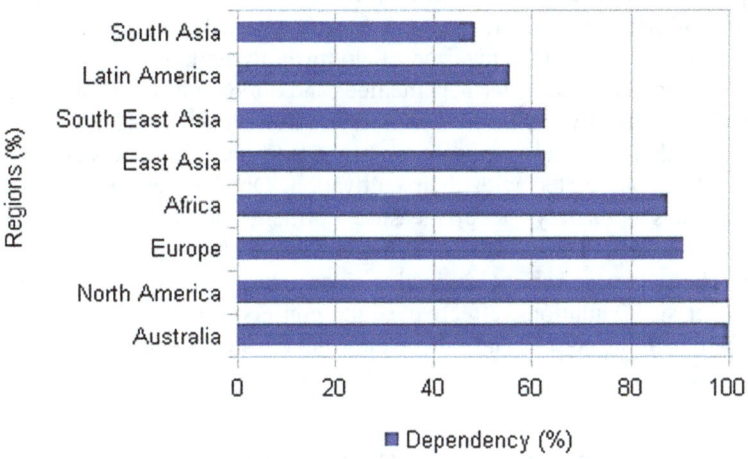

Fig. 12.1 Interdependence of Countries on Crop Varieties

Bangladesh happen to exhibit a dependence in the range of 15–20% (among the least in the world), with highest being North America, Australia and Central Africa (ranging from 90 to 100%). This dependence is likely to increase further as a result of climate change. The regional dependency of food crops is shown in the adjoining figure (Fig. 12.1).

This high level of interdependence has motivated development of international treaties to regulate and facilitate access to agricultural genetic resources by rule-based mechanisms, a scenario where ITPGRFA plays a pivotal role.

12.9.2 Sustainable Use of PGR Through Conservation

Conservation has a broad connotation and is often used to establish the extent to which a given germplasm is kept virile for the present and future generations amid various forms of human and environmental challenges. Thus, as we have discussed before, there are two approaches to conservation, namely in situ and ex situ. Article-5 of the ITPGRFA [16] elaborates that member countries should take measures for 'Conservation, Collection, Characterization, Evaluation and Documentation of Plant Genetic Resources for Food and Agriculture'. It elaborates on the importance of in situ conservation of genetic resources and the role played by farmers, indigenous and local communities in the process. Simultaneously, ITPGRFA also underpins the importance of ex situ conservation strategies and advocates establishment of appropriate networks through international collaboration.

ITPGRFA has not made a very clear definition of 'sustainable use'. It is interpreted that the interplay and complementary operation of in situ and ex situ strategies are instrumental in achieving sustainable use [15]. In situ approaches ensure crops are conserved through their propagation in farmers fields in the agricultural ecosystems in which they evolved; making use of farmers methods and often traditional knowledge of the communities. Thereby, on-farm conservation allows crops to adapt to local conditions through their constant exposure to such conditions; and to sustain local agricultural practices associated with their cultivation. On the one hand, ex situ conservation operates as a safety backup measure. Further it facilitates research and breeding of new varieties. The process assumes particular significance under rare circumstances when a certain variety is wiped out by a natural disaster or some other eventuality. Under such situations, effective ex situ conservation would enable the lost germplasm to be reintroduced and used again from the stored genebank facility.

12.9.3 What Is the Advantage of a Multilateral System?

Evolution of a multilateral system is at the heart of ITPGRFA. The system would allow any natural or legal person belonging to the jurisdiction of a contracting party to have facilitated access to a very vast reservoir of crop samples. It is pertinent to mention that the definition of natural and legal persons in the above connotation covers individuals (breeders, farmer), organizations (research establishments, non-governmental organizations, breeding companies etc). Interestingly national gene banks also fall in this category. The global gene pool contains over 1.5 million unique samples of crop varieties, that is being increased progressively. Stakeholders within the jurisdiction of contracting parties also have a share of benefits arising out of the utilization of the PGR. Thus, evolution of a multilateral system not only promotes ex situ conservation practices; it also ensures flow of benefits to the farmers; and more importantly provides the farmers and breeders with access to genetic material to continuous generation of new varieties through breeding. The large ambit of ITPGRFA and its legally binding status opens the gate of a vast resource pool that would have been impossible through national and/or bilateral mechanisms.

12.9.4 Expanding Scope of the Multilateral System

As per terms of the ITPGRFA, the coverage of the multilateral system is restricted to the 64 food crops that are listed in Annex-1 of the treaty that are generally referred to as the 'Annex-I Crops'. Two criteria are earmarked for determining inclusion under Annex-I crops, namely importance in global food security; and extent of interdependence among countries and regions for a given crop. Scope exists for inclusion of items in Annex-I, thereby achieving expansion of the scope of multilateral system. Newer challenges from climate change make it imperative to redefine the scope of Annex-I so as to accommodate the requirements arising from it.

12.9.5 Addressing a Policy Bottleneck: Unauthorized Access Versus Legitimate Exchange of PGR

Implementation of a multilateral system under the ITPGRFA encounters a major policy challenge, i.e. regulating unauthorized access to PGR while allowing free exchange under gene pools. Uncertainty exists in many South Asian countries about the degree to which the existing laws and policies can be tuned so as to make them compliant with the multilateral system. This has resulted in many countries not to opt for the system at all; instead make materials available through the standard material transfer agreement (SMTA). Lack of knowledge of stakeholders, e.g. farmers and communities, general public, seed companies, etc., on the need and benefits of a multilateral system also pose a major impediment. For instance, Seldom do people recognize the difference in conservation mechanisms through ABS systems for medicinal plants and agricultural products. While the former occurs in nature and is bioprospected from endemic sources, the latter has to be manipulated by humans. Thus, while regulated ABS through PIC and MAT suffice for conserving the former, the approach for the latter should be based on legitimate interchange of germplasm through appropriate SMTA; and breeding thereafter.

Agriculturally rich BIMSTEC countries have a particularly strong relevance of PGRs. With exception to Sri Lanka, all the remaining BIMSTEC countries have either ratified or acceded to the ITPGRFA. In their endeavour to evolve acceptable ABS norms, the countries would be benefited through multilateral systems. Thus, it is imperative that relevant application of PIC/MAT or SMTA be adopted in the national or regional set-ups.

12.10 Regional Imbalance as a Consequence of National Laws

Political segregation of countries through international borders seldom segregates flow of germplasm, flow of community knowledge or migration of humans. Scenarios emerge where established national governance frameworks and national laws that are aimed at protecting a given facet of natural wealth become major sources of regional imbalances. A good example of such a situation is observed between India and Bangladesh. The two countries have regularly witnessed arguments and counter-arguments with respect to protection of geographical indications. India has secured GI protection for Fazli Mango (an endemic local variety growing in the eastern state of West Bengal in India), which is also claimed by Bangladesh. The overlap is understandable given the very close geographical proximity of the two mango-growing regions (ironically they belonged to the same British India prior to partition). Similar disputes on the origin of products also exist for Jamdani Saree, one of the renowned traditional cultural expression for textiles. India had put in place its GI Law in 2002 whereas Bangladesh has adopted similar legislation during 2014. Both the laws are in compliance to the TRIPS provisions and significantly similar. Clearly however, they are in conflict when it comes to issues such as the ones described above. One of the probable means of addressing the discrepancy is to evolve a regional protocol that sets rule-based criteria on GI and appellations that supersedes national laws in the event of conflict.

12.11 Evolving Regional IPR Protocols

We have seen in the previous chapter the implication of FTAs in making undesirable introduction of TRIPS Plus standards of protection. This coupled with the issues of conflicts among national legislation described above has tempted the thought of evolving regional IPR protocols. Such protocols would offset much of the controversy while maintaining national sovereignty over natural resources. We do find examples of such protocols in other parts of the world.

12.11.1 Lessons from the MERCOSUR

MERCOSUR comprises of four countries of South America comprising of Brazil, Argentina, Paraguay and Uruguay that constitute a vibrant trade bloc, with intra-bloc trade amounting to around 16% of the total trade. MERCOSUR has evolved a 'Protocol on Harmonization of Intellectual Property Norms' that has been very effective in facilitating free trade among the countries. The Protocol envisages:

'the need to establish to such ends, rules and principles which shall serve to guide the administrative, legislative and judicial actions of each Party State with respect to the recognition and application of intellectual property rights regarding trademarks, indications of source and denominations of origin'

Without prejudice to the obligations under international agreements, the Protocol has ensured that the countries are accorded national treatment and *'exempt from legalization, whenever possible, the documents and signatures [included] in the procedures related to intellectual property rights regarding trademarks, indications of source and denominations of origin'*. The Protocol further ensures that the countries reciprocally protect the indications of source and denomination of origin thereby pre-empting disputes related to similar indications within their territories. (www.ipiba.org)

12.11.2 Lessons from the ASEAN

The ASEAN comprises of a group of ten Southeast Asian countries, three of which fall in the mega-diverse category. In their endeavour to evolve a harmonious regime, the countries have resorted to make use of TRIPS flexibility coupled with provisions available under CBD and ITPGRFA. In addition to national frameworks and legislation, Southeast Asia Regional Initiatives for Community Empowerment (SEARICE), a regional non-governmental development organization based in the Philippines, has developed an 'ASEAN Framework Agreement on Access to Biological and Genetic Resources' in 2000 [14]. The impetus for the agreement is the recognition to evolve measures to protect the rights of local and indigenous communities using multicountry cooperation. The Agreement envisages safeguarding access to genetic resources in ASEAN as a bloc. Moreover, it highlights the need to evolve a consensus and consistent protocol for access to genetic and biological resources in the entire ASEAN region. Such a framework would set a minimum standard for national implementation and maximize opportunities for conservation and sustainable use of biodiversity [14].

The ASEAN has also provided adequate space to non-governmental and community organizations to advance the mandate of conserving biodiversity through PVP and ABS. This is exemplified by SEARICE has been recognized by ASEAN as a regional organization. Such organizations have the ability of dovetailing stakeholder needs with policy frameworks for multiple governments thereby strengthening the regional cohesion in terms of evolving implementation regimes. Such an approach serves as a major lesson for similar blocs to develop their own systems keeping in view interest of the region to which they belong.

12.11.3 Prospects of the BIMSTEC

The multisectoral orientation of BIMSTEC raises its prospect of evolving a regional IPR protocol with respect to plant variety protection, protection of GI and ABS. The region is endowed with similar geographical and agro-climatic characters thereby making the conservation needs very similar. The following characteristics of the region are worth mentioning.

1. Parties to International Covenants: With exceptions of a few, most of the countries are parties to the international covenants governing natural wealth protection (list provided in Appendix) either through ratification or through accession. This makes prospects of harmonization of domestic regimes easier.
2. National laws in tune with conservation needs: Many countries have various points of time implemented national laws that mandate conservation and protection of natural resources and agriculture. In many cases, such laws transcend the TRIPS or CBD. Even countries like Bhutan, which is the only WTO non-member, have its own Biodiversity Act that provides for protection of plant varieties, tradi-

tional knowledge and ABS. Thus, harmonization into a regional regime could be strongly facilitated.
3. Availability of strong laws in some countries: Countries like India have put in place strong instruments such as those on PVP, ABS and GI. As needs in the group are similar to a large extent, the Indian law can be used as a model to evolve a regional protocol. Such an overarching protocol can be further naturalized to meet specific needs of the individual countries.
4. Benefit to lagging countries: Some countries in transition such as Myanmar or those like Bhutan or LDCs like Nepal or Bangladesh are yet to evolve national legislations. In absence of such instruments, many of these countries are prone to provisions under FTAs. Such instances mark specific cases where regional protocols can be evolved.

12.12 Policy Challenges for Agenda 21 Compliance

The evolution of regional protocols having a reasonable degree of orientation towards a multilateral system is likely to provide a suitable governance framework in shaping a seamless IPR regime among the countries. However, the adequate enforcement of the above would require building up of relevant institutional mechanisms and operating guidelines. In the previous discussions, we have seen that the BIMSTEC bloc is inherently capable of developing such a system. Also presence of India along a knowledge and experience sharing provision from SAARC and ASEAN is also expected to accelerate the mechanism. Nevertheless, it is felt that significant policy challenges would remain if a reasonable amount of Agenda 21 mandate is to be implemented. A few of them are given below.

Trans-boundary Technology Transfer:

Technology transfer and scientific capabilities is identified as a key vehicle for Agenda 21. India and Thailand could be the nucleating countries for such a milieu. Nevertheless, BIMSTEC is yet to develop an acceptable protocol for trans-boundary movement of technology, whether this be in the domain of transgenics or in agriculture.

Effective Institutions:

The region lacks adequate institutions and associated ancillary structures that are capable of driving the value chain; leverage the advantages of FTA, trade facilitation measures, FDI and so on; and translate technologies towards stakeholder requirements.

Capacity Building Measures:

Most of the countries, especially the LDC members, are severely deficient in capacity to make use of provisions of most legislations, e.g. the ones on PIC. MAT, SMTA.

Incidentally, this has been one of the chief causes of inordinate delay in many of the countries to comply with various TRIPS timelines.

Collaborative Arrangements:

The social, institutional and economic structures of the countries do not support large-scale collaborative arrangements among themselves. This is a major impediment in evolving a seamless regime that drive development.

Some of these regional measures might be undertaken within the ambit of WTO or other international set-ups or under the overall structures of BIMSTEC. However, for others it might be needed to adopt a totally new approach.

References

1. De P (2017) Big ideas to shape BIMSTEC's future. East Asia Forum, 15 Sept 2017
2. Kumar N (2009) South-South and triangular cooperation in Asia-Pacific: Towards a new paradigm in development cooperation. MPDD Working Paper WP/09/05, UNESCAP, Bangkok
3. Bhattacharya S (2007) Does BIMSTEC-Japan economic cooperation promote intra-regional trade? the case for free trade arrangement. Discussion Paper No 23, p 7
4. World Development Indicators (2017) World Bank. http://wdi.worldbank.org/tables. Accessed 25 Sept 2017
5. Herring R (2007) Stealth seeds: biosafety, biopiracy, biopolitics. J Dev Stud 43(1):130–157
6. Dhar B (2002) Sui generis systems of plant variety protection: Options under trips, Quaker United Nations Office. http://www.quno.org/. Accessed 25 Sept 2017
7. Rafi (1994) Conserving indigenous knowledge: integrating two systems of innovation, United Nations Development Programme
8. Kumar N (2011) Intellectual property rights, technology and economic development: Experiences of Asian countries, The Political Economy of IPRs (Ed: C May) vol III, pp 209–226
9. South Asian Association for Regional Cooperation (SAARC) (2017). http://www.saarc.org. Accessed 25 Sept 2017
10. Association for South East Asean Nations (ASEAN) (2017). http://www.asean.org. Accessed 25 Sept 2017
11. GRAIN/Kalpavriksh (2002) Traditional knowledge of biodiversity in Asia Pacific: problems of piracy and protection. GRAIN and Kalpavriksh
12. Convention for Biological Diversity, Statute of Convention of Biological Diversity Annex I (1992). http://www.cbd.int. Accessed 25 Sept 2017
13. Dhar B (2003) The Convention on Biological Diversity and the TRIPS Agreement: Compatibility or conflict. In: Bellmann C, Dutfield G, Melendez-Ortiz R (eds) Trading in knowledge: development perspectives on TRIPS, trade and sustainability. ICTSD, London, p 77–87
14. Adhikari K (2008) Protection of Farmers Rights over plant varieties in South East Asian Countries. South East Asian Council on Food Security and Trade, Kuala Lumpur
15. Halewood M, Brahmi P, Mathur PN, Bansal KC (eds) (2013) A roadmap for implementing the multilateral system of (ABS) in India. Bioversity International, Rome; ICAR and NBPGR, New Delhi
16. International Treary on Plant Genetic Resources for Food and Agriculture (2017) Food and Agricultural Organization, Rome. http://www.fao.org. Accessed 25 Sept 2017
17. FAO (2001) Crops proposed for the Multilateral System: Centres of Diversity, Locations of ex situ Collections, and Major Producing Countries. Background Study Paper No. 12. Commission on Genetic Resources for Food and Agriculture, Rome

Appendix A
Statistical Tables and Additional Information

A.1 Summary of Major International Treaties, Covenants and Protocols

A.1.1 Trade-Related Aspects of Intellectual Property Rights

Came Into Force

1994

Ratification and Accession

162 Member Countries

Administered by

WTO

Main Objectives

The TRIPS Agreement introduced intellectual property law into the international trading system for the first time and remains the most comprehensive international agreement on intellectual property to date.

Highlights

Developed as an annexe to the Agreement establishing the World Trade Organization that was negotiated during the Uruguay Round of GATT in 1994. It comprises of 73 articles in seven parts. The parts include: (1) general provisions and basic principles, (2) scope and use of intellectual property rights, (3) enforcement of intellectual property rights, (4) acquisition and maintenance of intellectual property rights, (5) dispute prevention and settlement, (6) transitional arrangement, (7) institutional arrangements and final provisions.

Points in Favour

Considered as a comprehensive multilateral agreement that aims towards creating a global intellectual property regime, thereby facilitating free trade among countries and providing a rule-based system for everyone to follow.

Points Against

Largely biased towards the interest of the developed countries especially the American TNCs. Leaves out the concerns and interest of the developing countries. Likely to increase the divide among developed and developing countries with expansion of Euro-American hegemony over other states. The harmonization of IPR laws is likely to damage industries in the developing countries and has deleterious effects on environment, biodiversity and traditional knowledge.

Conflict with Other Treaties

CBD

Access to Full Text

https://www.wto.org/trips

A.1.2 Convention on Biological Diversity

Came into Force

1993

Ratification and Accession

196 Member Countries

Administered by

United Nations Environment

Main Objectives

The objectives of CBD is the conservation of biological diversity, the sustainable use of its components and the fair and equitable sharing of the benefits arising out of the utilization of genetic resources. This includes appropriate access to genetic resources and appropriate transfer of relevant technologies, taking into account all rights over those resources and to technologies. Appropriate funding for implementation is also a part of the objective.

Highlights

The CBD is conceived as a practical tool for translating the principles of Agenda 21 into reality. In this regard the Convention recognizes that the scope of biological diversity is more than plants, animals and micro-organisms and their ecosystems; it also includes people and their need for food security, medicines, fresh air and water, shelter, and a clean and healthy environment. The convention recognized for the first time in international law that the conservation of biodiversity is 'a common concern of humankind' and is an integral part of the development process. The agreement covers all ecosystems, species, and genetic resources. It links traditional conservation efforts to the economic goal of using biological resources sustainably. It sets principles for the fair and equitable sharing of the benefits arising from the use of genetic resources, notably those destined for commercial use. It also encompass the rapidly expanding field of biotechnology through its Cartagena Protocol on Biosafety, addressing technology development and transfer, benefit-sharing and biosafety issues. Importantly, the Convention is legally binding; countries that join it ('Parties') are obliged to implement its provisions.

Points in Favour

The convention constitutes an important instrument in safeguarding the interests of the biodiversity-rich developing countries against the onslaught of globalization. The convention was a path setter by the fact that it had for the first time guaranteed sovereign rights to the countries over their natural resources which had thus far being considered as common heritage of mankind.

Points Against

Countries like USA have not ratified the convention as it is argued that the CBD would dilute and compromise on the strong intellectual property regime envisaged by the TRIPS in view of concessions given to the developing countries.

Conflict with Other Treaties

TRIPS and many other covenants of the WTO

Access of Full Text

https://www.cbd.int/convention/articles

A.1.3 Nagoya Protocol

Came into Force

2010

Ratification and Accession

102 Member Countries

Administered by

CBD

Main Objectives

Objective of the Nagoya Protocol is the fair and equitable sharing of benefits arising from the utilization of genetic resources, thereby contributing to the conservation and sustainable use of biodiversity.

Highlights

The protocol is a supplementary agreement to the Convention on Biological Diversity that provides a transparent legal framework for the effective implementation of one of the three objectives of the CBD, namely the fair and equitable sharing of benefits arising out of the utilization of genetic resources. The Nagoya Protocol applies to genetic resources that are covered by the CBD and to the benefits arising from their utilization. It also covers traditional knowledge (TK) associated with genetic resources that are covered by the CBD and the benefits arising from its utilization. The protocol sets out core obligations for its contracting parties to take measures in relation to access to genetic resources, benefit sharing and compliance against the parameters of access obligations; benefit-sharing obligations; and compliance obligations. Implementation of the Nagoya Protocol is through prior informed consent (PIC) and based upon mutually acceptable term (MAT).

Points in Favour

The Protocol is instrumental for the developing countries to safeguard access to its genetic resources that would otherwise have been subjected to piracy.

Points Against

Clear enumeration lacking in terms of fair exchange of genetic materials under certain special circumstances.

Conflict with Other Treaties

None in particular

Access of Full Text

https://www.cbd.int/abs/nagoya-protocol

Appendix A: Statistical Tables and Additional Information 157

A.1.4 Cartagena Protocol on Biosafety

Came into Force

2003

Ratification and Accession

103 Member Countries

Administered by

CBD

Main Objectives

The objective of this Protocol is to contribute to ensuring an adequate level of protection in the field of the safe transfer, handling and use of living modified organisms resulting from modern biotechnology that may have adverse effects on the conservation and sustainable use of biological diversity, taking also into account risks to human health and specifically focusing on trans-boundary movements.

Highlights

The Cartagena Protocol on Biosafety to the Convention on Biological Diversity is an international treaty governing the movements of living modified organisms (LMOs) resulting from modern biotechnology from one country to another.

Points in Favour

This is the first structural approach to biosafety by bringing stakeholders onto a common platform.

Points Against

None in particular. Some issues regarding R&D aspects of unknown entities whose safety protocols are not clear.

Conflict with Other Treaties

WTO Treaties

Access of Full Text

http://bch.cbd.int/protocol/text

A.1.5 Nagoya–Kuala Lumpur Supplementary Protocol on Liability and Redress

Came into Force

2010

Ratification and Accession

66 Member Countries

Administered by

CBD

Main Objectives

The objective of this Supplementary Protocol is to contribute to the conservation and sustainable use of biological diversity, taking also into account risks to human health, by providing international rules and procedures in the field of liability and redress relating to living modified organisms.

Highlights

Liability and redress in the context of the Protocol concerns the question of what would happen if the trans-boundary movement of living modified organisms (LMOs) has caused damage.

Points in Favour

Liability of use of GMO is pinpointed and scope defined, thus making it convenient for implementation.

Points Against

List of liabilities non-exhaustive.

Conflict with Other Treaties

TRIPS

Access of Full Text

http://bch.cbd.int/protocol/NKL_text

A.1.6 International Treaty on Plant Genetic Resources for Food and Agriculture

Came into Force

2004

Ratification and Accession

195 Member Countries

Administered by

FAO

Main Objectives

The objective of this Treaty is the conservation and sustainable use of plant genetic resources for food and agriculture and the fair and equitable sharing of the benefits arising out of their use, in harmony with the Convention on Biological Diversity, for sustainable agriculture and food security.

Highlights

The Treaty provides a truly innovative solution to access and benefit sharing. The Multilateral System puts 64 of our most important crops that together account for 80% of the food we derive from plants into an easily accessible global pool of Treaties for some uses. The Treaty facilitates access to the genetic materials of the 64 crops in the Multilateral System for research, breeding and training for food and agriculture. Those who access the materials must be from the Treaties ratifying nations, and they must agree to use the materials totally for research, breeding and training for food and agriculture. Those who access genetic materials through the Multilateral System agree to share any benefits from their use through four benefit-sharing mechanisms established by the Treaty. The Treaty recognizes the enormous contribution farmers have made to the ongoing development of the worlds' wealth of plant genetic resources. It calls for protecting the traditional knowledge of these farmers, increasing their participation in national decision-making processes and ensuring that they share in the benefits from the use of these resources. Most of the worlds' food comes from four main crops: rice, wheat, maize and potatoes. However, local crops, not among the main four, are a major food source for hundreds of millions of people and have potential to provide nutrition to countless others. The Treaty helps maximize the use and breeding of all crops and promotes development and maintenance of diverse farming systems.

Points in Favour

The ITPGRFA is the only overarching framework that takes into account the developing country interests during access to its genetic resources and enabling sustainable use of nature. The Treaty explicitly recognizes farmers' contribution to agriculture. Provisions laid down in this Treaty has been the foundation for evolving various plant variety protections and farmers' rights legislations in member countries.

Points Against

None in particular. However, some conflict with certain national legislation,

Conflict with Other Treaties

TRIPS, UPOV

Access of full text

http://www.fao.org/plant-treaty/overview/texts-treaty/en/

A.1.7 UPOV Convention

Came into Force

1961

Ratification and Accession

74 Member Countries

Administered by

UPOV

Main Objectives

The objective of UPOV is to encourage development of new varieties of plants for the benefit of the society. The UPOV represents an intergovernmental organization that was adopted in Paris in 1961 and subsequently revised in 1972, 1978 and 1991.

Highlights

UPOV incorporated different aspects of plant variety protection systems in its three versions. The UPOV 1961 version recognized the right of breeder through patent and applied to all genera of plants. Members were expected to apply for protection of at least five genera to start with and then increase them in a phased manner. The UPOV 1978 accorded protection to plant varieties that were new and which conformed to the criteria of distinctness, uniformity and stability, and unlike patents could be granted even if the variety was 'discovered'. The UPOV 1991 was characterized by stronger breeder rights, enhanced coverage of varieties that qualify for protection and requires a comprehensive coverage of plant varieties by the member states.

Points in Favour

The UPOV Convention is the only available multilateral instrument for a non-patent-based *sui generis* system for protection of new varieties of plants. It achieves harmonization of a IPR regime globally outside the ambit of patents.

Points Against

The convention is highly biased towards the developed countries and therefore is not ratified by many developing countries like India who envisage to develop effective *sui generis* systems. The UPOV does not benefit the rights to farmers and puts breeders at distinctly advantageous positions, thereby endangering the community knowledge, traditional knowledge, etc, of the developing countries.

Conflict with Other Treaties

ITPGRFA

Access of Full Text

www.upov.int

A.1.8 Lisbon Agreement on the Appellation of Origin and Their International Registration

Came into Force

1958

Ratification and Accession

28 Member Countries

Administered by

WIPO

Main Objectives

The objective of the Lisbon Agreement is securing protection for a special category of geographical indications called the appellation of origin in countries other than the country of origin through specific registration at the International Bureau.

Highlights

The Lisbon Agreement provides protection of appellation of origin, that is the "geographical denomination of a country, region, or locality, which serves to designate a product originating therein, the quality or characteristics of which are due exclusively or essentially to the geographic environment, including natural and human factors". A Contracting State may declare, within one year of receiving the notice of registration, that it cannot ensure the protection of a registered appellation within its territory. The Lisbon Agreement, concluded in 1958, was revised at Stockholm in 1967 and amended in 1979.

Points in Favour

First instrument to provide a framework for dealing with appellation and denomination of origin, that allowed registration.

Points Against

Provisions and outcomes are somewhat beneficial to large farmers with less impact on small and marginal farmers/farming communities. More institutionalized mechanisms are needed for implementation of this agreement.

Conflict with Other Treaties

TRIPS and UPOV

Access of Full Text

http://www.wipo.int/treaties/en/registration/lisbon/

A.1.9 Geneva Act of the Lisbon Agreement on Appellation of Origin and Geographical Indications

Came into Force

2015

Ratification and Accession

28 Member Countries

Administered by

WIPO

Main Objectives

The Geneva Act formally introduces GIs under its scope of application and provides a solid level of protection for both GIs and appellation of origin.

Highlights

The Geneva Act introduces a number of flexibilities compared to the previous version of the Lisbon Agreement, which makes the new international system for the registration and the protection of GIs and appellation of Origin. Elements of flexibility in the Lisbon System include aspects such as the possibility for GI beneficiaries to file an application for international registration; is instrumental to attract a large number of Contracting parties; accords coverage to all categories of GI.

Points in Favour

It is an instrument that creates the enforcement mechanism for Lisbon Agreement.

Points Against

Not yet determined

Conflict with Other Treaties

Not yet determined

Access of Full Text

www.wipo.int/edocs/lexdocs/treaties/en/lisbon/

Appendix A: Statistical Tables and Additional Information 163

A.2 Some Other International Instruments Not Directly Connected with Natural Resource IPR Protection

1. *Nice Agreement Concerning the International Classification of Goods and Services for the Purposes of the Registration of Marks (1957)*:
   The Nice Agreement, concluded at Nice in 1957, was revised at Stockholm in 1967 and further at Geneva in 1977. It was amended in 1979. The Agreement establishes a classification of goods and services for the purposes of registering trademarks and service marks (the Nice Classification) which is open to State party to the Paris Convention for the Protection of Industrial Property (1883). The agreement is administered by WIPO.
   Nice Classification is mandatory not only for the national registration of marks in countries' party to the Nice Agreement, but also for the international registration of marks effected by the African Intellectual Property Organization (OAPI), the African Regional Intellectual Property Organization (ARIPO), the Benelux Office for Intellectual Property (BOIP), the European Union Intellectual Property Office (EUIPO) and the International Bureau of WIPO. The Nice Classification is also applied in a number of countries, not party to the Nice Agreement.

2. *Hague Agreement Concerning the International Registration of Industrial Designs (1925)*:
   The Hague Agreement comprises of two Acts that are in operation currently, namely the 1999 Act and the 1960 Act. In September 2009, it was decided to freeze the application of the 1934 Act of the Hague Agreement, thus simplifying and streamlining overall administration of the international design registration system.
   According to the Act, an international design registration may be obtained only by a natural person or legal entity having a connection through establishment, domicile, and nationality or, under the 1999 Act, habitual residence with a Contracting Party to either of the two Acts. The Hague Agreement allows applicants to register an industrial design by filing a single application with the International Bureau of WIPO.

3. *The Strasbourg Agreement Concerning the International Patent Classification (1971)*:
   The Strasbourg Agreement establishes the International Patent Classification (IPC) which divides technology into eight sections with approximately 70,000 subdivisions. Each subdivision is denoted by a symbol consisting of Arabic numerals and letters of the Latin alphabet.
   The appropriate IPC symbols are indicated on patent documents (published patent applications and granted patents), and appropriate symbols are allotted by the national or regional industrial property office that publishes the patent document. For PCT applications, IPC symbols are allotted by the International Searching Authority.

4. *Budapest Treaty on the International Recognition of the Deposit of Microorganisms for the Purposes of Patent Procedure (1977)*:

The main feature of the Treaty is that a contracting State which allows or requires the deposit of micro-organisms for the purposes of patent procedure must deposit the micro-organism with any 'international depositary authority', irrespective of whether such authority is on or outside the territory of the said State.

However, in order to eliminate the need to deposit in each country in which protection is sought, the Treaty provides that the deposit of a micro-organism with any 'international depositary authority' suffices for the purposes of patent procedure before the national patent offices of all of the contracting States and before any regional patent. The European Patent Office (EPO), the Eurasian Patent Organization (EAPO) and the African Regional Intellectual Property Organization (ARIPO) have made such declarations.

5. *Patent Cooperation Treaty (PCT)*:
The Patent Cooperation Treaty (PCT) makes it possible to seek patent protection for an invention simultaneously in each of a large number of countries by filing an 'international' patent application. Such an application may be filed by anyone who is a national or resident of a PCT Contracting State. It may generally be filed with the national patent office of the Contracting State of which the applicant is a national or resident or, at the applicant's option, with the International Bureau of WIPO in Geneva.

A.3 Selected Economic Indicators

Tables A.1, A.2 and A.3

Table A.1 Economy

	Year	Bangladesh	Bhutan	India	Myanmar	Nepal	Sri Lanka	Thailand
GDP (current Billion US$)	2005	69.44	0.82	808.9	11.98	8.13	24.40	189.32
	2015	195.07	2.06	2111.75	62.60	21.31	80.61	399.23
GDP growth (annual %)	2005	6.53	7.12	9.28	13.56	3.47	6.24	4.18
	2015	6.55	6.49	8.01	7.29	2.72	4.83	2.94
GDP per capita (constant 2010 US$)	2005	598.62	1534.82	971.22	603.83	502.23	2149.04	4337.26
	2015	971.64	2625.57	1758.04	1346.04	686.08	3642.21	5733.92
GDP per capita growth (annual %)	2005	4.96	4.45	7.56	12.61	2.14	5.45	3.51
	2015	5.36	5.01	6.75	6.31	1.53	3.86	2.58
GNI (current US$)	2005	72.52	0.801	803.002	11.97	8.15	24.11	180.83
	2015	207.74	1.87	2087.09	58.79	21.65	78.54	378.53
GNI growth (annual %)	2005	6.63	8.06	9.26		4.08	6.01	4.06
	2015	6.39	4.29	8.02	5.09	2.69	3.57	2.67
GNI & Atlas method (current US$)	2005	76.59	0.79	804.73	13.24	8.01	23.68	182.74
	2015	191.31	1.84	2099.70	62.40	20.97	78.62	390.48
Population growth (annual %)	2005	1.49	2.52	1.58	0.84	1.29	0.75	0.65
	2015	1.12	1.39	1.16	0.91	1.16	0.93	0.35
Rural population (% of total population)	2005	73.19	69.03	70.76	71.07	84.82	81.62	62.48
	2015	65.72	61.35	67.25	65.90	81.38	81.64	49.63

(continued)

Table A.1 (continued)

	Year	Bangladesh	Bhutan	India	Myanmar	Nepal	Sri Lanka	Thailand
Rural population growth (annual %)	2005	0.54	0.89	1.12	0.24	0.93	0.76	−1.35
	2015	−0.03	0.19	0.60	0.09	0.71	0.89	−2.04
Total natural resources rents (% of GDP)	2005	1.14	2.58	3.71	10.16	0.79	0.12	2.17
	2015	1.03	5.52	1.87	4.84	1.46	0.15	1.24
Trade (% of GDP)	2005	34.39	101.81	42.48	0.27	44.06	73.60	137.85
	2015	42.08	92.85	42.19	47.32	53.33	49.55	126.58
Adjusted net national income (annual % growth)	2005	6.29	9.25	9.04		3.48	4.56	2.41
	2015	6.52	−0.37	6.81	5.43	3.91	8.32	7.15
Foreign direct investment & net inflows (% of GDP)	2005	1.09	0.75	0.89	1.95	0.03	1.12	4.34
	2015	1.73	0.52	2.08	6.52	0.24	0.84	2.25
Foreign direct investment & net outflows (% of GDP)	2005	0.002		0.33			0.16	0.29
	2015	0.03		0.35			0.06	1.25

Source: World Development Indicators 2017, World Bank, accessed on 25th September, 2017

Table A.2 Trade

	Year	Bangladesh	Bhutan	India	Myanmar	Nepal	Sri Lanka	Thailand
Merchandize exports (current Billion US$)	2005	9.30	0.26	99.62	3.77	0.86	6.35	110.94
	2015	32.38	0.55	267.44	11.43	0.72	10.50	214.35
Merchandize exports to high-income economies (% of total merchandize exports)	2005	78.24		68.92	21.53	28.13	70.09	67.66
	2015	72.16		63.40	19.51	31.04	75.92	55.29
Merchandize exports to low- and middle-income economies in East Asia & Pacific (% of total merchandize exports)	2005	1.57		11.61	55.98		1.79	23.55
	2015	3.17		10.77	67.65		2.13	32.82
Merchandize exports to low- and middle-income economies in South Asia (% of total merchandize exports)	2005	2.20		5.41	13.99	67.36	10.26	2.55
	2015	2.22		6.65	8.27	59.85	9.15	3.57
Merchandize exports to low- and middle-income economies outside region (% of total merchandize exports)	2005	4.46		25.29	14.72		10.79	8.41
	2015	7.93		28.87	9.06		14.86	11.30
Merchandize exports to low- and middle-income economies within region (% of total merchandize exports)	2005	2.21		5.41	55.98	67.36	10.26	23.54
	2015	2.22		6.64	67.65	59.85	9.15	32.82
Merchandize imports (current Billion US$)	2005	13.89	0.38	142.87	1.90	2.28	8.83	118.17
	2015	39.46	1.06	392.86	16.88	6.65	18.93	202.65
Merchandize imports from high-income economies (% of total merchandize imports)	2005	49.36		49.49	32.84	20.60	50.18	68.25
	2015	35.11		52.15	25.74	17.55	53.56	57.41

(continued)

Table A.2 (continued)

	Year	Bangladesh	Bhutan	India	Myanmar	Nepal	Sri Lanka	Thailand
Merchandize imports from low- and middle-income economies in East Asia & Pacific (% of total merchandize imports)	2005	20.56		12.41	62.27		16.18	23.27
	2015	31.28		24.34	68.96		11.61	35.54
Merchandize imports from low- and middle-income economies in South Asia (% of total merchandize imports)	2005	15.32		0.94	3.63	59.72	22.35	1.22
	2015	15.58		0.77	3.99	62.11	30.67	1.42
Merchandize trade (% of GDP)	2005	33.38	78.71	29.97	47.42	38.70	62.19	121.02
	2015	36.83	78.22	31.26	45.23	34.59	36.52	104.45
Export value index (2000 = 100)	2005	145.52	250.67	235.06	233.08	107.36	116.88	160.86
	2015	506.78	429.88	630.37	685.48	82.11	193.45	310.85
Export volume index (2000 = 100)	2005	144.99	154.11	189.04	170.05	94.05	113.27	143.26
	2015	437.41	224.41	415.49	368.35	50.37	156.48	200.99
Exports as a capacity to import (constant LCU $\times 10^9$)	2005	638.88	12.01	10558.85	15196.25	71.56	1146.66	4793.81
	2015	1237.42	18.34	22499.62		103.56	1875.97	7783.30
Import value index (2000 = 100)	2005	156.35	220.48	277.29	80.48	145.15	140.63	190.84
	2015	444.22	569.06	760.78	738.35	413.90	301.44	327.26
Import volume index (2000 = 100)	2005	125.36	183.28	195.83	62.58	106.02	155.91	164.31
	2015	255.03	358.58	523.46	444.04	218.21	267.51	220.82

Source: World Development Indicators 2017, World Bank, accessed on 25th September, 2017

Appendix A: Statistical Tables and Additional Information

Table A.3 Agriculture

	Year	Bangladesh	Bhutan	India	Myanmar	Nepal	Sri Lanka	Thailand
Agricultural land (% of land area)	2005	71.53	15.55	60.58	17.24	29.31	40.02	38.38
	2013	69.97	13.63	60.63	19.27	28.75	43.69	43.27
Agriculture and value added (% of GDP)	2005	69.97	23.18	19.51	46.68	36.34	11.82	9.19
	2013	15.50	17.43	17.46	26.74	33.003	8.81	8.72
Arable land (% of land area)	2005	60.77	4.38	53.63	15.39	15.90	17.54	29.75
	2013	58.98	2.63	52.80	16.49	14.75	20.73	32.90
Food exports (% of merchandize exports)	2005	6.22	10.64	8.97			22.23	11.63
	2015			11.55		26.89	25.66	13.78
Food imports (% of merchandize imports)	2005	13.9	14.49	3.67		18.30	12.46	4.01
	2015			5.76			13.15	6.56
Food production index (2004–2006 = 100)	2005	102.81	105.78	99.94	100.28	102.33	98.24	97.9
	2013	155.56	97.13	138.76	130.07	130.36	141.52	128.49
Cereal yield (kg per hectare)	2005	3681.6	2334.9	3493.7	2311.6	3467.2	3015.7	3018.9
	2014	4405.8	3130.9	2981.1	3706.6	2747.9	3801.4	3102.9
Crop production index (2004–2006 = 100)	2005	103.06	107.31	99.9	98.78	100.25	101.92	97.91
	2013	137.79	97.46	141.87	121.47	130.09	136.22	128.62
Permanent cropland (% of land area)	2005	6.15	0.49	3.44	1.37	0.93	15.46	7.06
	2013	6.38	0.33	4.37	2.31	1.48	15.94	8.80

Source: World Development Indicators 2017, World Bank, accessed on 25th September, 2017

Glossary

ABS Access and benefit sharing (ABS) is referred to as a protocol by which an outsider get regulated access to a given community or a given endemic region with the aim of commercially exploiting a given natural resource in return of sharing the benefits arising out of its utilization with the community in a fair and equitable way. Access and benefit sharing under international protocols is usually required to be done through prior informed consent (PIC) and under mutually agreed terms (MATs).

AIA AIA or the advance informed agreement procedure is designed to ensure that before an LMO is imported into a country for the first time for intentional introduction into the environment, the party of import: (a) is notified about the proposed import and (b) receives full information about the LMO and its intended use.

Appellation of origin An appellation of origin is a special kind of geographical indication generally consisting of a geographical name or a traditional designation used on products which have a specific quality or characteristics that are essentially due to the geographical environment in which they are produced.

ASEAN Association for Southeast Asian Nations (ASEAN) is an intergovernmental organization in Southeast Asia that essentially constitutes a trading bloc in Asia that makes up 8.8% of the total world population. Currently, it comprises of ten southeast Asian countries, namely Brunei, Cambodia, Indonesia, Laos, Malaysia, Myanmar, Philippines, Singapore, Thailand and Vietnam. East Timor and Papua New Guinea are present as observers.

Biodiversity Biodiversity refers to the variety of plant and animal life in the world or in a particular habitat, a high level of which is usually considered to be important and desirable. In a more extended connotation, biodiversity also encompasses agricultural diversity, diversity of crops, genetic diversity and even diversity of practices that originate from the surrounding natural habitats such as those practices by local communities.

Biopiracy Biopiracy is the practice of commercially exploiting naturally occurring biochemical or genetic material, especially by obtaining patents that restrict its future use, while failing to pay fair compensation to the community from which it originates.

Cartagena Protocol The Cartagena Protocol on Biosafety is an instrument developed under the Convention on Biological Diversity. It is an international agreement which aims to ensure the safe handling, transport and use of living modified organisms (LMOs) resulting from modern biotechnology that may have adverse effects on biological diversity and the environment. It also takes into account effects on human health.

Certification marks A certification mark is a sign certifying that the goods or services in respect of which it is used are of a particular origin, material, mode of manufacture, quality, accuracy, performance or other characteristic.

Community intellectual rights Community intellectual rights (CIRs) are referred to as the intellectual property rights that are owned by a given community (usually indigenous community) over some of its practices or product or process that is held by the community usually across generations.

Essentially biological process A process for the production of plants or animals which is based on the sexual crossing of whole genomes and on the subsequent selection of plants is referred to as an essentially biological process of production of plants and animals. Under current patent laws, this is excluded from patentability.

Essentially derived varieties Essentially derived variety is a variety which is predominantly derived from another variety (protected or otherwise) and conforms to the initial variety in all aspects except for the differences which result from the act of derivation and yet is clearly distinguishable from such initial variety.

Ex situ conservation Ex situ conservation means "off-site conservation". It is the process of protecting an endangered species, variety or breed, of plant or animal outside of its natural habitat, for example by removing part of the population from a threatened habitat and placing it in a new location, which may be a wild area or within the care of humans. Ex situ management can occur within or outside a species' natural geographic range. Individuals maintained ex situ exist outside of an ecological niche. Agricultural biodiversity is also conserved in ex situ collections which occurs primarily in the form of gene banks where samples are stored in order to conserve the genetic resources of major crop plants and their wild counterparts.

Farmers' rights Farmers' rights consist of the customary rights of farmers to save, use, exchange and sell farm-saved seed and propagating material, their rights to be recognized, rewarded and supported for their contribution to the global pool of genetic resources as well as to the development of commercial varieties of plants, and to participate in decision-making on issues related to crop genetic resources.

Flora and fauna They are main elements of the natural world. Flora constitutes the plant resources, while fauna refers to the animal resources.

Glossary

Food security Food security is a condition related to the supply of food and individuals' access to it. Food security indicators and measures are derived from country-level household income and expenditure surveys to estimate per capita caloric availability.

FTA A free trade area (FTA) is the region encompassing a trade bloc whose member countries have signed a free trade agreement (also known as FTA). Such agreements involve cooperation between two or more countries to reduce trade barriers—import quotas and tariffs—and to increase trade of goods and services among themselves. FTAs are crucial for economic integration.

GDP The gross domestic product (GDP) is one of the primary indicators used to gauge the health of a country's economy. It represents the total dollar value of all goods and services produced over a specific time period; it actually represents the size of the economy.

GM crops Genetically modified crops (GM crops) are plants used in agriculture, the DNA of which has been modified using genetic engineering methods. In most cases, the aim is to introduce a new trait to the plant which does not occur naturally in the species.

In situ conservation In situ conservation refers to the on-site conservation. It is thus the conservation of genetic resources in natural populations of plant or animal species, such as forest genetic resources in natural populations of tree species. It is the process of protecting an endangered plant or animal species in its natural habitat, either by protecting or restoring the habitat itself, or by defending the species from predators. It is also applied to conservation of agricultural biodiversity in agro-ecosystems by farmers, especially those using unconventional farming practices.

Indigenous knowledge Indigenous knowledge usually refers to the knowledge held by indigenous communities. It is a subset of traditional knowledge.

Informal and formal seed sector The informal seed sector is usually defined as the total of seed production activities of farmers, mostly small-scale farmers. In contrast, the formal sector refers to seed production activities by the public and commercial sector.

IPR Intellectual property rights (IPRs) is referred to the creation of human mind and covers patents, trademarks, copyrights and so on. Of late, geographical indications, plant variety protection and protection of traditional knowledge have also become important aspects of intellectual property rights.

ITPGRFA The International Treaty on Plant Genetic Resources for Food and Agriculture (also known as the International Seed Treaty) is a comprehensive international agreement in harmony with the Convention on Biological Diversity. It aims at guaranteeing food security through the conservation, exchange and sustainable use of the world's plant genetic resources for food and agriculture (PGRFA), as well as the fair and equitable benefit sharing arising from its use. The basic elements of farmers' rights, traditional knowledge protection in agriculture and so on are incorporated into the Treaty which makes it an enabling instrument for developing countries.

Landraces A landrace is a domesticated, locally adapted, traditional variety of a species of animal or plant that has developed over time, through adaptation to its natural and cultural environment of agriculture and pastoralism, and due to isolation from other populations of the species. Landraces are important elements of agricultural diversity of a region.

Materials transfer agreement A Material transfer agreement (MTA) is a contract that governs the transfer of tangible research materials between two organizations, when the recipient intends to use it for his or her own research purposes. The MTA defines the rights of the provider and the recipient with respect to the materials and any derivatives.

MERCOSUR Mercosul or emby emuha (Spanish: Mercado Comn del Sur, Portuguese: Mercado Comum do Sul, Guarani: emby emuha, Southern Common Market) is a subregional bloc in South America that forms a trade bloc. Its full members are Argentina, Brazil, Paraguay and Uruguay.

MFN A most favoured nation (MFN) clause is a level of status given to one country by another and enforced by the World Trade Organization. A country grants this clause to another nation if it is interested in increasing trade with that country.

Misappropriation Misappropriation is the intentional, illegal use of the property of another person for one's own use or other unauthorized purpose, particularly by a public official, a trustee of a trust, that causes loss or damage to the actual owner of the property. In natural wealth terminology, it is used in much the similar way as biopiracy.

Nagoya Protocol The Nagoya Protocol on Access to Genetic Resources and the Fair and Equitable Sharing of Benefits Arising from their Utilization to the Convention on Biological Diversity is an international agreement which aims at sharing the benefits arising from the utilization of genetic resources in a fair and equitable way.

Plant breeders' rights Plant breeders' rights (PBR) are rights granted to the breeder of a new variety of plant that give the breeder exclusive control over the propagating material (including seed, cuttings, divisions, tissue culture) and harvested material (cut flowers, fruit, foliage) of a new variety for a number of years.

Plant genetic resources Plant genetic resources (PBR)include all our agricultural crops and some of their wild relatives because they possess valuable traits. Genetic resource according to the CBD implies any genetic material of actual and potential value that has the capability of inheritance. Plant genetic resources are used by farmers and scientists as the raw material for breeding new plant varieties. They are also a reservoir of genetic diversity which acts as a buffer against environmental and economic change.

Prior informed consent Prior informed consent is a mechanism where the owner of a traditional or indigenous knowledge (usually a community) is informed in advance that their knowledge is being used for a given commercial or other activity and the purpose for which it is being used. The community also has to give the consent to the organization or individual to the use of their knowledge.

SAARC South Asian Association for Regional Cooperation (SAARC) is a regional economic bloc in South Asia comprising of Afghanistan, Bangladesh, Bhutan, India, Maldives, Nepal, Pakistan and Sri Lanka.

Sharecroppers Sharecropper is a tenant farmer who gives a part of each crop as rent.

South–south cooperation South–south cooperation is a term historically used by policy makers and academics to describe the exchange of resources, technology and knowledge between developing countries, also known as countries of the global south. The name owes its origin from the fact that most of the developing countries are usually located south of the developed countries of the north (i.e. Europe and North America).

Sui generis systems A *sui generis* system simply means 'one that is of its own kind'. *Sui generis* system refers to the creation of a new national law or the establishment of international norms that would afford protection to intellectual property dealing with genetic resources—or biodiversity—and the biotechnology that might result.

Sustainable development Sustainable development is a developmental paradigm that is envisaged to meet human development goals while sustaining the ability of natural systems to provide the natural resources and ecosystem services upon which the economy and society depend. The desirable end result is a state of society where living and conditions and resource use continue to meet human needs without undermining the integrity and stability of the natural systems.

TKDL Traditional Knowledge Digital Library (TKDL) is a database of traditional medicinal practices and products in India that are documented and submitted to the international patent offices in a form and language that is comprehensible to them. This is a pioneer initiative of India to prevent misappropriation of country's traditional medicinal knowledge.

TKRC Traditional knowledge resource classification (TKRC) is a system of classification of traditional knowledge information in databases for easier storage, access and retrieval. It is a similar system as International Patent Classification.

Traditional cultural expressions Traditional cultural expressions (TCEs), also called "expressions of folklore", may include music, dance, art, designs, names, signs and symbols, performances, ceremonies, architectural forms, handicrafts and narratives, or many other artistic or cultural expressions. They are usually held by indigenous and local communities and are currently being protected as intellectual property rights.

Traditional knowledge Traditional knowledge refers to the tacit knowledge held by communities. Traditional knowledge is normally undocumented and passed on from generation to generation through oral communication.

TRIPS The Agreement on Trade-Related Aspects of Intellectual Property Rights (TRIPS) is an international legal agreement between all the member nations of the

World Trade Organization (WTO) that evolved as an annex to the last meeting of General Agreement of Tariff and Trade, the so-called Uruguay Round. The TRIPS Agreement introduced intellectual property law into the international trading system for the first time and remains the most comprehensive international agreement on intellectual property to date.

TRIPS Plus TRIPS Agreement stipulates minimum standards in the international rules governing intellectual property rights. TRIPS Plus is higher level of protection norms demanded by the developed countries that are not prescribed by the WTO TRIPs regime. Although they are named as TRIPS Plus, they are not formally related to TRIPs. Rather, the term is used to indicate that these requirements go beyond the minimum standards imposed by TRIPs.

UPOV The International Union for Protection of New Plant Varieties (French: Union internationale pour la protection des obtentions vtales—UPOV) is an intergovernmental organization headquartered in Geneva that was established by the International Convention for the Protection of New Varieties of Plants. The UPOV represents an international instrument that envisages to accord protection to new plant varieties other than by plant patents.

WTO WTO refers to the World Trade Organization that comprises of the institutional structure coordinating the rule-based trading system in the world. The goal is to help producers of goods and services, exporters and importers conduct their business in a seamless manner.

Index

A
ABS, 97
Access to Genetic Resources, 12
Act on the protection and promotion of Thai traditional medicinal intelligence, 67
Advanced Informed Agreement, 82
Agenda-21, 4
Agreement on Agriculture, 126
Agricultural IPR, 22
Amla, 61
Andean Subregional Integration Agreement, 9
Annex-I Crops, 146
Appellations of origin, 16
ARIPO, 9
Article 15 of the Convention of Biological Diversity, 93
Article-22 of the CBD, 18
Article 27.3(b), 25
Article 8(j), 47
Article 9.1, 47
ASEAN, 31
ASSINSEL, 27
Ayahuasca vine, 23

B
Bangladesh, 36
Bangladesh Biodiversity Act, 99
Bangui Agreement, 9
Basmati patent, 75
Berne Convention, 8
Bhutan, 37
Bhutan Biodiversity Act, 51
Bhutanese Red Rice, 72
BIMSTEC, 31

Biodiversity and community knowledge protection act, 64
Biodiversity Conservation Action Plan, 66
Biodiversity hot spots, 42
Biopiracy, 122
Bioprospecting, 126
Biosafety, 13
Biosafety Clearing House, 82
Biosafety guidelines, 86
Biosafety Rules of Bangladesh (2012), 87
Bonn Guidelines, 95
Breeders, 28
Bt cotton, 123
Budapest Treaty, 15

C
Cartagena Protocol, 12
CBD, 11
CBRs, 63
Certification marks and labels, 68
Ceylon Tea, 72
CGIAR, 14
Chia Tai, 55
CIRs, 29
Climate change, 121
Code of Intellectual Property Act No 59 of Sri Lanka, 66
COICA, 94
Common heritage, 122
Community Biodiversity Register, 65
Community Forestry Acts, 29
Community rights, 112
Community-based biodiversity management, 65
Compulsory licensing, 18
Conservation issues, 1

Containment and use of LMOs, 13
Convention on Biological Diversity, 1
CSIR, 62

D
Da Vine, 94
Darjeeling Tea, 72
Defensive rights, 124
Depleting water resources, 120
Development lobby, 137
Distinctness, 27
Doha declaration, 129
Draft Access to Genetic Resources and Benefit-Sharing Bill, 102
Draft Act on Biosafety, 90
Draft Bangladesh Biodiversity Act, 50
Draft Biosafety Law of Myanmar, 88
Draft National Biosafety Framework (2007), 89
Draft national guidelines for import and planned release of GMOs and products thereof, 90
Draft Patent Act, 50
Draft Plant Variety and Farmers Rights Protection Act, 50

E
Earth Summit, 4
Endogenous communities, 93
Equitable sharing of benefits, 23
Essentially biological processes, 16
European Patent Convention, 9
Ex situ Conservatio, 12

F
Farmers Rights, 13
Farmers Rights Act, 28
Fazli Mango, 147
Folklore, 3
Food security, 22
Forage species, 13
Foreign Prior Use, 95
Framework Agreement on Access to Biological and Genetic Resources, 139

G
GATT, 10
GDP annual growth rate, 108
GEAC, 123
Gene polymorphisms, 17

Genetic diversity, 17
Genetic engineering, 17
Geographical indications, 71
Geographical indications of goods (registration and protection) act, 76
Geographical indications protection act, 79
Geographical location of the BIMSTEC, 36
GI Act of Bangladesh, 77
GI registry, 74
Globalization, 7
GM products, 13
GM technology, 43
Guidelines for research in transgenic plants, 85

H
Hagahai tribesmen, 23
Hague Agreement, 8
Harmonization of intellectual property norms, 128
HDI, 35
Himalayan GI, 114
Homogenization, 23

I
IGC, 24
India, 38
In situ Conservation, 12
Indigenous human communities, 23
Indigenous knowledge, 3
Industrial Revolution, 7
Informal breeding, 46
Intellectual property rights, 1
Interdependence of countries on crop varieties, 145
International Depository Authority, 16
Inward technology flow, 27
ITPGRFA, 13, 47

J
Jamdani Saree, 148

K
Kani Tribal Model, 99

L
Land races, 84
Land use, 34
LDC, 50

Legitimate exchange of PGR, 147
Lisbon Agreement, 16, 72
Livelihood practices, 120
LMOs, 12
Locally adapted varieties, 25
Look East policy, 5
Look West policy, 5

M
Madrid Agreement, 8
Marrakesh Agreement, 10
MDGs, 136
MERCOSUR, 9
MFN, 129
Ministerial Regulation, 79
Misappropriation, 24
Monsanto seeds, 47
Multilateral system, 146
Multilateral treaties, 8
Multisectoral set-up, 32
Myanmar, 39

N
NAFTA, 9
Nagoya–Kuala Lumpur Supplementary Protocol, 83
Nagoya Protocol, 96
Nap Hal, 61
National Biodiversity Act (2002), 98
National Biosafety Framework (2006), 86
National Biosafety Framework (2007), 87
National treatment, 11
Natural mineral water, 113
Natural wealth, 3
Neem, 60
Nepal, 40
Nice Agreement, 8

O
OAPI, 9
OECD, 43

P
Padma Hilsha, 72
Paris Convention, 8, 21
Patent Act, 45
Patentability of life forms, 10
Patterns of land use, 120
PBRs, 63
Plant Quarantine Order, 85

Plant Registry, 45
Plant Varieties and Farmers Rights Act, 48
Plant Varieties and Farmers Rights Act of Bangladesh, 64
Plant Variety Protection Act of Thailand, 55
Positive rights, 124
Principle-15 of the Rio Declaration, 12
Proprietary knowledge, 17
Protectionist lobby, 137
Protocol on Harmonization of intellectual property norms, 148
PVP, 47

R
Regional Protocols, 132
Regional Value Chains, 135

S
SAARC, 31
SACEP, 121
SDGs, 136
SEARICE, 149
Sectoral composition of GDP, 127
Seed policy, 85
Seeds Act of Bhutan, 52
Sharecroppers, 51
SMTA, 131
South Asian Region, 31
Sri Lanka, 41
SRISTI, 63
Stability, 27
Stealth seeds, 126
Strassborg Agreement, 45
Strassborg Convention, 45
Sui generis system, 10
Sustainable development, 31
Sustainable use of PGR, 144

T
Tacit knowledge, 93
TCE, 68
Thailand, 42
Thailand's National Biosafety Framework, 90
TKDL, 62
TKRC, 63
Total exports from the BIMSTEC, 33
Total imports into the BIMSTEC, 33
Traditional cultural expressions, 24
Trans-boundary movement, 13, 109
Transgenic crops, 81

Transgenic seeds, 123
TRIPS, 1
TRIPS Council, 25
TRIPS plus, 73
Turmeric, 60

U
Uniformity, 27
Unpaid royalties, 138
UPOV, 14
UPOV-61, 15

UPOV-78, 15
UPOV-91, 15
Uruguay Round, 10

V
Vienna Congress, 8

W
Wise use, 125
WTO, 1

GPSR Compliance

The European Union's (EU) General Product Safety Regulation (GPSR) is a set of rules that requires consumer products to be safe and our obligations to ensure this.

If you have any concerns about our products, you can contact us on

ProductSafety@springernature.com

In case Publisher is established outside the EU, the EU authorized representative is:

Springer Nature Customer Service Center GmbH
Europaplatz 3
69115 Heidelberg, Germany

www.ingramcontent.com/pod-product-compliance
Lightning Source LLC
LaVergne TN
LVHW020412070526
838199LV00054B/3584